MORTGAGE MARKETS AND THE ROLE OF NONPRIME LOANS

ECONOMIC ISSUES, PROBLEMS AND PERSPECTIVES

Additional books in this series can be found on Nova's website under the Series tab.

Additional E-books in this series can be found on Nova's website under the E-book tab.

ECONOMIC ISSUES, PROBLEMS AND PERSPECTIVES

MORTGAGE MARKETS AND THE ROLE OF NONPRIME LOANS

ERIC J. CARLSON
EDITOR

Nova Science Publishers, Inc.
New York

NOTICE TO THE READER

The Publisher has taken reasonable care in the preparation of this book, but makes no expressed or implied warranty of any kind and assumes no responsibility for any errors or omissions. No liability is assumed for incidental or consequential damages in connection with or arising out of information contained in this book. The Publisher shall not be liable for any special, consequential, or exemplary damages resulting, in whole or in part, from the readers' use of, or reliance upon, this material. Any parts of this book based on government reports are so indicated and copyright is claimed for those parts to the extent applicable to compilations of such works.

Independent verification should be sought for any data, advice or recommendations contained in this book. In addition, no responsibility is assumed by the publisher for any injury and/or damage to persons or property arising from any methods, products, instructions, ideas or otherwise contained in this publication.

This publication is designed to provide accurate and authoritative information with regard to the subject matter covered herein. It is sold with the clear understanding that the Publisher is not engaged in rendering legal or any other professional services. If legal or any other expert assistance is required, the services of a competent person should be sought. FROM A DECLARATION OF PARTICIPANTS JOINTLY ADOPTED BY A COMMITTEE OF THE AMERICAN BAR ASSOCIATION AND A COMMITTEE OF PUBLISHERS.

Additional color graphics may be available in the e-book version of this book.

LIBRARY OF CONGRESS CATALOGING-IN-PUBLICATION DATA

Mortgage markets and the role of nonprime loans / editor, Eric J. Carlson.
    p. cm. -- (Economic issues, problems, and perspectives)
  Includes bibliographical references and index.
  ISBN 978-1-61122-918-9 (hardcover : alk. paper)
  1. Mortgages--United States. 2. Subprime mortgage loans--United States.
I. Carlson, Eric J.
  HG4655.M667 2011
  332.7'20973--dc22
                        2010044740

Published by Nova Science Publishers, Inc. † New York

CONTENTS

PREFACE

During the first part of this decade, the number of mortgage originations grew rapidly, particularly in the nonprime segment of the mortgage market. This new book examines the evolution and condition of the nonprime market segment.

Chapter 1- During the first part of this decade, the number of mortgage originations grew rapidly, particularly in the nonprime segment of the mortgage market, which includes subprime and Alt-A loans. In dollar terms, nonprime loans accounted for an increasing share of the overall mortgage market, rising from 12 percent in 2000 to 34 percent in 2006. Over this period, the dollar volume of nonprime mortgages originated annually climbed from $100 billion to $600 billion in the subprime market and from $25 billion to $400 billion in the Alt-A market. However, these market segments contracted sharply in the summer of 2007, partly in response to a dramatic increase in default and foreclosure rates for these mortgages. As we reported in 2007, a loosening of underwriting standards for subprime and Alt-A loans contributed to this increase. As of the first quarter of 2009, approximately 1 in 8 nonprime mortgages were in the foreclosure process. The negative repercussions from nonprime lending practices has prompted greater scrutiny of this market segment, a number of government efforts to modify troubled loans, and proposals to strengthen federal regulation of the mortgage industry.

Chapter 2- As reported in July 2009, the number of nonprime mortgage originations (including subprime and Alt-A loans) grew rapidly from 2000 through 2006, a period during which average house prices appreciated dramatically. In dollar terms, the nonprime share of mortgage originations rose from about 12 percent ($125 billion) in 2000 to approximately 34 percent ($1 trillion) in 2006. These mortgages have been associated with what was subsequently recognized as a speculative housing bubble. As house prices subsequently fell, the subprime and Alt-A market segments contracted sharply, and very few nonprime originations were made after mid-2007. Borrowers who had obtained nonprime mortgages earlier in the decade increasingly fell behind on their mortgage payments, helping to push default and foreclosure rates to historical highs.

Chapter 3- The decline of home prices in many parts of the country has left millions of homeowners with negative home equity, meaning that their outstanding mortgage balances exceed the current value of their homes. A substantial proportion of borrowers with active nonprime mortgages (including subprime and Alt-A loans) had negative equity in their homes as of June 30, 2009. For example, among the 16 metropolitan areas examined, it is estimated that the percentage of nonprime borrowers with negative equity ranged from about 9 percent

(Denver, Colorado) to more than 90 percent (Las Vegas, Nevada). Research indicates that negative home equity substantially increases the risk of mortgage delinquency, making it an important dimension of ongoing problems in the nonprime market.

Chapter 4- The surge in mortgage foreclosures that began in late 2006 and continues today was initially driven by deterioration in the performance of nonprime (subprime and Alt-A) loans. Nonprime mortgage originations increased dramatically from 2000 through 2006, rising from about 12 percent ($125 billion) of all mortgage originations to about 34 percent ($1 trillion). The nonprime market contracted sharply in mid-2007, partly in response to increasing defaults and foreclosures for these loans.

This chapter (1) provides information on the performance of nonprime loans through December 31, 2009; (2) examines how loan and borrower characteristics and economic conditions influenced the likelihood of default (including foreclosure) of nonprime loans; and (3) describes the features and limitations of primary sources of data on nonprime loan performance and borrower characteristics, and discusses federal government efforts to improve the availability or use of such data. To do this work, GAO analyzed a proprietary database of securitized nonprime loans and Home Mortgage Disclosure Act data, and reviewed information on mortgage data sources maintained by private firms and the federal government.

In: Mortgage Markets and the Role of Nonprime Loans   ISBN: 978-1-61122-918-9
Editor: Eric J. Carlson   © 2011 Nova Science Publishers, Inc.

Chapter 1

CHARACTERISTICS AND PERFORMANCE OF NONPRIME MORTGAGES

United States Government Accountability Office

July 28, 2009

The Honorable Carolyn B. Maloney
Chair
Joint Economic Committee
House of Representatives

The Honorable Charles E. Schumer
Vice Chairman
Joint Economic Committee
United States Senate

Subject: Characteristics and Performance of Nonprime Mortgages

During the first part of this decade, the number of mortgage originations grew rapidly, particularly in the nonprime segment of the mortgage market, which includes subprime and Alt-A loans.[1] In dollar terms, nonprime loans accounted for an increasing share of the overall mortgage market, rising from 12 percent in 2000 to 34 percent in 2006. Over this period, the dollar volume of nonprime mortgages originated annually climbed from $100 billion to $600 billion in the subprime market and from $25 billion to $400 billion in the Alt-A market.[2] However, these market segments contracted sharply in the summer of 2007, partly in response to a dramatic increase in default and foreclosure rates for these mortgages. As we reported in 2007, a loosening of underwriting standards for subprime and Alt-A loans contributed to this increase.[3] As of the first quarter of 2009, approximately 1 in 8 nonprime mortgages were in the foreclosure process. The negative repercussions from nonprime lending practices has prompted greater scrutiny of this market segment, a number of government efforts to modify troubled loans, and proposals to strengthen federal regulation of the mortgage industry.

To inform congressional oversight and decision making about efforts to address current problems in the mortgage market, you requested that we examine the evolution and condition of the nonprime market segment. Accordingly, this report discusses (1) trends in the loan and borrower characteristics of nonprime mortgages originated from 2000 through 2007 and (2) the performance of these mortgages as of March 31, 2009. Additionally, this report provides supplemental information, including detailed statistics by annual loan cohort, state, and congressional district. We provide this additional information in enclosures I through VI.

As agreed with your offices, in two subsequent reports we will provide information on the extent of negative home equity in metropolitan areas, the influence of nonprime loan and borrower characteristics and economic conditions on the likelihood of default, and sources of data on nonprime loans. Also, the information provided in this report will be updated in these subsequent reports to reflect the most recent available data and additional analyses.

To conduct our work, we analyzed data from Loan Performance's (LP) Asset-backed Securities database for nonprime loans originated from 2000 through 2007.[4] The database contains loan-level data on nonagency securitized mortgages in subprime and Alt-A pools.[5] About three-quarters of nonprime mortgages have been securitized in recent years, and the LP database covers the vast majority of them. For example, for the period 2001 through July 2007 the LP database contains information covering (in dollar terms) an estimated 87 percent of securitized subprime loans and 98 percent of securitized Alt-A loans. Research has found that nonprime mortgages that were not securitized (i.e., mortgages that lenders held in their portfolios) may have different characteristics and performance histories than those that were securitized. For purposes of our analysis, we defined a subprime loan as a loan in a subprime pool and an Alt-A loan as a loan in an Alt-A pool.[6] We focused our analysis on first-lien purchase and refinance mortgages for 1-4 family residential units.

To determine trends in nonprime loan and borrower characteristics, we calculated the numbers and percentages of subprime and Alt-A mortgage originations. We then disaggregated them by loan purpose (e.g., purchase, refinance), loan type (e.g., adjustable-rate mortgages [ARM], fixed-rate mortgages), and other characteristics, including interest rates at origination, borrowers' credit scores, and loan features such as low or no documentation of borrower income or assets and prepayment penalites. To determine the performance of nonprime mortgages, we calculated the number and percentage of mortgages that were in different performance categories—for example, current (up to date on payments), delinquent (30-89 days behind), in default (90 or more days behind), in the foreclosure process, or had completed the foreclosure process as of March 31, 2009.[7] We also examined the performance of specific loan cohorts and loans for homes in different geographic areas, including Census divisions, states, and congressional districts.[8] To estimate loan performance by congressional district, we linked ZIP code–level information in the LP database to congressional districts.[9] Specifically, we (1) calculated for each ZIP code area the total number of loans and the number of loans either in default or in the foreclosure process (seriously delinquent), (2) used mapping software to determine the proportion of each ZIP code area that fell within a given congressional district, and (3) used information from the first two steps to estimate for each congressional district the total number of loans and the number and percentage of loans that were seriously delinquent. Our analysis assumed that the loans in each ZIP code area were evenly distributed across the area. For example, if 80 percent of a ZIP code area fell within a given congressional district, we assumed that 80 percent of the loans in that ZIP code area were in the congressional district.

We reviewed documentation on the process LP uses to collect and ensure the reliability and integrity of its data. We discussed this process and the interpretation of different data fields with LP representatives. In addition, we conducted reasonableness checks on data elements to identify any missing, erroneous, or outlying data. We concluded that the data we used were sufficiently reliable for our purposes. We conducted our work in Washington, D.C., from September 2008 through June 2009 in accordance with all sections of GAO's Quality Assurance Framework that are relevant to our objectives. The framework requires that we plan and perform the engagement to obtain sufficient and appropriate evidence to meet our stated objectives and to discuss any limitations in our work. We believe that the evidence obtained provides a reasonable basis for our findings based on our audit objectives.

RESULTS IN BRIEF

Nonprime mortgage originations grew rapidly from 2000 through 2005 before sharply contracting in mid-2007. Subprime mortgages accounted for approximately two-thirds of the increase in nonprime originations over that period—rising from 457,000 in 2000 to 2.3 million in 2005—before declining somewhat in 2006. Alt-A originations, although a smaller share of the nonprime market, increased at an even faster rate than subprime originations, increasing 18-fold from 2000 through 2005. From 2000 through 2007, an increasing proportion of subprime and Alt-A mortgages had loan and borrower characteristics that have been associated with a higher likelihood of default and foreclosure. These characteristics include adjustable interest rates, less than full documentation of borrower income and assets, and higher debt service-to-income (DTI) ratios.[10]

Approximately 1.6 million of the 14.4 million nonprime loans originated from 2000 through 2007 had completed the foreclosure process as of March 31, 2009. Of the 5.2 million loans that were still active (i.e., not foreclosed or prepaid), almost one-quarter were either in default or in the foreclosure process (seriously delinquent), indicating that hundreds of thousands of additional nonprime borrowers are at risk of losing their homes in the near future.[11] Within the subprime market segment, about 28 percent of active loans were seriously delinquent, and within the active Alt-A segment, the serious delinquency rate was about 17 percent. Within both segments, serious delinquency rates were even higher for certain loan products with adjustable interest rates. Most of the serious delinquencies involved mortgages originated from 2004 through 2007. The rates varied widely across states and Census divisions, with the highest rate occurring in Florida (38 percent) and the lowest rate occurring in Wyoming (9 percent).

BACKGROUND

The mortgage market has four major segments that are defined, in part, by the credit quality of the borrowers and the types of mortgage institutions that serve them.

- *Prime*—Serves borrowers with strong credit histories and provides the most attractive interest rates and mortgage terms.
- *Nonprime*—Encompasses two categories of loans:
  - *Alt-A*—Generally serves borrowers whose credit histories are close to prime, but loans have one or more high-risk features such as limited documentation of income or assets or the option of making monthly payments that are lower than required for a fully amortizing loan.
  - *Subprime*—Generally serves borrowers with blemished credit and features higher interest rates and fees than the prime market.
- *Government-insured or government-guaranteed*—Primarily serves borrowers who may have difficulty qualifying for prime mortgages but features interest rates competitive with prime loans in return for payment of insurance premiums or guarantee fees. The Federal Housing Administration and Department of Veterans Affairs operate the two main federal programs that insure or guarantee mortgages.

Across all of these market segments, two types of loans are common: fixed-rate mortgages, which have interest rates that do not change over the life of the loan; and adjustable-rate mortgages (ARM), which have interest rates that can change periodically based on changes in a specified index. Additionally, loans are used for two general purposes: to finance the purchase of a home or refinance an existing loan.

The following categories are commonly used to describe the performance status of mortgages:

- *Current*—The borrower is meeting scheduled payments.
- *Delinquent*—The borrower has missed one or more scheduled monthly payments.
- *Default*—The borrower is 90 or more days delinquent.12 At this point, foreclosure proceedings against the borrower become a strong possibility.
- *Foreclosure*—A legal, and often lengthy, process with several possible outcomes, including that the borrower sells the property or the lender repossesses the home.
- *Prepaid*—The borrower has paid off the entire loan balance before it is due. Prepayment often occurs as a result of the borrower selling the home or refinancing into a new mortgage.

The nonprime market segment featured a number of nontraditional products and characteristics:[13]

- *Hybrid ARM*—Interest rate is fixed during an initial period then "resets" to an adjustable rate for the remaining term of the loan.
- *Payment-option ARM*—Borrower has multiple payment options each month, which may include minimum payments lower than what would be needed to cover any of the principal or all of the accrued interest. This feature is known as "negative amortization" because the outstanding loan balance may increase over time.
- *Interest-only*—Allows the borrower to pay just the interest on the loan for a specified period, usually the first 3 to 10 years, thereby deferring principal payments.

- *Low and no documentation loans*—Requires little or no verification of a borrower's income or assets.
- *High loan-to-value (LTV) ratios*—Borrower makes a small down payment, causing the ratio of the loan amount to the home value to be relatively high.
- *Prepayment penalties*—Borrower incurs a fee if he or she pays off the loan balance before it is due.

The nation's economy has been in recession since December 2007. The rising rate of unemployment and declining home prices has worsened the financial circumstances for many families and, with it, their ability to make their mortgage payments. According to the Bureau of Labor Statistics, as of June 2009, the nationwide unemployment rate was 9.5 percent, the highest rate since 1983. Additionally, over the past 2 years, house prices have declined in many areas of the country. For example, according to the Federal Housing Finance Agency's (FHFA) house price index, from the first quarter of 2008 through the first quarter of 2009, home prices in California and Florida both fell 22 percent.[14]

NONPRIME MORTGAGE LENDING INCREASED FROM 2000 THROUGH 2006 AND INCLUDED MANY LOANS WITH FEATURES ASSOCIATED WITH POOR LOAN PERFORMANCE

Nonprime Mortgage Originations Increased Rapidly from 2000 to 2005

As shown in figure 1, nonprime lending increased rapidly earlier in the decade before abruptly declining in 2007 as the nation entered a financial crisis. In the data we analyzed, about two-thirds of the nonprime mortgages originated from 2000 through 2007 were subprime loans.[15] The number of subprime originations increased more than five-fold from 2000 through 2005—rising from approximately 457,000 to about 2.3 million—before declining somewhat in 2006 and falling off sharply in 2007. Despite this generally rising trend, subprime loans accounted for a declining share of the nonprime market over this period because the volume of Alt-A originations increased at an even faster rate. Specifically, Alt-A originations grew 18-fold from 2000 through 2005—rising from approximately 78,000 to about 1.4 million—before declining in 2006 and declining further in 2007. As a result, the Alt-A share of the nonprime market increased from about 15 percent in 2000 to 43 percent in 2006, and continued to increase to 57 percent in 2007.

The majority of nonprime loans originated from 2000 through 2007 were used to refinance an existing loan rather than to purchase a home. The combination of rising home values and historically low interest rates provided homeowners with opportunities to reduce their mortgage payments and access the equity in their homes through refinancing. A substantial proportion of nonprime borrowers refinanced their mortgages at a higher amount than the loan balance to convert their home equity into money for personal use (known as "cash-out refinancing"). Of the subprime mortgages originated from 2000 through 2007, 55 percent were for cash-out refinancing, 9 percent were for no-cash-out refinancing, and 36 percent were for a home purchase. In 2003, for example, the number of subprime mortgages for cash-out refinancing totaled more than 740,000, the number of no-cash-out refinance loans was about 152,000, and the number of home purchase loans was just over 380,000 (see Figure 2). In contrast, about one-third of Alt-A loans originated from 2000 through 2007 were for cash-out refinancing, 16 percent were for no-cash-out refinancing, and 50 percent were for home purchases.

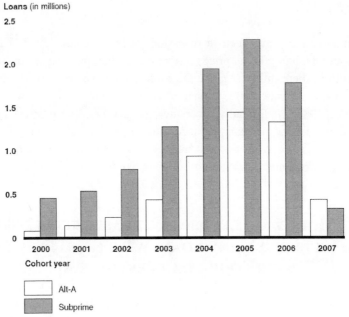

Source: GAO analysis of LP data.

Figure 1. Number of Subprime and Alt-A Originations by Cohort Year, 2000-2007.

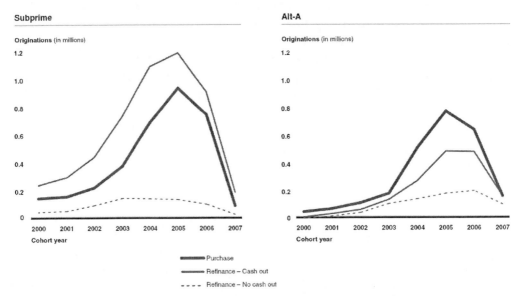

Source: GAO analysis of LP data.

Figure 2. Number of Nonprime Purchase and Refinance Loans by Cohort Year, 2000-2007.

Loan and Borrower Features Associated with a Higher Likelihood of Default and Foreclosure Became Common in 2000-2007

As we reported in 2007, more aggressive lending practices—that is, an easing of underwriting standards and wider use of certain loan features associated with poorer loan performance—contributed to recent increases in default and foreclosure rates.[16] Many loans were originated with a number of these features, a practice known as risk layering. These practices reduced the likelihood that some borrowers would be able to meet their mortgage obligations, particularly in times of economic stress or declining house prices. Because nonprime loans were often considered more profitable than prime loans, mortgage market participants had incentives to originate and securitize these loans despite their higher risks. Additionally, research suggests that some borrowers did not understand the true costs and risks of these loans, while others were willing to take on these risks to tap accumulated home equity or to obtain larger homes.

Loan-to-Value Ratios

A substantial amount of research indicates that loan-to-value (LTV) ratio is one of the most important factors in assessing the default risk of the borrower.[17] The higher the LTV ratio when a loan is originated, the less equity borrowers will have in their homes and the more likely they are to default on mortgage obligations, especially during times of financial stress. In recent years many borrowers used second liens, or "piggyback loans," to finance all or part of their down payment. Piggyback loans can result in higher combined loan-to-value (CLTV) ratios—that is, the LTV ratio taking both the first mortgage and piggyback loan into account.[18] As shown in figure 3, the average CLTV ratio for subprime loans rose from 78.0 percent in 2000 to 85.8 percent in 2006, before dropping slightly to 82.9 percent in 2007. In 2000 and 2001, average CLTV ratios for Alt-A loans were higher than those for subprime loans, but in 2002 and thereafter the reverse was true. Average CLTV ratios for Alt-A loans trended downward from 2000 through 2003 (from 81.3 percent to 76.3 percent) but rose to 82.4 percent by 2006, before declining to 80.3 percent in 2007. Furthermore, the percentage of loans with a CLTV ratio of at least 100 percent increased over the time period we examined in both the subprime and Alt-A markets. In 2000, 2.4 percent of subprime loans had a CLTV ratio of at least 100 percent. By 2006, this percentage had increased to 29.3 percent before falling to 17.5 percent in 2007. Likewise, 8.6 percent of Alt-A loans had a CLTV ratio of at least 100 percent in 2000. This percentage reached 19.5 percent by 2006 before falling to 14.5 percent in 2007.

Debt Service-to-Income Ratios

The debt service-to-income (DTI) ratio represents the percentage of a borrower's income that goes toward all recurring debt payments, including the mortgage payment. The higher the ratio, the greater the risk that the borrower will have cash flow problems and will miss mortgage payments. In the subprime market, average DTI ratios rose from 38.8 percent to 41.5 percent from 2000 through 2007. In the Alt-A market, average DTI ratios increased somewhat from 2000 through 2002, then decreased in 2003 before increasing to 37.3 percent in 2007 (see Figure 4). Additionally, the percentage of subprime and Alt-A loans with DTI ratios over 41 percent—the value used as a guideline in underwriting mortgages insured by the Federal Housing Administration—rose over the period we examined. Specifically, in the subprime market this percentage increased from 47.1 percent in 2000 to 59.3 percent in 2007. In the Alt-A market this percentage rose from 22.9 percent to 36.8 percent over the same time frame.[19]

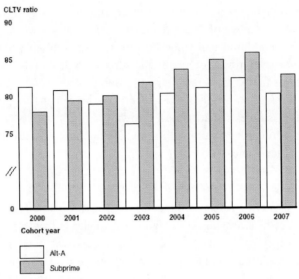

Source: GAO analysis of LP data.
Note: The LP data do not capture all second liens. As a result, the average CLTV ratios presented are likely lower than the actual averages.

Figure 3. Average CLTV Ratios for Nonprime Loans by Cohort Year, 2000-2007.

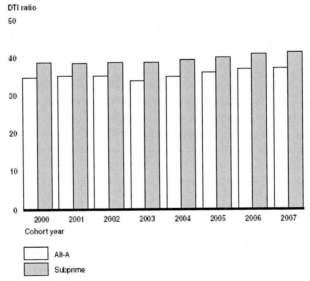

Source: GAO analysis of LP data.
Note: The figures presented are for the 61 percent of nonprime loans for which the data contained DTI information.

Figure 4. Average DTI Ratio for Nonprime Loans by Cohort Year, 2000-2007.

Adjustable Interest Rates

Mortgages with adjustable interest rates are generally considered to carry a higher default risk than comparable fixed-rate mortgages, in part because monthly payments increase when interest rates rise. In 2000, the number of subprime ARMs originated was about 262,000. [20] This number grew seven-fold to about 1.8 million originations in 2005, which represented the peak of the market for subprime ARMs. Likewise, originations of Alt-A ARMs increased substantially, growing from about 10,000 loans in 2000 to more than 893,000 in 2005. The largest increase occurred from 2003 to 2004, when the number of Alt-A ARMs grew almost five-fold, rising from about 117,000 to approximately 584,000 (see Figure 5).

Some of these ARMs were "short-term hybrid" loans that can lead to payment shock— that is, large increases in monthly payments as a result of higher interest rates. In this type of mortgage, the interest rate is fixed and relatively low during an initial period and then "resets" to an adjustable rate for the remaining term of the loan. In the subprime market, 2/28 and 3/27 mortgages—that is, fixed rate for 2 or 3 years and adjustable rate for the next 28 or 27 years—were common types of short-term hybrids. As the number of subprime loans nearly doubled from 2003 through 2005, the share of short-term hybrids grew as well, reaching nearly 80 percent of all subprime originations in 2005, or more than 1.7 million mortgages (see Figure 6). Over the entire 2000 through 2007 period, 70 percent of subprime mortgage originations were short-term hybrids. In contrast, short-term hybrids were not a common product in the Alt-A market segment.

Although short-term hybrid ARMs have the potential to produce payment shock, research suggests that most of the defaults for these loans have occurred well before the interest rate reset.[21] Nonetheless, interest rate resets may cause difficulties going forward, especially for borrowers whose loans were originated in more recent years. These borrowers may not be able to refinance to avoid payment shock because falling house prices and tightened underwriting standards may make it difficult for them to qualify for a new loan.

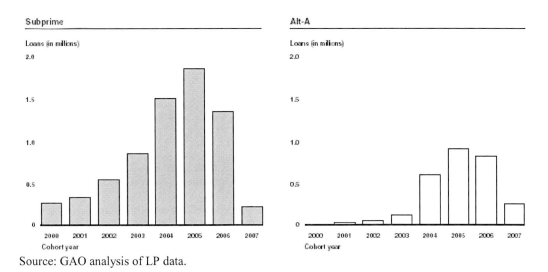

Source: GAO analysis of LP data.

Figure 5. Number of Subprime and Alt-A Loans with Adjustable Interest Rates by Cohort Year, 2000-2007.

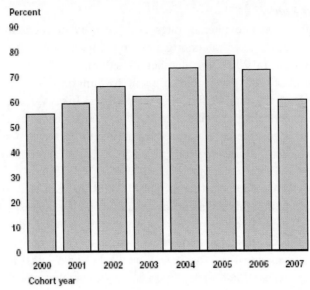

Source: GAO analysis of LP data.

Figure 6. Short-Term Hybrid ARMs as a Share of Subprime Mortgages by Cohort Year, 2000-2007.

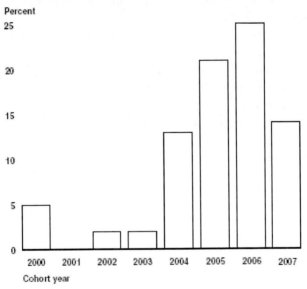

Source: GAO analysis of LP data.

Figure 7. Payment-Option ARMs as a Share of Alt-A Loans by Cohort Year, 2000-2007.

Approximately 17 percent of Alt-A loans originated from 2000 through 2007 were another type of ARM known as payment-option ARMs. For an initial period of typically 5 years or when the loan balance reaches a specified cap, this product provides the borrower with multiple payment options each month, including minimum payments that are lower than what would be needed to cover any of the principal or all of the accrued interest. After the initial period, payments are "recast" to include an amount that will fully amortize the outstanding balance over the remaining loan term. Consequently, payment-option ARMs can result in payment shock, especially if the loan balance increased because the borrower was making only the minimum payment. As we reported in 2006, payment-option ARMs were once specialized products for financially sophisticated borrowers but ultimately became more widespread. According to federal banking regulators and a range of industry participants, as home prices increased rapidly in some areas of the country, lenders began marketing payment-option ARMs as affordability products and made them available to less-creditworthy and lower-income borrowers.[22] As shown in figure 7, the percentage of Alt-A loans that were payment-option ARMs was 5 percent or less from 2000 to 2003, before rising sharply in 2004. From 2004 to 2006, that percentage increased from 13 percent to 25 percent, before dropping to 14 percent in 2007.

Prepayment Penalties

Prepayment penalties are another mortgage feature that some research has associated with a higher likelihood of default.[23] Prepayment penalties can be an obstacle to refinancing into a more affordable loan because borrowers must pay the penalty if they pay off the original loan before the prepayment period expires. Further, research indicates that many borrowers may not have realized that their mortgages include a prepayment penalty. For the entire 8-year period we examined, the percentage of subprime loans with prepayment penalties exceeded 60 percent each year. In contrast, only 21 percent of Alt-A mortgages had prepayment penalties in 2000, but this percentage increased to 46 percent by 2006 (see Figure 8).

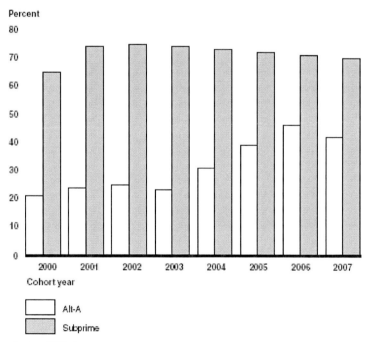

Source: GAO analysis of LP data.

Figure 8. Percentage of Nonprime Loans with Prepayment Penalties by Cohort Year, 2000-2007.

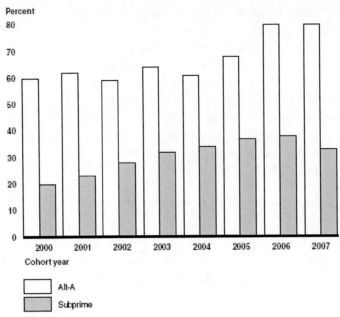

Source: GAO analysis of LP data.

Figure 9. Percentage of Nonprime Loans with Low or No Documentation.

Low or No Documentation

Low or no documentation of income or assets allows borrowers to provide less detailed financial information than is traditionally required. This feature was originally intended for borrowers who may have difficulty documenting income, such as the self-employed, but eventually became more widespread.[24] Such loans can be problematic if borrowers or loan originators overstate income or assets to qualify borrowers for mortgages they cannot afford. From 2000 through 2007, the percentage of Alt-A mortgages that did not have full documentation of borrower income, assets, or both rose from 60 percent to 80 percent.[25] For subprime loans, the proportion of low and no documentation mortgages grew from 20 percent to 38 percent, then decreased to 33 percent over the same period (see Figure 9).

Enclosures I and II provide more detailed information about the characteristics of nonprime loans originated from 2000 through 2007.

SERIOUS DELINQUENCY RATES WERE HIGHEST FOR SUBPRIME LOANS, CERTAIN ADJUSTABLE-RATE MORTGAGES, AND RECENT LOAN COHORTS AND VARIED WIDELY ACROSS STATES AND REGIONS

As of March 31, 2009, approximately 1.6 million of the 14.4 million nonprime loans (11 percent) originated from 2000 through 2007 had completed the foreclosure process. Subprime mortgages accounted for about 80 percent of these loans and Alt-A mortgages accounted for the remaining 20 percent. Additionally, about 7.6 million of the 14.4 million loans (53 percent) originated had prepaid as of March 31, 2009 (see Figure 10). Because many of these prepaid loans were due to borrowers refinancing into new nonprime mortgages, the total number of originations over the period we examined far exceeds the number of individual borrowers. For the majority of the 5.2 million nonprime loans that were still active as of March 31, 2009, the borrowers were current on their payments. However, about 1.2 million, or 23 percent, of these active loans were seriously delinquent (either in default or in the foreclosure process), indicating that hundreds of thousands of additional nonprime borrowers are at risk of losing their homes in the near future. [26] Specifically, about 594,000 (11 percent) of active nonprime loans were in default and about 613,000 (12 percent) were in the foreclosure process, as shown in figure 10. Within the subprime market segment, about 775,000 loans (28 percent) were seriously delinquent. Among active Alt-A mortgages, approximately 433,000 (17 percent) were seriously delinquent.

Serious delinquency rates were higher for certain adjustable-rate products common in the subprime and Alt-A market segments than they were for the market segments as a whole. As previously discussed, short-term hybrid ARMs accounted for the majority of subprime mortgage originations in recent years (e.g., 72 percent in 2006). As of March 31, 2009, 38 percent (about 584,000) of active short-term hybrid ARMs were seriously delinquent, a rate 10 percentage points higher than that for the entire subprime market (see Figure 11). In the Alt-A market segment, payment-option ARMs became a prominent product, accounting for about 25 percent of Alt-A loans originated in 2006. As of March 31, 2009, approximately 30 percent (about 122,000) of active payment-option ARMs were seriously delinquent, a rate about 13 percentage points higher than for the Alt-A market segment as a whole.

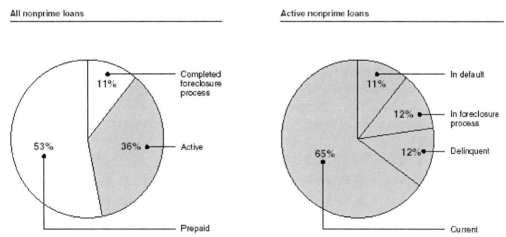

Source: GAO analysis of LP data.

Note: We considered a loan to be delinquent if the borrower was 30 to 89 days late on his or her mortgage payments. We considered a loan to be in default if the borrower was 90 or more days late.

Figure 10. Percentage of All Nonprime Loans and All Active Nonprime Loans Originated from 2000 through 2007, by Performance Status as of March 31, 2009.

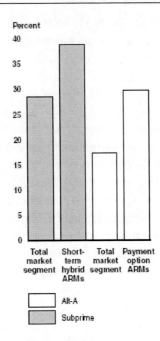

Source: GAO analysis of LP data.

Figure 11. Percentage of Short-Term Hybrid ARMs and Payment-Option ARMs That Were Seriously Delinquent as of March 31, 2009.

Performance of Nonprime Loans by Cohort

Mortgages originated from 2004 through 2007 accounted for the majority of troubled loans. Of the active subprime loans originated from 2000 through 2007, 92 percent of those that were seriously delinquent as of March 31, 2009, were from those four cohorts. Furthermore, loans from those cohorts made up 71 percent of the subprime mortgages that had completed the foreclosure process. This pattern was even more pronounced in the Alt-A market. Among active Alt-A loans, almost all (98 percent) of the loans that were seriously delinquent as of March 31, 2009, were from the 2004 through 2007 cohorts. Likewise, 93 percent of the loans that had completed the foreclosure process as of that date were from those cohorts.

Cumulative foreclosure rates show that the percentage of mortgages completing the foreclosure process increased for each successive loan cohort (see Figure 12). Within 2 years of loan origination, 2 percent of the subprime loans originated in 2004 had completed the foreclosure process, compared with 3 percent of the 2005 cohort, 6 percent of the 2006 cohort, and 8 percent of the 2007 cohort. Within 3 years of loan origination, 5 percent of the 2004 cohort had completed the foreclosure process, compared with 8 percent and 16 percent of the 2005 and 2006 cohorts, respectively. The trend was similar for Alt-A loans, although Alt-A loans foreclosed at a slower rate than subprime loans. For example, within 3 years of origination, 1 percent of Alt-A loans originated in 2004 had completed the foreclosure process, compared with 2 percent of the loans originated in 2005, and 8 percent of the loans originated in 2006.[27]

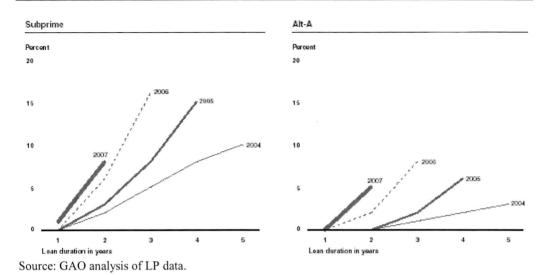

Source: GAO analysis of LP data.

Figure 12. Cumulative Percentage of Subprime and Alt-A Loans That Completed the Foreclosure Process by Cohort Year, 2004-2007.

This trend is partly attributable to a stagnation or decline in home prices in much of the country beginning in 2005 and worsening in subsequent years. This situation made it more difficult for some borrowers to sell or refinance their homes to avoid default or foreclosure. In addition, borrowers who purchased homes (particularly for investment purposes) but now owed more than the properties were worth, had incentives to stop making mortgage payments in order to minimize their financial losses. The deterioration in credit quality for the successive cohorts may also reflect an increase in riskier loan and borrower characteristics, such as less than full documentation of borrower income and higher DTI ratios.

Enclosures III and IV provide more detailed information about the performance of nonprime loans by cohort year and product type.

Performance of Nonprime Loans by Census Division, State, and Congressional District

The proportion of active nonprime mortgages that were seriously delinquent as of March 31, 2009, varied across Census divisions and states (see Figure 13). Among the nine Census divisions, the South Atlantic had the highest rate of seriously delinquent loans (28 percent) and the West South Central had the lowest rate (13 percent).[28] Only three regions—West South Central, West North Central, and East South Central—had serious delinquency rates of less than 20 percent.

At the state level, six states—California, Florida, Illinois, Massachusetts, Nevada, and New Jersey—had the highest serious delinquency rates as of March 31, 2009 (see Figure 14). Each state had rates above 25 percent, and Florida's rate of 38 percent was the highest in the country. Twelve states had serious delinquency rates between 20 and 25 percent, and 21 states and the District of Columbia had serious delinquency rates between 15 and 20 percent. The remaining 12 states had serious delinquency rates of less than 15 percent, including Wyoming's rate of 9 percent, which was the lowest in the country.

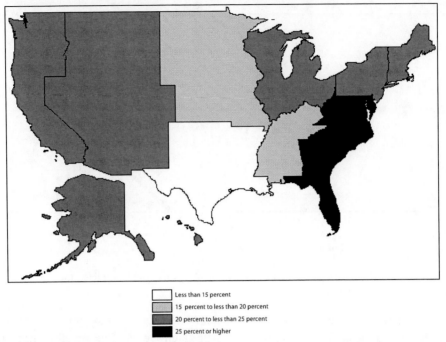

Less than 15 percent
15 percent to less than 20 percent
20 percent to less than 25 percent
25 percent or higher

Source: GAO analysis of LP data, map (MapInfo).

Figure 13. Serious Delinquency Rates by Census Division as of March 31, 2009.

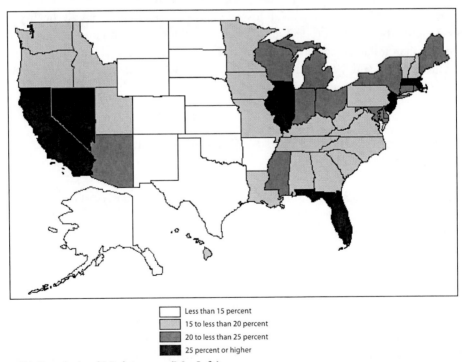

Less than 15 percent
15 to less than 20 percent
20 to less than 25 percent
25 percent or higher

Source: GAO analysis of LP data, map (MapInfo).

Figure 14. Serious Delinquency Rates by State as of March 31, 2009.

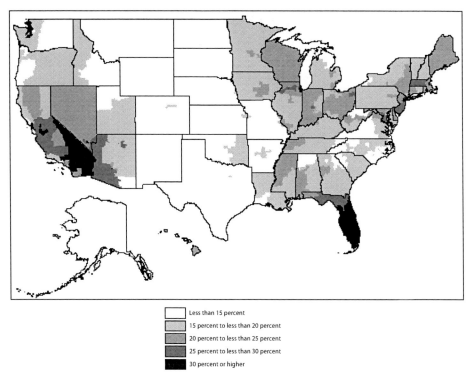

Less than 15 percent

15 percent to less than 20 percent

20 percent to less than 25 percent

25 percent to less than 30 percent

30 percent or higher

Source: GAO analysis of LP data, map (MapInfo).

Figure 15. Estimated Serious Delinquency Rates by Congressional District as of March 31, 2009.

Of the 6 states with the highest serious delinquency rates, the "Sunbelt" states—California, Florida, and Nevada—have been more dramatically affected by the changes in the nonprime mortgage market than other regions of the country. These states experienced particularly large drop-offs in house price appreciation after a period of strong growth. In addition to high rates of seriously delinquent loans, these states accounted for a substantial proportion of active nonprime loans nationwide. More specifically, as of March 31, 2009, these three states combined represented 34 percent of all active nonprime loans and 45 percent of all seriously delinquent nonprime loans. In contrast, Illinois, Massachusetts, and New Jersey together accounted for about 7 percent of active nonprime loans and 9 percent of seriously delinquent nonprime loans as of March 31, 2009.

Serious delinquency rates also varied by congressional district within each state, as shown in figure 15 below.[29] For more detailed data on the performance of nonprime loans by Census division, state, and congressional district, see enclosures V and VI.

William B. Shear
Director, Financial Markets and Community Investment Enclosures

ENCLOSURES I. CHARACTERISTICS OF NONPRIME LOANS BY COHORT YEAR, 2000-2007

This enclosure contains the results of our analysis of LoanPerformance (LP) data on loan and borrower characteristics for nonprime mortgages originated from 2000 through 2007. Tables 1 and 2 show the percentage and number, respectively, of nonprime mortgages that were subprime and Alt-A loans.[30] Tables 3 and 4 provide the percentage and number, respectively, of nonprime mortgages by loan purpose (purchase or refinance) and loan type (adjustable-rate mortgage [ARM] or fixed-rate mortgage). Table 5 shows the proportion of subprime loans that were short-term hybrid ARMs and the proportion of Alt-A loans that were payment-options ARMs. Tables 6 and 7 provide the percentage and number, respectively, of nonprime mortgages with selected loan and borrower characteristics, as well as mean values for a number of variables such as loan amount at origination and borrower FICO score at origination.

Table 1. Percentage of Nonprime Loans by Market Segment, 2000-2007.

Market segment	2000	2001	2002	2003	2004	2005	2006	2007	Total
Subprime	85%	80%	77%	75%	68%	61%	57%	43%	65%
Alt-A	15%	20%	23%	25%	32%	39%	43%	57%	35%
Total	100%	100%	100%	100%	100%	100%	100%	100%	100%

Source: GAO analysis of LP data.

Table 2. Number of Nonprime Loans by Market Segment, 2000-2007.

Market segment	2000	2001	2002	2003	2004	2005	2006	2007	Total
Subprime	456,631	537,734	784,963	1,281,732	1,947,427	2,284,420	1,782,677	330,514	9,406,098
Alt-A	78,183	138,645	231,404	435,703	936,667	1,447,782	1,329,629	436,078	5,034,091
Total	534,814	676,379	1,016,367	1,717,435	2,884,094	3,732,202	3,112,306	766,592	14,440,189

Source: GAO analysis of LP data.

Table 3. Percentage of Nonprime Loans by Purpose and Type, 2000-2007.

		2000	2001	2002	2003	2004	2005	2006	2007	Total
Loan purpose										
Purchase		39%	36%	34%	33%	42%	46%	45%	34%	41%
	Subprime share of purchase	74%	68%	66%	68%	58%	55%	54%	37%	58%
	Alt-A share of purchase	26%	32%	34%	32%	42%	45%	46%	63%	42%
Refinance		61%	64%	66%	67%	58%	54%	55%	66%	59%
	Subprime share of refinance	93%	86%	83%	78%	75%	67%	60%	46%	70%
	Cash out	81%	81%	81%	82%	88%	89%	89%	84%	86%
	No cash out	18%	16%	18%	17%	12%	11%	11%	16%	14%
	Unknown	2%	3%	1%	1%	0%	0%	0%	0%	0%
	Alt-A share of refinance	7%	14%	17%	22%	25%	33%	40%	54%	30%
	Cash out	67%	63%	59%	56%	65%	73%	70%	61%	67%
	No cash out	31%	36%	41%	44%	34%	27%	29%	39%	33%
	Unknown	2%	0%	0%	0%	1%	0%	0%	0%	0%
Loan type										
ARM		51%	52%	58%	56%	72%	73%	69%	60%	66%
	Subprime share of ARM	96%	93%	91%	88%	72%	67%	62%	46%	71%
	Alt-A share of ARM	4%	7%	9%	12%	28%	33%	38%	54%	29%
Fixed-rate mortgage		42%	43%	40%	43%	28%	26%	27%	35%	32%
	Subprime share of fixed rate	70%	62%	57%	58%	57%	43%	42%	33%	51%
	Alt-A share of fixed rate	30%	38%	43%	42%	43%	57%	58%	67%	49%
Other		8%	5%	2%	1%	0%	0%	4%	4%	2%
	Subprime share of other	96%	90%	83%	51%	36%	92%	77%	79%	80%
	Alt-A share of other	4%	10%	17%	49%	64%	8%	23%	21%	20%

Source: GAO analysis of LP data.

Note: Percentages for ARMs and fixed-rate mortgages do not include balloon mortgages, which account for most of the "other" category. Balloon mortgages can have fixed or adjustable interest rates.

Table 4. Number of Nonprime Loans by Purpose and Type, 2000-2007.

		2000	2001	2002	2003	2004	2005	2006	2007	Total
Loan purpose										
Purchase		206,020	240,156	345,338	567,899	1,210,349	1,719,131	1,396,567	264,018	5,949,478
	Subprime share of purchase	152,312	164,460	228,531	383,789	698,278	943,877	754,552	98,913	3,424,712
	Alt-A share of purchase		75,696	116,807	184,110	512,071	775,254	642,015	165,105	2,524,766
Refinance		328,794	436,223	671,029	1,149,536	1,673,745	2,013,071	1,715,739	502,574	8,490,711
	Subprime share of refinance	304,319	373,274	556,432	897,943	1,249,149	1,340,543	1,028,125	231,601	5,981,386
	Cash out	246,366	303,143	448,038	740,493	1,098,668	1,196,493	917,552	194,871	5,145,624
	No cash out	53,348	60,752	101,679	152,131	149,906	143,723	109,995	36,705	808,239
	Unknown	4,605	9,379	6,715	5,319	575	327	578	25	27,523
	Alt-A share of refinance	24,475	62,949	114,597	251,593	424,596	672,528	687,614	270,973	2,509,325
	Cash out	16,484	39,958	67,923	140,426	276,758	487,753	482,900	165,237	1,677,439
	No cash out	7,611	22,969	46,524	110,523	144,656	183,841	202,696	105,728	824,548
	Unknown	380	22	150	644	3,182	934	2,018	8	7,338
Loan type										
ARM		272,048	349,910	590,558	958,430	2,066,473	2,737,410	2,146,756	462,172	9,583,757
	Subprime share of ARM	261,975	325,047	537,833	841,067	1,482,569	1,844,167	1,339,129	213,672	
	Alt-A share of ARM	10,073	24,863	52,725	117,363	583,904	893,243	807,627	248,500	2,738,298
Fixed-rate mortgage		222,649	291,084	403,665	738,662	807,994	977,629	851,171	271,284	4,564,138
	Subprime share of fixed rate	155,992	180,742	228,828	430,208	461,372	424,407	355,315	90,698	2,327,562
	Alt-A share of fixed rate	66,657	110,342	174,837	308,454	346,622	553,222	495,856	180,586	2,236,576
Other		40,117	35,385	22,144	20,343	9,627	17,163	114,379	33,136	292,294
	Subprime share of other	38,664	31,945	18,302	10,457	3,486	15,846	88,233	26,144	233,077
	Alt-A share of other	1,453	3,440	3,842	9,886	6,141	1,317	26,146	6,992	59,217

Source: GAO analysis of LP data.

Note: Numbers for ARMs and fixed-rate mortgages do not include balloon mortgages, which account for most of the "other" category. Balloon mortgages can have fixed or adjustable interest rates.

Table 5. Short-term Hybrid ARMs as a Percentage of Subprime Market and Payment-option ARMs as a Percentage of Alt-A Market, 2000-2007.

	2000	2001	2002	2003	2004	2005	2006	2007	Total
Number of subprime short term hybrid ARMsA	248,964	316,119	516,804	798,136	1,429,475	1,787,984	1,290,983	198,240	6,586,705
Short-term hybrid ARMsas a percentage of subprime market	55%	59%	66%	62%	73%	78%	72%	60%	70%
Number of Alt-A payment-option ARMs	4,217	682	4,570	7,572	123,202	310,140	326,298	60,523	837,204
Payment-option ARMsas a percentage of Alt-A market	5%	0%	2%	2%	13%	21%	25%	14%	17%

Source: GAO analysis of LP data.

Table 6. Percentage of Subprime and Alt-A Loans with Selected Loan and Borrower Characteristics and Mean Values for Key Variables, 2000-2007.

	2000	2001	2002	2003	2004	2005	2006	2007	Total
Low or no documentation of borrower assets or income									
Subprime	20%	23%	28%	32%	34%	37%	38%	33%	33%
Alt-A	60%	62%	59%	64%	61%	68%	80%	80%	70%
Prepayment penalty									
Subprime	65%	74%	75%	74%	73%	72%	71%	70%	72%
Alt-A	21%	24%	25%	23%	31%	39%	46%	42%	37%
Negative amortization feature									
Subprime	0%	0%	0%	0%	0%	0%	0%	0%	0%
Alt-A	7%	3%	2%	2%	15%	25%	30%	31%	21%
Owner-occupant									
Subprime	91%	92%	92%	92%	92%	92%	92%	92%	92%
Alt-A	78%	85%	77%	69%	73%	74%	76%	76%	75%

Table 6. (Continued)

	2000	2001	2002	2003	2004	2005	2006	2007	Total
Mean loan amount at origination									
Subprime	$103,607	$125,545	$145,213	$164,204	$179,520	$199,488	$211,773	$218,462	$180,130
Alt-A	$219,543	$263,053	$250,274	$228,621	$259,784	$290,963	$324,220	$378,106	$292,350
Mean unpaid balance as of March 31, 2009									
Subprime	$68,745	$80,927	$95,081	$126,088	$146,205	$183,110	$204,672	$217,694	$183,026
Subprime number	62,050	59,788	79,755	180,689	362,823	740,157	986,353	246,744	2,718,359
Alt-A	$129,663	$186,629	$186,854	$180,395	$225,842	$279,133	$322,093	$379,044	$295,237
Alt A number	9,982	16,720	37,621	144,142	313,548	747,545	882,924	354,027	2,506,509
Mean borrower FICO score at origination									
Subprime	592	600	608	618	618	621	618	614	616
Alt-A	700	701	705	711	708	711	706	712	709
Mean combined loan-to-value ratio at origination									
Subprime	78.0	79.5	80.1	81.9	83.6	84.9	85.8	82.9	83.3
Alt-A	81.3	80.8	79.0	76.3	80.4	81.1	82.4	80.3	80.7
Mean debt service-to-income ratio at origination									
Subprime	38.8	38.5	38.9	38.9	39.4	40.2	41.1	41.5	39.9
Alt-A	34.8	35.2	35.3	33.9	35.1	36.1	37.0	37.3	36.1

Source: GAO analysis of LP data

Note: The LP data do not capture all second liens. As a result, the average combined loan-to-value ratios presented are likely lower than the actual averages. Also, 29 percent of the subprime loans and 56 percent of the Alt-A loans in the LP database did not contain information on the debt service-to-income ratio.

Table 7. Number of Subprime and Alt-A Loans with Selected Loan and Borrower Characteristics and Mean Values for Key Variables, 2000-2007.

	2000	2001	2002	2003	2004	2005	2006	2007	Total
Low or no documentation of borrower assets or income									
Subprime	91,351	122,431	220,782	405,280	652,803	836,791	672,090	109,920	**3,111,448**
Alt-A	46,836	85,732	136,499	276,760	571,862	991,704	1,061,630	348,937	**3,519,960**
Prepayment penalty									
Subprime	298,079	399,587	587,047	944,735	1,416,438	1,655,200	1,266,061	231,417	**6,798,564**
Alt-A	16,041	32,955	57,956	102,275	293,737	565,703	612,818	182,073	**1,863,558**
Negative amortization feature									
Subprime	168	92	124	94	140	588	269	22	**1,497**
Alt-A	5,761	4,402	5,276	10,131	136,390	355,230	397,196	136,954	**1,051,340**
Owner-occupant									
Subprime	415,913	492,220	721,559	1,177,982	1,785,929	2,094,208	1,635,348	303,421	**8,626,580**
Alt-A	60,715	117,252	178,180	299,683	686,744	1,074,917	1,014,307	331,494	**3,763,292**

Source: GAO analysis of LP data.

This enclosure contains the results of our analysis of LoanPerformance (LP) data on the distribution of initial interest rates at loan origination for nonprime mortgages originated from 2000 through 2007. Tables 8 and 9 provide information in percentages and total numbers, respectively.

Table 8. Percentage of Nonprime Loans in Different Initial Interest Rate Ranges by Cohort Year, 2000-2007.

Interest rate range	2000	2001	2002	2003	2004	2005	2006	2007	Totals
Subprime fixed rate	34%	34%	29%	34%	24%	19%	20%	27%	25%
0.1% – 5.0%	0%	1%	0%	2%	2%	1%	0%	0%	1%
5.1% - 6.0%	0%	1%	3%	16%	24%	20%	4%	4%	13%
6.1% - 7.0%	1%	9%	20%	34%	35%	34%	22%	18%	26%
7.1% - 8.0%	5%	18%	30%	27%	23%	26%	30%	25%	25%
8.1% - 9.0%	14%	21%	23%	13%	10%	12%	24%	23%	16%
9.1% - 10.0%	21%	21%	13%	5%	3%	4%	13%	17%	9%
Greater than 10%	59%	29%	11%	2%	1%	2%	7%	13%	10%
Subprime short-term hybrid ARM	55%	59%	66%	62%	73%	78%	72%	60%	70%
0.1% – 5.0%	3%	1%	2%	1%	3%	1%	0%	1%	1%
5.1% - 6.0%	0%	0%	2%	12%	21%	16%	2%	3%	11%
6.1% - 7.0%	0%	3%	13%	30%	34%	34%	16%	15%	25%
7.1% - 8.0%	2%	14%	27%	31%	26%	28%	33%	28%	27%
8.1% - 9.0%	12%	26%	29%	17%	11%	14%	28%	28%	19%
9.1% - 10.0%	29%	28%	17%	6%	3%	5%	14%	17%	10%
Greater than 10%	54%	29%	10%	3%	1%	2%	6%	8%	7%

Table 8. (Continued)

Interest rate range	2000	2001	2002	2003	2004	2005	2006	2007	Totals
Subprime other ARM	**3%**	**2%**	**3%**	**3%**	**3%**	**2%**	**3%**	**5%**	**3%**
0.1% – 5.0%	4%	5%	11%	18%	15%	7%	1%	1%	9%
5.1% - 6.0%	2%	6%	9%	17%	32%	33%	10%	10%	20%
6.1% - 7.0%	4%	11%	14%	27%	31%	34%	30%	20%	27%
7.1% - 8.0%	8%	15%	22%	22%	16%	17%	30%	22%	20%
8.1% - 9.0%	13%	21%	23%	11%	5%	6%	17%	20%	12%
9.1% - 10.0%	23%	19%	13%	3%	1%	2%	8%	14%	7%
Greater than 10%	45%	23%	8%	1%	0%	1%	4%	13%	6%
Subprime other	**8%**	**6%**	**2%**	**1%**	**0%**	**1%**	**5%**	**8%**	**2%**
0.1% – 5.0%	0%	0%	0%	1%	10%	1%	0%	0%	0%
5.1% - 6.0%	0%	0%	2%	10%	30%	19%	4%	4%	4%
6.1% - 7.0%	0%	2%	10%	28%	33%	41%	30%	20%	19%
7.1% - 8.0%	1%	10%	27%	33%	16%	26%	36%	29%	24%
8.1% - 9.0%	7%	21%	28%	17%	6%	9%	20%	24%	18%
9.1% - 10.0%	21%	26%	19%	8%	3%	3%	7%	14%	13%
Greater than 10%	70%	40%	14%	3%	1%	1%	3%	8%	20%
Alt-A fixed rate	**85%**	**80%**	**76%**	**71%**	**37%**	**38%**	**37%**	**41%**	**44%**
0.1% – 5.0%	0%	0%	0%	11%	5%	1%	0%	0%	3%
5.1% - 6.0%	0%	2%	15%	53%	57%	61%	12%	26%	37%
6.1% - 7.0%	0%	22%	40%	27%	31%	29%	57%	53%	37%
7.1% - 8.0%	10%	42%	30%	8%	6%	7%	23%	15%	15%
8.1% - 9.0%	47%	25%	11%	2%	1%	1%	6%	4%	6%
9.1% - 10.0%	35%	7%	3%	0%	0%	0%	1%	2%	2%
Greater than 10%	8%	2%	1%	0%	0%	0%	0%	1%	0%

Table 8. (Continued)

Interest rate range	2000	2001	2002	2003	2004	2005	2006	2007	Totals
Alt-A payment-option ARM	**5%**	**0%**	**2%**	**2%**	**13%**	**21%**	**25%**	**14%**	**17%**
0.1% – 5.0%	100%	100%	100%	97%	99%	100%	94%	91%	97%
5.1% - 6.0%	0%	0%	0%	2%	0%	0%	0%	0%	0%
6.1% - 7.0%	0%	0%	0%	1%	1%	0%	2%	0%	1%
7.1% - 8.0%	0%	0%	0%	0%	0%	0%	4%	5%	2%
8.1% - 9.0%	0%	0%	0%	0%	0%	0%	1%	4%	1%
9.1% - 10.0%	0%	0%	0%	0%	0%	0%	0%	0%	0%
Greater than 10%	0%	0%	0%	0%	0%	0%	0%	0%	0%
Alt-A other ARM	**7%**	**17%**	**21%**	**25%**	**49%**	**40%**	**36%**	**43%**	**38%**
0.1% – 5.0%	28%	19%	22%	44%	44%	19%	12%	26%	26%
5.1% - 6.0%	2%	13%	34%	36%	41%	47%	18%	17%	34%
6.1% - 7.0%	5%	34%	27%	14%	12%	25%	45%	34%	28%
7.1% - 8.0%	13%	22%	13%	5%	2%	7%	20%	17%	10%
8.1% - 9.0%	33%	9%	4%	1%	0%	1%	3%	5%	2%
9.1% - 10.0%	13%	3%	1%	0%	0%	0%	0%	1%	0%
Greater than 10%	6%	1%	0%	0%	0%	0%	0%	1%	0%
Alt-A other	**2%**	**2%**	**2%**	**2%**	**1%**	**0%**	**2%**	**2%**	**1%**
0.1% – 5.0%	0%	0%	1%	37%	64%	13%	33%	18%	30%
5.1% - 6.0%	0%	0%	1%	32%	25%	16%	4%	11%	11%
6.1% - 7.0%	0%	2%	15%	17%	8%	38%	31%	41%	24%
7.1% - 8.0%	1%	30%	43%	11%	2%	23%	23%	22%	20%
8.1% - 9.0%	21%	42%	29%	2%	1%	7%	8%	6%	10%
9.1% - 10.0%	53%	18%	9%	0%	0%	2%	2%	2%	4%
Greater than 10%	25%	8%	2%	0%	1%	1%	0%	0%	1%

Source: GAO analysis of LP data.

Table 9. Number of Nonprime Loans in Different Initial Interest Rate Ranges by Cohort Year, 2000-2007.

Interest rate range	2000	2001	2002	2003	2004	2005	2006	2007	Total
Subprime fixed rate	155,992	180,742	228,828	430,208	461,372	424,407	355,315	90,698	2,327,562
0.1% – 5.0%	100	1,908	910	8,216	8,087	3,734	1,326	58	24,339
5.1% – 6.0%	213	1,484	7,980	69,875	112,784	84,258	14,951	3,456	295,001
6.1% – 7.0%	1,229	16,956	45,172	146,914	163,308	145,963	76,904	15,967	612,413
7.1% – 8.0%	7,813	32,520	67,808	117,937	108,385	110,702	107,444	22,492	575,101
8.1% – 9.0%	21,407	37,394	52,410	55,851	47,449	52,721	83,535	21,165	3 71,932
9.1% – 10.0%	32,768	38,007	29,877	21,511	15,423	19,069	45,188	15,598	217,441
Greater than 10%	92,462	52,473	24,671	9,904	5,936	7,960	25,967	11,962	231,335
Subprime short-term hybrid ARM	248,964	316,119	516,804	798,136	1,429,475	1,787,984	1,290,983	198,240	6,586,705
0.1% – 5.0%	6,655	1,966	8,915	9,382	43,131	21,154	525	2,370	94,098
5.1% – 6.0%	813	400	11,702	94,297	296,382	283,511	26,126	5,536	718,767
6.1% – 7.0%	911	10,225	68,333	240,971	491,613	612,667	209,368	29,640	1,663,728
7.1% – 8.0%	4,973	43,088	139,553	244,252	371,576	501,701	427,209	56,040	1,788,392
8.1% – 9.0%	30,236	81,772	148,706	138,028	162,516	254,383	366,393	54,950	1,236,984
9.1% – 10.0%	71,264	88,211	87,993	50,074	47,272	86,912	186,433	33,723	651,882
Greater than 10%	134,112	90,457	51,602	21,132	16,985	27,656	74,929	15,981	432,854
Subprime other ARM	13,011	8,928	21,029	42,931	53,094	56,183	48,146	15,432	258,754
0.1% – 5.0%	468	444	2,237	7,623	7,726	3,791	464	148	22,901
5.1% – 6.0%	309	506	1,890	7,485	16,952	18,635	4,662	1,526	51,965
6.1% – 7.0%	540	941	3,014	11,667	16,235	19,146	14,338	3,048	68,929
7.1% – 8.0%	1,058	1,381	4,606	9,386	8,472	9,422	14,328	3,393	52,046
8.1% – 9.0%	1,751	1,876	4,901	4,712	2,743	3,430	8,388	3,132	3 0,933
9.1% – 10.0%	2,982	1,713	2,791	1,490	758	1,279	3,978	2,235	17,226
Greater than 10%	5,903	2,067	1,590	568	208	480	1,988	1,950	14,754
Subprime other	38,664	31,945	18,302	10,457	3,486	15,846	88,233	26,144	233,077

Table 9. (Continued)

Interest rate range	2000	2001	2002	2003	2004	2005	2006	2007	Total
Subprime other									
0.1% – 5.0%	40	16	30	113	356	130	28	12	725
5.1% - 6.0%	13	119	277	1,056	1,033	2,975	3,748	1,023	10,244
6.1% - 7.0%	74	746	1,870	2,910	1,150	6,568	26,615	5,293	45,226
7.1% - 8.0%	485	3,299	5,031	3,441	571	4,111	31,923	7,592	56,453
8.1% - 9.0%	2,751	6,606	5,197	1,816	223	1,504	17,300	6,338	41,735
9.1% - 10.0%	8,112	8,299	3,406	808	107	432	6,229	3,679	3 1,072
Greater than 10%	27,189	12,860	2,491	313	46	126	2,390	2,207	47,622
Alt-A fixed rate	66,657	110,342	174,837	308,454	3 46,622	553,222	495,856	180,586	2,236,576
0.1% – 5.0%	105	111	708	32,749	17,411	8,239	637	648	60,608
5.1% - 6.0%	62	1,863	26,000	162,263	197,470	338,058	61,088	46,551	833,355
6.1% - 7.0%	328	24,335	69,550	81,877	107,620	160,787	283,500	94,851	8 22,848
7.1% - 8.0%	6,706	46,239	52,651	25,634	19,674	38,611	113,852	26,795	33 0,162
8.1% - 9.0%	31,279	27,830	19,523	5,359	3,771	6,792	29,767	7,862	132,183
9.1% - 10.0%	23,128	8,086	5,438	523	528	664	5,647	2,949	46,963
Greater than 10%	5,049	1,878	967	49	148	71	1,365	930	10,457
Payment-option ARM	4,217	682	4,570	7,572	123,202	310,140	326,298	60,523	837,204
0.1% – 5.0%	4,207	679	4,549	7,368	121,817	309,147	305,422	55,039	8 08,228
5.1% - 6.0%	7	3	8	157	614	658	662	21	2,130
6.1% - 7.0%	2	-	13	46	769	283	5,005	209	6,327
7.1% - 8.0%	1	-	-	-	2	43	12,266	2,911	15,223
8.1% - 9.0%	-	-	-	-	-	9	2,891	2,283	5,183
9.1% - 10.0%	-	-	-	-	-	-	52	60	112
Greater than 10%	-	-	-	1	-	-	-	-	1
Alt-A other ARM	5,856	24,181	48,155	109,791	460,702	583,103	481,329	187,977	1,901,094
0.1% – 5.0%	1,648	4,541	10,374	48,411	202,178	113,296	60,083	48,640	489,171
5.1% - 6.0%	131	3,076	16,246	39,905	190,345	276,396	88,778	32,369	647,246
6.1% - 7.0%	274	8,297	13,095	15,617	56,519	148,557	218,100	63,486	523,945

Table 9. (Continued)

	Interest rate range	2000	2001	2002	2003	2004	2005	2006	2007	Total
Alt-A other ARM	7.1% - 8.0%	778	5,231	6,032	5,042	9,966	39,470	96,715	31,227	**194,461**
	8.1% - 9.0%	1,913	2,102	1,876	714	1,458	4,828	15,390	8,672	**3 6,953**
	9.1% - 10.0%	745	675	443	93	194	484	1,933	2,553	**7,120**
	Greater than 10%	367	259	89	9	42	72	330	1,030	**2,198**
Alt-A other		**1,453**	**3,440**	**3,842**	**9,886**	**6,141**	**1,317**	**26,146**	**6,992**	**59,217**
	0.1% – 5.0%	1	-	20	3,648	3,920	176	8,732	1,277	**17,774**
	5.1% – 6.0%	3	11	30	3,132	1,507	207	1,053	763	**6,706**
	6.1% – 7.0%	-	54	575	1,720	480	506	7,978	2,862	**14,175**
	7.1% – 8.0%	9	1,028	1,670	1,107	134	298	5,896	1,508	**11,650**
	8.1% – 9.0%	310	1,450	1,110	239	42	97	1,987	454	**5,689**
	9.1% – 10.0%	766	634	354	37	22	23	434	123	**2,393**
	Greater than 10%	364	263	83	3	36	10	66	5	**83 0**

Source: GAO analysis of LP data.

ENCLOSURE III. STATUS OF NONPRIME LOANS ORIGINATED FROM 2000 THROUGH 2007 BY COHORT YEAR AND PRODUCT TYPE AS OF MARCH 31, 2009

This enclosure contains the results of our analysis of LoanPerformance (LP) data on the status of nonprime mortgages originated from 2000 through 2007, as of March 31, 2009. Tables 10 and 11 provide information in percentages and total numbers, respectively.

Table 10. Percentage of Nonprime Loans in Different Status Categories by Cohort Year as of March 31, 2009.

Subprime — ARM (excluding short-term hybrids)

Cohort year	Prepaid	Current	Delinquent	In default	In foreclosure process	Completed foreclosure process	Total
2000	73%	9%	2%	1%	1%	14%	100%
2001	79%	6%	2%	1%	1%	11%	100%
2002	80%	7%	2%	1%	1%	9%	100%
2003	81%	9%	1%	1%	1%	7%	100%
2004	72%	16%	2%	2%	2%	7%	100%
2005	46%	30%	5%	4%	5%	10%	100%
2006	23%	36%	9%	9%	10%	14%	100%
2007	15%	41%	11%	16%	10%	8%	100%
Total	56%	22%	4%	4%	4%	10%	100%

Subprime — Short-term hybrid ARM

Cohort year	Prepaid	Current	Delinquent	In default	In foreclosure process	Completed foreclosure process	Total
2000	72%	5%	2%	1%	1%	19%	100%
2001	76%	4%	1%	1%	1%	17%	100%
2002	81%	3%	1%	1%	1%	13%	100%
2003	84%	3%	1%	1%	1%	10%	100%
2004	78%	5%	2%	2%	1%	12%	100%
2005	57%	11%	4%	5%	5%	18%	100%
2006	29%	20%	8%	10%	11%	21%	100%
2007	17%	32%	12%	14%	13%	13%	100%
Total	61%	10%	4%	4%	4%	16%	100%

Subprime — Fixed rate

Cohort year	Prepaid	Current	Delinquent	In default	In foreclosure process	Completed foreclosure process	Total
2000	64%	13%	4%	2%	1%	16%	100%
2001	69%	13%	3%	1%	1%	13%	100%
2002	72%	15%	3%	1%	1%	9%	100%
2003	65%	24%	3%	1%	1%	6%	100%
2004	52%	34%	5%	3%	2%	6%	100%
2005	34%	43%	8%	5%	3%	7%	100%
2006	21%	47%	11%	8%	6%	7%	100%
2007	13%	52%	13%	11%	6%	5%	100%
Total	49%	32%	6%	4%	2%	8%	100%

Subprime — Other

Cohort year	Prepaid	Current	Delinquent	In default	In foreclosure process	Completed foreclosure process	Total
2000	60%	11%	3%	2%	1%	23%	100%
2001	67%	10%	2%	1%	1%	18%	100%
2002	69%	14%	2%	1%	1%	13%	100%
2003	64%	21%	3%	1%	1%	9%	100%
2004	53%	35%	3%	2%	2%	5%	100%
2005	32%	37%	8%	6%	6%	11%	100%
2006	18%	38%	11%	9%	10%	14%	100%
2007	11%	43%	15%	10%	13%	9%	100%
Total	38%	28%	7%	6%	6%	15%	100%

Table 10. (Continued)

Subprime

ARM (excluding short-term hybrids)

Cohort year	Prepaid	Current	Delinquent	In default	In foreclosure process	Completed foreclosure process	Total
2000	87%	9%	1%	1%	0%	3%	100%
2001	87%	8%	1%	0%	0%	3%	100%
2002	83%	13%	1%	0%	0%	2%	100%
2003	81%	14%	1%	1%	0%	2%	100%
2004	72%	20%	2%	1%	1%	4%	100%
2005	45%	33%	4%	3%	5%	9%	100%
2006	24%	39%	6%	7%	10%	14%	100%
2007	12%	52%	8%	8%	12%	9%	100%
Total	47%	31%	4%	4%	6%	8%	100%

Payment-option ARM

Cohort year	Prepaid	Current	Delinquent	In default	In foreclosure process	Completed foreclosure process	Total
2000	86%	13%	0%	0%	0%	1%	100%
2001	94%	4%	0%	0%	0%	1%	100%
2002	92%	7%	0%	0%	0%	0%	100%
2003	84%	12%	1%	1%	1%	1%	100%
2004	77%	16%	2%	2%	2%	2%	100%
2005	54%	25%	4%	6%	6%	6%	100%
2006	25%	37%	7%	10%	11%	9%	100%
2007	12%	51%	9%	10%	12%	6%	100%
Total	44%	30%	5%	7%	7%	7%	100%

Fixed rate

Cohort year	Prepaid	Current	Delinquent	In default	In foreclosure process	Completed foreclosure process	Total
2000	82%	11%	1%	1%	1%	5%	100%
2001	83%	11%	1%	0%	0%	4%	100%
2002	79%	16%	1%	0%	0%	4%	100%
2003	58%	38%	1%	1%	0%	2%	100%
2004	47%	46%	2%	1%	1%	2%	100%
2005	31%	56%	4%	2%	3%	4%	100%
2006	23%	54%	6%	4%	6%	7%	100%
2007	12%	66%	6%	5%	6%	4%	100%
Total	42%	46%	3%	2%	3%	4%	100%

Other

Cohort year	Prepaid	Current	Delinquent	In default	In foreclosure process	Completed foreclosure process	Total
2000	80%	9%	2%	0%	0%	9%	100%
2001	80%	8%	1%	1%	0%	9%	100%
2002	82%	8%	1%	1%	0%	7%	100%
2003	74%	21%	1%	1%	1%	3%	100%
2004	66%	28%	1%	1%	1%	2%	100%
2005	37%	33%	4%	5%	7%	15%	100%
2006	19%	39%	8%	9%	13%	12%	100%
2007	9%	53%	9%	8%	14%	8%	100%
Total	41%	32%	5%	5%	8%	9%	100%

Source: GAO analysis of LP data.

Table 11. Number of Nonprime Loans in Different Status Categories by Cohort Year as of March 31, 2009.

Subprime

ARM (excluding short-term hybrids)

Cohort year	Prepaid	Current	Delinquent	In default	In foreclosure process	Completed foreclosure process	Total
2000	9,463	1,159	302	155	98	1,832	13,009
2001	7,038	570	161	104	53	1,000	8,926
2002	16,916	1,513	365	185	169	1,876	21,024
2003	34,742	3,804	635	444	326	2,907	42,858
2004	38,020	8,310	1,322	999	855	3,534	53,040
2005	26,024	16,809	2,737	2,168	2,710	5,664	56,112
2006	11,033	17,144	4,106	4,203	4,700	6,941	48,127
2007	2,271	6,324	1,672	2,415	1,529	1,218	15,429
Total	145,507	55,633	11,300	10,673	10,440	24,972	258,525

Short-term hybrid ARM

Cohort year	Prepaid	Current	Delinquent	In default	In foreclosure process	Completed foreclosure process	Total
2000	179,375	13,140	4,161	3,226	2,260	46,742	248,904
2001	239,938	12,973	4,150	3,014	1,912	54,099	316,086
2002	419,956	15,664	6,050	4,554	3,088	67,357	516,669
2003	668,013	25,843	8,843	7,285	4,908	82,976	797,868
2004	1,110,764	75,796	27,470	29,199	20,601	164,379	1,428,209
2005	1,010,676	202,322	77,351	86,690	90,136	319,050	1,786,225
2006	377,417	263,574	103,539	130,521	144,233	270,324	1,289,608
2007	33,351	63,065	23,731	26,765	26,079	25,234	198,225
Total	4,039,490	672,377	255,295	291,254	293,217	1,030,161	6,581,794

Fixed rate

Cohort year	Prepaid	Current	Delinquent	In default	In foreclosure process	Completed foreclosure process	Total
2000	99,773	20,887	5,538	2,874	1,803	24,925	155,800
2001	124,281	22,822	5,145	2,653	1,583	24,192	180,676
2002	164,268	34,282	5,883	2,957	1,686	19,700	228,776
2003	279,722	102,619	13,075	6,225	3,890	24,547	430,078
2004	238,370	156,218	21,557	11,772	7,253	26,056	461,226
2005	146,167	183,160	32,612	21,115	13,410	27,759	424,223
2006	74,715	167,737	37,397	29,725	19,683	25,859	355,116
2007	12,240	46,831	11,953	9,532	5,822	4,313	90,691
Total	1,139,536	734,556	133,160	86,853	55,130	177,351	2,326,586

Other

Cohort year	Prepaid	Current	Delinquent	In default	In foreclosure process	Completed foreclosure process	Total
2000	23,196	4,179	1,099	635	534	9,013	38,656
2001	21,426	3,270	699	406	273	5,860	3 1,934
2002	12,646	2,478	436	265	180	2,297	183 , 02
2003	6,741	2,161	34	152	132	920	10,453
2004	1,849	1,219	115	72	65	164	3,484
2005	5,111	5,803	1,341	915	878	1,793	15,841
2006	15,870	33,714	9,461	7,883	8,733	12,520	88,181
2007	2,756	11,257	3,901	2,575	3,293	2,353	26,135
Total	89,595	64,081	17,399	12,903	14,088	34,920	232,986

Alt-A

ARM (excluding payment-option ARMs)

Cohort year	Prepaid	Current	Delinquent	In default	In foreclosure process	Completed foreclosure process	Total
2000	5,095	514	50	30	7	158	5,854

Fixed rate

Cohort year	Prepaid	Current	Delinquent	In default	In foreclosure process	Completed foreclosure process	Total
2000	54,812	7,020	866	370	404	3,133	66,605

Table 11. (Continued)

ARM (excluding payment-option ARMs)

Cohort year	Prepaid	Current	Delinquent	In default	In foreclosure process	Completed foreclosure process	Total
2001	21,066	1,969	157	102	72	715	24,081
2002	40,161	6,125	379	209	143	1,102	48,119
2003	89,229	15,740	976	624	544	2,578	109,691
2004	329,623	91,257	7,058	5,763	6,770	19,659	460,130
2005	264,475	193,809	20,398	20,215	29,018	54,241	582,156
2006	113,795	188,761	28,715	34,963	49,421	65,254	480,909
2007	22,329	97,102	14,299	15,396	21,622	17,218	187,966
Total	885,773	595,277	72,032	77,302	107,597	160,925	1,898,906

Payment-option ARM

Cohort year	Prepaid	Current	Delinquent	In default	In foreclosure process	Completed foreclosure process	Total
2000	3,636	539	6	9	2	25	4,217
2001	642	30	2	-	1	7	682
2002	4,203	322	7	6	11	20	4,569
2003	6,326	940	107	51	63	77	7,564
2004	94,676	19,175	2,270	2,343	2,203	2,522	123,189
2005	166,421	76,092	11,581	19,182	17,145	19,680	310,101
2006	82,726	121,819	22,703	32,503	35,696	30,761	326,208
2007	7,199	31,080	5,173	6,115	7,131	3,805	60,503
Total	365,829	249,997	41,849	60,209	62,252	56,897	837,033

Fixed rate

Cohort year	Prepaid	Current	Delinquent	In default	In foreclosure process	Completed foreclosure process	Total
2001	91,319	11,936	1,113	545	439	4,804	110,156
2002	137,930	27,099	1,534	809	583	6,874	174,829
2003	179,367	115,671	3,862	1,849	1,424	6,188	308,361
2004	163,933	159,743	7,372	4,050	3,619	7,868	346,585
2005	171,696	310,079	19,862	13,005	16,517	21,945	553,104
2006	112,250	267,654	28,667	22,274	31,705	33,196	495,746
2007	22,540	118,565	11,407	9,162	11,148	7,762	180,584
Total	933,847	1,017,767	74,683	52,064	65,839	91,770	2,235,970

Other

Cohort year	Prepaid	Current	Delinquent	In default	In foreclosure process	Completed foreclosure process	Total
2000	1,164	127	24	7	7	124	1,453
2001	2,761	267	51	22	14	325	3,440
2002	3,159	310	40	28	16	288	3,841
2003	7,307	2,036	119	66	70	273	9,871
2004	4,078	1,735	89	40	61	138	6,141
2005	482	437	47	63	95	193	1,317
2006	4,938	10,180	2,007	2,406	3,450	3,153	26,134
2007	612	3,674	662	547	944	553	6,992
Total	24,501	18,766	3,039	3,179	4,657	5,047	59,189

Source: GAO analysis of LP data.

Enclosure IV. Status of Nonprime Loans Originated from 2004 through 2007 by Year and Quarter as of March 31, 2009

This enclosure contains the results of our analysis of LoanPerformance (LP) data on the annual and quarterly status of nonprime mortgages originated from 2004 through 2007, as of March 31, 2009. Tables 12 and 13 provide information in percentages and total numbers, respectively.

Table 12. Percentage of Nonprime Loans Originated in 2004 through 2007 in Different Status Categories as of March 31, 2009.

Status date	Subprime							Alt-A						
	Prepaid (cumulative)	Current	Delinquent	In default	In foreclosure process	Completed foreclosure process (cumulative)	Total	Prepaid (cumulative)	Current	Delinquent	In default	In foreclosure process	Completed foreclosure process (cumulative)	Total
2007 Cohort														
December 31, 2007	5%	71%	15%	4%	4%	1%	100%	5%	87%	5%	1%	2%	0%	100%
December 31, 2008	13%	41%	16%	11%	10%	8%	100%	11%	63%	8%	6%	7%	5%	100%
March 31, 2009	15%	39%	13%	13%	11%	10%	100%	12%	58%	7%	7%	9%	7%	100%
2006 Cohort														
December 31, 2006	7%	78%	11%	2%	2%	0%	100%	6%	90%	3%	0%	0%	0%	100%
December 31, 2007	18%	50%	13%	6%	7%	6%	100%	17%	70%	6%	2%	3%	2%	100%
December 31, 2008	25%	28%	11%	9%	10%	16%	100%	22%	48%	7%	6%	8%	8%	100%
March 31, 2009	26%	27%	9%	10%	10%	18%	100%	23%	45%	6%	7%	9%	10%	100%
2005 Cohort														
December 31, 2005	7%	83%	8%	1%	1%	0%	100%	6%	92%	2%	0%	0%	0%	100%
December 31, 2006	28%	54%	9%	3%	3%	3%	100%	23%	72%	3%	0%	1%	0%	100%
December 31, 2007	46%	28%	8%	4%	5%	8%	100%	36%	55%	4%	1%	2%	2%	100%
December 31, 2008	51%	19%	6%	5%	5%	15%	100%	40%	43%	4%	3%	4%	6%	100%
March 31, 2009	51%	18%	5%	5%	5%	16%	100%	41%	40%	4%	4%	4%	7%	100%
2004 Cohort														
December 31, 2004	6%	86%	6%	1%	1%	0%	100%	5%	93%	2%	0%	0%	0%	100%

Table 12. (Continued)

Status date	Subprime							Alt-A						
	Prepaid (cumulative)	Current	Delinquent	In default	In foreclosure process	Completed foreclosure process (cumulative)	Total	Prepaid (cumulative)	Current	Delinquent	In default	In foreclosure process	Completed foreclosure process (cumulative)	Total
December 31, 2005	34%	52%	7%	2%	2%	2%	100%	28%	69%	2%	0%	0%	0%	100%
December 31, 2006	60%	26%	5%	2%	2%	5%	100%	47%	50%	2%	0%	0%	1%	100%
December 31, 2007	69%	16%	4%	2%	2%	8%	100%	58%	37%	2%	1%	1%	2%	100%
December 31, 2008	71%	12%	3%	2%	1%	10%	100%	62%	30%	2%	1%	1%	3%	100%
March 31, 2009	71%	12%	3%	2%	1%	10%	100%	63%	29%	2%	1%	1%	3%	100%

Source: GAO analysis of LP data.

Table 13. Number of Nonprime Loans Originated in 2004 through 2007 in Different Status Categories as of March 31, 2009.

2007 Cohort

Status date	Subprime							Alt-A						
	Prepaid (cumulative)	Current	Delinquent	In default	In foreclosure process	Completed foreclosure process (cumulative)	Total	Prepaid (cumulative)	Current	Delinquent	In default	In foreclosure process	Completed foreclosure process (cumulative)	Total
December 31, 2007	16,702	231,732	48,916	14,677	13,944	2,575	328,546	20,613	376,372	21,186	6,506	8,089	1,199	433,965
December 31, 2008	44,058	135,117	51,296	37,274	32,844	27,904	328,493	46,301	273,614	35,286	25,035	32,185	22,524	434,945
March 31, 2009	47,707	126,116	40,744	41,125	36,439	33,755	325,886	50,918	250,421	31,541	31,220	40,845	30,000	434,945
December 31, 2006	91,519	1,048,577	152,186	27,941	24,897	5,257	1,350,377	58,318	946,169	35,999	3,879	4,536	1,047	1,049,948
December 31, 2007	308,751	882,179	234,132	109,507	132,283	97,330	1,764,182	222,661	920,896	78,839	30,737	42,176	26,384	1,321,693

Table 13. (Continued)

Status date	Subprime							Alt-A						
	Prepaid (cumulative)	Current	Delinquent	In default	In foreclosure process	Completed foreclosure process (cumulative)	Total	Prepaid (cumulative)	Current	Delinquent	In default	In foreclosure process	Completed foreclosure process (cumulative)	Total
2006 Cohort														
December 31, 2008	445,971	499,686	198,891	165,708	167,881	285,050	1,763,187	293,261	640,299	97,729	80,107	99,861	110,817	1,322,074
March 31, 2009	455,898	479,918	153,826	171,915	176,813	318,993	1,757,363	304,578	588,414	82,092	92,146	120,272	134,572	1,322,074
2005 Cohort														
December 31, 2005	122,108	1,438,997	140,861	22,176	14,074	2,925	1,741,141	69,322	1,073,961	25,836	2,592	862	177	1,172,750
December 31, 2006	627,811	1,211,085	210,943	63,501	70,422	59,164	2,242,926	332,557	1,035,786	40,776	7,152	10,284	7,125	1,433,680
December 31, 2007	1,051,097	642,590	180,328	99,140	112,350	176,696	2,262,201	513,319	795,283	51,354	20,839	27,134	32,349	1,440,278
December 31, 2008	1,150,054	417,954	138,513	108,056	104,624	332,524	2,251,725	580,129	611,351	59,875	44,682	52,883	84,045	1,432,965
March 31, 2009	1,149,483	402,072	112,319	110,044	105,757	353,621	2,233,296	595,903	580,417	51,888	52,465	62,775	97,339	1,440,787
December 31, 2004	93,670	1,294,270	97,242	11,653	8,467	1,282	1,506,584	37,168	667,091	12,295	968	548	133	718,203
December 31, 2005	661,304	1,002,601	142,532	46,017	36,363	32,192	1,921,009	260,603	631,707	19,096	4,375	2,663	2,756	921,200
December 31, 2006	1,145,083	503,451	100,791	41,055	40,637	91,913	1,922,930	432,908	459,055	16,964	3,830	4,430	8,832	926,019
December 31, 2007	1,329,305	306,046	69,058	40,023	36,250	149,350	1,930,032	540,157	344,041	16,853	5,921	6,110	16,885	929,967
December 31, 2008	1,369,206	240,074	59,395	41,400	27,986	189,629	1,927,690	576,517	281,903	18,657	10,129	10,637	28,001	925,844
March 31, 2009	1,362,146	236,097	49,766	41,807	28,399	193,652	1,911,867	586,386	271,699	16,775	12,195	12,643	30,444	930,142

Source: GAO analysis of LP data.

ENCLOSURE V. STATUS OF NONPRIME LOANS ORIGINATED FROM 2000 THROUGH 2007 BY CENSUS DIVISION AND STATE AS OF MARCH 31, 2009

This enclosure contains the results of our analysis of LoanPerformance (LP) data on the status of nonprime mortgages by Census division and state. The analysis covers mortgages originated from 2000 through 2007, as of March 31, 2009. Tables 14 and 15 provide information in percentages and total numbers, respectively.

Table 14. Percentage of 2000-2007 Nonprime Loans in Different Status Categories by Census Division and State as of March 31, 2009.

State	Market segment	Prepaid	Current	Delinquent	In default	In foreclosure process	Completed foreclosure process	Unknown	Total
Connecticut	Subprime	61.50%	16.45%	4.53%	3.70%	3.98%	9.12%	0.72%	123,057
	Alt-A	46.10%	40.00%	4.01%	2.52%	3.69%	3.28%	0.41%	44,759
Maine	Subprime	62.21%	16.28%	4.41%	2.99%	4.81%	8.24%	1.06%	36,312
	Alt-A	46.73%	38.84%	3.96%	1.99%	4.71%	3.27%	0.50%	9,706
Massachusetts	Subprime	65.55%	11.76%	3.62%	4.75%	2.97%	10.06%	1.29%	201,130
	Alt-A	50.71%	33.78%	3.56%	3.25%	3.33%	4.53%	0.85%	85,185
New Hampshire	Subprime	60.91%	16.61%	4.80%	4.07%	2.07%	10.88%	0.65%	41,435
	Alt-A	46.67%	39.03%	3.99%	2.45%	1.76%	5.52%	0.57%	15,602
Rhode Island	Subprime	69.07%	10.53%	3.12%	2.71%	2.40%	11.04%	1.14%	52,816
	Alt-A	50.18%	32.24%	3.97%	2.87%	3.23%	6.87%	0.65%	15,764
Vermont	Subprime	63.92%	17.70%	4.18%	3.08%	3.97%	6.13%	1.02%	9,758
	Alt-A	47.93%	41.47%	3.04%	1.94%	3.01%	1.74%	0.87%	3,914
New England	**Subprime**	**64.17%**	**13.77%**	**3.98%**	**4.01%**	**3.26%**	**9.77%**	**1.04%**	**464,508**
	Alt-A	**48.84%**	**36.15%**	**3.76%**	**2.86%**	**3.34%**	**4.38%**	**0.67%**	**174,930**
New Jersey	Subprime	67.69%	11.54%	3.58%	3.69%	5.42%	6.62%	1.46%	264,731
	Alt-A	50.66%	33.04%	3.83%	2.91%	6.00%	2.90%	0.66%	143,788

Table 14. (Continued)

State	Market segment	Prepaid	Current	Delinquent	In default	In foreclosure process	Completed foreclosure process	Unknown	Total
New York	Subprime	57.61%	18.78%	4.85%	5.01%	5.37%	7.51%	0.86%	384,925
	Alt-A	40.82%	42.65%	4.43%	4.47%	4.60%	2.65%	0.37%	166,080
Pennsylvania	Subprime	50.80%	24.58%	6.13%	5.21%	3.48%	9.16%	0.62%	262,683
	Alt-A	42.14%	46.18%	3.71%	2.37%	2.47%	2.73%	0.41%	81,623
Mid Atlantic	**Subprime**	**58.58%**	**18.35%**	**4.85%**	**4.69%**	**4.84%**	**7.73%**	**0.97%**	**912,339**
	Alt-A	**44.71%**	**39.86%**	**4.06%**	**3.46%**	**4.67%**	**2.76%**	**0.48%**	**391,491**
Illinois	Subprime	61.49%	13.01%	3.90%	3.50%	4.45%	12.38%	1.27%	450,147
	Alt-A	50.23%	32.75%	3.52%	2.75%	4.81%	5.13%	0.81%	147,636
Indiana	Subprime	41.53%	21.08%	5.35%	4.44%	4.38%	22.67%	0.55%	176,216
	Alt-A	36.49%	43.34%	3.58%	2.70%	4.15%	9.37%	0.37%	38,381
Michigan	Subprime	47.07%	14.74%	4.97%	4.74%	1.94%	25.78%	0.76%	373,310
	Alt-A	35.94%	40.41%	4.42%	3.29%	2.37%	13.12%	0.44%	94,707
Ohio	Subprime	43.56%	19.89%	5.05%	4.51%	4.80%	21.47%	0.72%	319,389
	Alt-A	34.31%	46.41%	3.76%	2.75%	4.27%	8.17%	0.34%	73,621
Wisconsin	Subprime	62.05%	13.26%	3.69%	3.31%	3.93%	12.78%	0.98%	131,066
	Alt-A	45.79%	39.72%	3.14%	2.30%	3.49%	4.91%	0.66%	29,608
East North Central	**Subprime**	**51.45%**	**15.97%**	**4.58%**	**4.14%**	**3.82%**	**19.12%**	**0.91%**	**1,450,128**
	Alt-A	**41.94%**	**38.85%**	**3.76%**	**2.84%**	**3.94%**	**8.09%**	**0.57%**	**383,953**
Iowa	Subprime	55.11%	17.72%	4.34%	2.89%	3.47%	15.85%	0.62%	52,627
	Alt-A	41.13%	46.93%	2.73%	1.48%	2.44%	4.80%	0.48%	10,536
Kansas	Subprime	53.72%	19.40%	4.70%	3.32%	2.30%	15.85%	0.71%	49,747
	Alt-A	41.53%	47.95%	2.60%	1.45%	1.48%	4.68%	0.31%	16,854
Minnesota	Subprime	59.31%	12.19%	3.48%	2.88%	2.52%	18.70%	0.91%	162,906
	Alt-A	36.96%	40.80%	3.84%	2.93%	3.53%	11.54%	0.39%	67,357

Table 14. (Continued)

State	Market segment	Prepaid	Current	Delinquent	In default	In foreclosure process	Completed foreclosure process	Unknown	Total
Missouri	Subprime	53.19%	16.22%	4.95%	4.10%	1.47%	19.29%	0.78%	180,305
	Alt-A	43.24%	41.86%	3.16%	2.11%	1.28%	7.88%	0.47%	48,859
Nebraska	Subprime	49.52%	22.70%	5.05%	3.71%	2.41%	16.23%	0.39%	29,602
	Alt-A	38.41%	49.61%	3.05%	1.52%	1.80%	5.30%	0.31%	6,987
North Dakota	Subprime	57.13%	22.87%	4.82%	2.91%	2.37%	9.34%	0.56%	4,465
	Alt-A	41.33%	49.89%	2.33%	1.08%	2.00%	3.14%	0.22%	1,846
South Dakota	Subprime	55.28%	20.23%	4.48%	2.72%	2.91%	13.88%	0.51%	7,321
	Alt-A	41.94%	46.94%	2.32%	1.90%	1.90%	4.80%	0.21%	2,418
West North Central	**Subprime**	**55.35%**	**15.87%**	**4.36%**	**3.43%**	**2.21%**	**18.01%**	**0.77%**	**486,973**
	Alt-A	**39.92%**	**42.93%**	**3.34%**	**2.31%**	**2.40%**	**8.69%**	**0.41%**	**154,857**
Delaware	Subprime	58.48%	18.91%	5.49%	4.62%	4.68%	7.09%	0.73%	24,645
	Alt-A	44.89%	42.40%	3.46%	2.30%	3.60%	2.82%	0.54%	11,764
District of Columbia	Subprime	68.90%	11.44%	3.66%	3.95%	2.62%	7.90%	1.54%	17,372
	Alt-A	49.31%	38.25%	3.27%	2.64%	2.17%	3.68%	0.69%	15,469
Florida	Subprime	54.97%	14.76%	4.35%	4.69%	10.21%	10.25%	0.76%	935,244
	Alt-A	35.88%	35.23%	4.39%	5.07%	13.72%	5.20%	0.51%	528,708
Georgia	Subprime	47.11%	17.53%	6.09%	6.14%	2.55%	19.82%	0.76%	267,382
	Alt-A	36.67%	43.60%	4.55%	3.25%	2.37%	9.16%	0.41%	157,997
Maryland	Subprime	68.36%	12.26%	3.98%	4.18%	3.11%	6.66%	1.46%	255,118
	Alt-A	47.50%	36.28%	4.15%	4.42%	3.45%	3.56%	0.64%	135,923
North Carolina	Subprime	51.34%	20.14%	6.43%	5.00%	1.96%	14.32%	0.79%	179,453
	Alt-A	43.12%	44.15%	3.69%	2.41%	1.51%	4.68%	0.45%	86,627
South Carolina	Subprime	48.76%	20.80%	6.04%	3.95%	3.64%	16.10%	0.71%	94,146
	Alt-A	43.77%	41.75%	3.52%	2.06%	3.14%	5.15%	0.60%	48,943

Table 14. (Continued)

State	Market segment	Prepaid	Current	Delinquent	In default	In foreclosure process	Completed foreclosure process	Unknown	Total
Virginia	Subprime	63.49%	14.77%	4.25%	4.05%	1.90%	10.52%	1.03%	213,215
	Alt-A	42.53%	37.82%	3.62%	3.47%	2.75%	9.10%	0.70%	162,599
West Virginia	Subprime	50.41%	22.79%	6.79%	4.80%	2.73%	11.64%	0.83%	16,904
	Alt-A	37.60%	43.45%	4.92%	3.40%	3.26%	6.83%	0.54%	4,819
South Atlantic	**Subprime**	**56.04%**	**15.67%**	**4.82%**	**4.74%**	**6.16%**	**11.69%**	**0.89%**	**2,003,479**
	Alt-A	**39.46%**	**37.96%**	**4.17%**	**4.12%**	**7.74%**	**6.02%**	**0.54%**	**1,152,849**
Alabama	Subprime	47.86%	21.96%	6.74%	6.32%	1.79%	14.80%	0.54%	84,284
	Alt-A	41.08%	44.79%	3.70%	2.37%	1.63%	5.98%	0.45%	27,202
Kentucky	Subprime	47.30%	21.56%	5.42%	3.74%	3.94%	17.46%	0.58%	71,589
	Alt-A	38.94%	46.58%	3.27%	1.98%	3.07%	5.84%	0.33%	18,430
Mississippi	Subprime	40.70%	24.15%	7.69%	7.61%	2.45%	16.64%	0.75%	53,230
	Alt-A	38.86%	44.97%	4.45%	2.84%	1.96%	6.20%	0.72%	9,470
Tennessee	Subprime	44.30%	22.26%	6.56%	6.96%	1.75%	17.60%	0.57%	168,271
	Alt-A	38.97%	47.05%	3.68%	2.42%	1.37%	6.14%	0.38%	46,066
East South Central	**Subprime**	**45.16%**	**22.33%**	**6.54%**	**6.30%**	**2.27%**	**16.81%**	**0.59%**	**377,374**
	Alt-A	**39.52%**	**46.16%**	**3.68%**	**2.36%**	**1.80%**	**6.05%**	**0.42%**	**101,168**
Arkansas	Subprime	43.77%	27.28%	6.62%	5.39%	2.16%	14.26%	0.51%	37,687
	Alt-A	35.78%	50.64%	3.39%	2.17%	1.77%	5.93%	0.32%	11,345
Louisaina	Subprime	49.75%	24.62%	6.27%	5.22%	3.28%	10.21%	0.65%	89,817
	Alt-A	44.17%	44.17%	3.25%	2.27%	2.22%	3.47%	0.44%	19,390
Oklahoma	Subprime	42.64%	26.73%	5.93%	3.77%	3.52%	16.93%	0.49%	66,160
	Alt-A	34.51%	53.97%	2.91%	1.34%	2.26%	4.75%	0.25%	18,235
Texas	Subprime	39.30%	31.57%	7.11%	4.94%	2.09%	14.54%	0.45%	570,001
	Alt-A	34.34%	52.39%	3.27%	1.98%	1.32%	6.44%	0.25%	185,969

Table 14. (Continued)

State	Market segment	Prepaid	Current	Delinquent	In default	In foreclosure process	Completed foreclosure process	Unknown	Total
West South Central	**Subprime**	**41.04%**	**30.12%**	**6.88%**	**4.89%**	**2.36%**	**14.23%**	**0.48%**	**763,665**
	Alt-A	**35.23%**	**51.75%**	**3.25%**	**1.97%**	**1.49%**	**6.04%**	**0.27%**	**234,939**
Arizona	Subprime	59.83%	12.70%	3.93%	4.59%	3.98%	14.08%	0.88%	300,678
	Alt-A	45.06%	33.62%	3.86%	3.56%	4.31%	8.83%	0.77%	233,624
Colorado	Subprime	53.47%	15.91%	3.67%	2.95%	2.22%	21.03%	0.74%	188,769
	Alt-A	43.87%	42.07%	2.66%	1.75%	2.10%	7.10%	0.45%	138,558
Idaho	Subprime	59.83%	17.02%	4.49%	3.72%	3.16%	11.19%	0.60%	38,247
	Alt-A	45.77%	40.86%	3.30%	2.40%	3.32%	3.88%	0.47%	31,997
Montana	Subprime	62.31%	17.50%	4.12%	3.44%	2.40%	9.63%	0.60%	12,973
	Alt-A	50.51%	41.08%	2.54%	1.60%	1.67%	2.27%	0.32%	8,848
Nevada	Subprime	56.73%	12.06%	3.70%	5.07%	4.64%	16.92%	0.88%	152,588
	Alt-A	36.40%	33.88%	4.87%	5.92%	6.29%	12.07%	0.57%	152,154
New Mexico	Subprime	61.98%	17.44%	4.25%	2.69%	2.64%	10.01%	0.99%	40,494
	Alt-A	48.11%	41.64%	2.72%	1.59%	2.88%	2.58%	0.48%	22,328
Utah	Subprime	64.23%	14.06%	3.77%	2.91%	2.17%	12.12%	0.74%	80,323
	Alt-A	52.74%	35.04%	2.71%	1.80%	2.69%	4.44%	0.58%	56,996
Wyoming	Subprime	63.58%	20.34%	4.22%	2.41%	1.24%	7.83%	0.38%	9,748
	Alt-A	51.91%	42.33%	1.93%	1.02%	0.69%	1.95%	0.18%	4,519
Mountain	**Subprime**	**58.42%**	**14.05%**	**3.86%**	**3.96%**	**3.36%**	**15.53%**	**0.82%**	**823,820**
	Alt-A	**43.71%**	**36.41%**	**3.64%**	**3.40%**	**4.00%**	**8.24%**	**0.60%**	**649,024**
Alaska	Subprime	61.76%	19.19%	4.55%	3.21%	2.12%	8.70%	0.47%	9,435
	Alt-A	45.05%	45.15%	3.07%	1.52%	1.34%	3.50%	0.36%	3,942
California	Subprime	65.94%	10.36%	2.68%	3.55%	3.39%	12.90%	1.17%	1,745,539
	Alt-A	46.87%	32.39%	3.82%	5.04%	4.61%	6.80%	0.47%	1,530,897

Table 14. (Continued)

State	Market segment	Prepaid	Current	Delinquent	In default	In foreclosure process	Completed foreclosure process	Unknown	Total
Hawaii	Subprime	64.27%	19.51%	3.60%	3.40%	4.09%	4.42%	0.71%	42,054
	Alt-A	46.51%	42.40%	3.13%	2.64%	3.45%	1.51%	0.35%	28,469
Oregon	Subprime	62.13%	17.14%	4.03%	3.31%	3.12%	9.69%	0.58%	106,926
	Alt-A	47.44%	41.27%	3.02%	2.09%	2.67%	3.11%	0.41%	78,525
Washington	Subprime	63.91%	15.86%	3.85%	3.70%	2.54%	9.46%	0.68%	204,705
	Alt-A	48.73%	40.74%	3.05%	2.37%	2.20%	2.50%	0.43%	144,262
Pacific	**Subprime**	**65.50%**	**11.46%**	**2.89%**	**3.55%**	**3.30%**	**12.22%**	**1.08%**	**2,108,659**
	Alt-A	**47.03%**	**33.64%**	**3.71%**	**4.65%**	**4.30%**	**6.20%**	**0.46%**	**1,786,095**
United States	**Subprime**	**56.62%**	**16.25%**	**4.44%**	**4.28%**	**3.97%**	**13.55%**	**0.89%**	**9,390,945**
	Alt-A	**43.44%**	**37.34%**	**3.80%**	**3.83%**	**4.78%**	**6.30%**	**0.50%**	**5,029,306**
	Total Nonprime	**52.02%**	**23.61%**	**4.22%**	**4.12%**	**4.25%**	**11.02%**	**0.76%**	**14,420,251**

Source: GAO analysis of LP data.

Note: For some loans, the data were insufficient to classify into a status category. These "unknown" loans are included in the total column. This table does not include data for Guam, Puerto Rico, and the Virgin Islands.

Table 15. Number of 2000-2007 Nonprime Loans in Different Status Categories by Census Division and State as of March 31, 2009.

State	Market segment	Prepaid	Current	Delinquent	In default	In foreclosure process	Completed foreclosure process	Unknown	Total
Connecticut	Subprime	75,685	20,245	5,576	4,550	4,900	11,221	880	123,057
	Alt-A	20,633	17,904	1,794	1,127	1,652	1,466	183	44,759
Maine	Subprime	22,590	5,911	1,601	1,086	1,745	2,993	386	36,312
	Alt-A	4,536	3,770	384	193	457	317	49	9,706

Table 15. (Continued)

State	Market segment	Prepaid	Current	Delinquent	In default	In foreclosure process	Completed foreclosure process	Unknown	Total
Massachusetts	Subprime	131,848	23,656	7,278	9,552	5,980	20,229	2,587	201,130
	Alt-A	43,195	28,772	3,029	2,768	2,838	3,860	723	85,185
New Hampshire	Subprime	25,238	6,884	1,989	1,688	856	4,509	271	41,435
	Alt-A	7,281	6,090	623	383	275	861	89	15,602
Rhode Island	Subprime	36,480	5,561	1,647	1,431	1,265	5,830	602	52,816
	Alt-A	7,910	5,082	626	452	509	1,083	102	15,764
Vermont	Subprime	6,237	1,727	408	301	387	598	100	9,758
	Alt-A	1,876	1,623	119	76	118	68	34	3,914
New England	**Subprime**	**298,078**	**63,984**	**18,499**	**18,608**	**15,133**	**45,380**	**4,826**	**464,508**
	Alt-A	**85,431**	**63,241**	**6,575**	**4,999**	**5,849**	**7,655**	**1,180**	**174,930**
New Jersey	Subprime	179,200	30,541	9,482	9,763	14,353	17,536	3,856	264,731
	Alt-A	72,842	47,514	5,507	4,183	8,624	4,176	942	143,788
New York	Subprime	221,768	72,301	18,665	19,303	20,665	28,897	3,326	384,925
	Alt-A	67,797	70,833	7,355	7,431	7,642	4,405	617	166,080
Pennsylvania	Subprime	133,454	64,577	16,110	13,691	9,138	24,073	1,640	262,683
	Alt-A	34,392	37,691	3,025	1,934	2,015	2,232	334	81,623
Mid Atlantic	**Subprime**	**534,422**	**167,419**	**44,257**	**42,757**	**44,156**	**70,506**	**8,822**	**912,339**
	Alt-A	**175,031**	**156,038**	**15,887**	**13,548**	**18,281**	**10,813**	**1,893**	**391,491**
Illinois	Subprime	276,788	58,563	17,549	15,769	20,022	55,737	5,719	450,147
	Alt-A	74,160	48,349	5,196	4,062	7,098	7,569	1,202	147,636
Indiana	Subprime	73,177	37,150	9,429	7,826	7,712	39,947	975	176,216
	Alt-A	14,006	16,634	1,375	1,035	1,591	3,597	143	38,381
Michigan	Subprime	175,708	55,012	18,547	17,712	7,242	96,238	2,851	373,310
	Alt-A	34,038	38,267	4,189	3,120	2,249	12,430	414	94,707

Table 15. (Continued)

State	Market segment	Prepaid	Current	Delinquent	In default	In foreclosure process	Completed foreclosure process	Unknown	Total
Ohio	Subprime	139,124	63,540	16,125	14,407	15,325	68,568	2,300	319,389
	Alt-A	25,262	34,166	2,765	2,024	3,141	6,016	247	73,621
Wisconsin	Subprime	81,332	17,382	4,834	4,338	5,153	16,745	1,282	131,066
	Alt-A	13,557	11,759	929	681	1,034	1,454	194	29,608
East North Central	**Subprime**	**746,129**	**231,647**	**66,484**	**60,052**	**55,454**	**277,235**	**13,127**	**1,450,128**
	Alt-A	**161,023**	**149,175**	**14,454**	**10,922**	**15,113**	**31,066**	**2,200**	**383,953**
Iowa	Subprime	29,004	9,324	2,284	1,519	1,827	8,343	326	52,627
	Alt-A	4,333	4,945	288	156	257	506	51	10,536
Kansas	Subprime	26,725	9,650	2,336	1,652	1,145	7,884	355	49,747
	Alt-A	6,999	8,081	438	244	250	789	53	16,854
Minnesota	Subprime	96,626	19,862	5,661	4,698	4,109	30,463	1,487	162,906
	Alt-A	24,897	27,482	2,585	1,972	2,380	7,775	266	67,357
Missouri	Subprime	95,912	29,242	8,920	7,384	2,659	34,775	1,413	180,305
	Alt-A	21,128	20,454	1,543	1,033	624	3,848	229	48,859
Nebraska	Subprime	14,658	6,720	1,494	1,098	714	4,803	115	29,602
	Alt-A	2,684	3,466	213	106	126	370	22	6,987
North Dakota	Subprime	2,551	1,021	215	130	106	417	25	4,465
	Alt-A	763	921	43	20	37	58	4	1,846
South Dakota	Subprime	4,047	1,481	328	199	213	1,016	37	7,321
	Alt-A	1,014	1,135	56	46	46	116	5	2,418
West North Central	**Subprime**	**269,523**	**77,300**	**21,238**	**16,680**	**10,773**	**87,701**	**3,758**	**486,973**
	Alt-A	**61,818**	**66,484**	**5,166**	**3,577**	**3,720**	**13,462**	**630**	**154,857**
Delaware	Subprime	14,413	4,660	1,352	1,138	1,154	1,748	180	24,645
	Alt-A	5,281	4,988	407	270	423	332	63	11,764

Table 15. (Continued)

State	Market segment	Prepaid	Current	Delinquent	In default	In foreclosure process	Completed foreclosure process	Unknown	Total
District of Columbia	Subprime	11,970	1,987	635	686	455	1,372	267	17,372
	Alt-A	7,627	5,917	506	408	336	569	106	15,469
Florida	Subprime	514,128	138,079	40,673	43,849	95,513	95,878	7,124	935,244
	Alt-A	189,699	186,239	23,222	26,792	72,561	27,514	2,681	528,708
Georgia	Subprime	125,957	46,883	16,289	16,412	6,809	52,996	2,036	267,382
	Alt-A	57,942	68,880	7,191	5,140	3,737	14,465	642	157,997
Maryland	Subprime	174,396	31,268	10,147	10,667	7,936	16,983	3,721	255,118
	Alt-A	64,565	49,311	5,646	6,004	4,683	4,839	875	135,923
North Carolina	Subprime	92,134	36,149	11,542	8,980	3,522	25,702	1,424	179,453
	Alt-A	37,350	38,247	3,198	2,089	1,307	4,050	386	86,627
South Carolina	Subprime	45,907	19,582	5,691	3,718	3,427	15,157	664	94,146
	Alt-A	21,422	20,433	1,725	1,007	1,538	2,523	295	48,943
Virginia	Subprime	135,376	31,496	9,051	8,629	4,047	22,421	2,195	213,215
	Alt-A	69,161	61,489	5,893	5,650	4,478	14,797	1,131	162,599
West Virginia	Subprime	8,522	3,853	1,148	811	461	1,968	141	16,904
	Alt-A	1,812	2,094	237	164	157	329	26	4,819
South Atlantic	**Subprime**	**1,122,803**	**313,957**	**96,528**	**94,890**	**123,324**	**234,225**	**17,752**	**2,003,479**
	Alt-A	**454,859**	**437,598**	**48,025**	**47,524**	**89,220**	**69,418**	**6,205**	**1,152,849**
Alabama	Subprime	40,340	18,506	5,677	5,329	1,507	12,471	454	84,284
	Alt-A	11,175	12,184	1,006	644	443	1,628	122	27,202
Kentucky	Subprime	33,862	15,436	3,881	2,679	2,818	12,500	413	71,589
	Alt-A	7,177	8,585	602	364	565	1,076	61	18,430
Mississippi	Subprime	21,667	12,857	4,096	4,049	1,306	8,858	397	53,230
	Alt-A	3,680	4,259	421	269	186	587	68	9,470

Table 15. (Continued)

State	Market segment	Prepaid	Current	Delinquent	In default	In foreclosure process	Completed foreclosure process	Unknown	Total
Tennessee	Subprime	74,550	37,465	11,037	11,705	2,940	29,610	964	168,271
	Alt-A	17,951	21,673	1,695	1,114	630	2,830	173	46,066
East South Central	**Subprime**	**170,419**	**84,264**	**24,691**	**23,762**	**8,571**	**63,439**	**2,228**	**377,374**
	Alt-A	**39,983**	**46,701**	**3,724**	**2,391**	**1,824**	**6,121**	**424**	**101,168**
Arkansas	Subprime	16,495	10,282	2,495	2,033	814	5,374	194	37,687
	Alt-A	4,059	5,745	385	246	201	673	36	11,345
Louisaina	Subprime	44,686	22,109	5,629	4,684	2,950	9,174	585	89,817
	Alt-A	8,565	8,565	631	441	430	672	86	19,390
Oklahoma	Subprime	28,210	17,684	3,923	2,491	2,327	11,202	323	66,160
	Alt-A	6,292	9,842	531	245	413	867	45	18,235
Texas	Subprime	223,983	179,930	40,519	28,153	11,940	82,898	2,578	570,001
	Alt-A	63,863	97,432	6,088	3,688	2,452	11,981	465	185,969
West South Central	**Subprime**	**313,374**	**230,005**	**52,566**	**37,361**	**18,031**	**108,648**	**3,680**	**763,665•**
	Alt-A	**82,779**	**121,584**	**7,635**	**4,620**	**3,496**	**14,193**	**632**	**234,939**
Arizona	Subprime	179,889	38,185	11,813	13,807	11,982	42,347	2,655	300,678
	Alt-A	105,273	78,546	9,007	8,306	10,066	20,628	1,798	233,624
Colorado	Subprime	100,940	30,026	6,932	5,578	4,189	39,700	1,404	188,769
	Alt-A	60,787	58,288	3,684	2,422	2,906	9,843	628	138,558
Idaho	Subprime	22,883	6,509	1,718	1,421	1,207	4,281	228	38,247
	Alt-A	14,644	13,075	1,055	769	1,062	1,243	149	31,997
Montana	Subprime	8,084	2,270	535	446	311	1,249	78	12,973
	Alt-A	4,469	3,635	225	142	148	201	28	8,848
Nevada	Subprime	86,561	18,400	5,647	7,736	7,079	25,825	1,340	152,588•
	Alt-A	55,379	51,552	7,407	9,009	9,578	18,363	866	152,154

Table 15. (Continued)

State	Market segment	Prepaid	Current	Delinquent	In default	In foreclosure process	Completed foreclosure process	Unknown	Total
New Mexico	Subprime	25,098	7,062	1,722	1,090	1,068	4,052	402	40,494
	Alt-A	10,741	9,298	608	355	643	576	107	22,328
Utah	Subprime	51,593	11,290	3,030	2,335	1,743	9,739	593	80,323
	Alt-A	30,058	19,973	1,543	1,027	1,534	2,528	333	56,996
Wyoming	Subprime	6,198	1,983	411	235	121	763	37	9,748
	Alt-A	2,346	1,913	87	46	31	88	8	4,519
Mountain	**Subprime**	**481,246**	**115,725**	**31,808**	**32,648**	**27,700**	**127,956**	**6,737**	**823,820**
	Alt-A	**283,697**	**236,280**	**23,616**	**22,076**	**25,968**	**53,470**	**3,917**	**649,024**
Alaska	Subprime	5,827	1,811	429	303	200	821	44	9,435
	Alt-A	1,776	1,780	121	60	53	138	14	3,942
California	Subprime	1,151,089	180,836	46,811	62,001	59,237	225,176	20,389	1,745,539
	Alt-A	717,507	495,851	58,497	77,151	70,519	104,149	7,223	1,530,897
Hawaii	Subprime	27,028	8,203	1,516	1,429	1,721	1,858	299	42,054
	Alt-A	13,242	12,071	892	752	982	431	99	28,469
Oregon	Subprime	66,431	18,324	4,313	3,540	3,333	10,364	621	106,926
	Alt-A	37,249	32,408	2,369	1,641	2,093	2,446	319	78,525
Washington	Subprime	130,836	32,457	7,872	7,581	5,196	19,372	1,391	204,705
	Alt-A	70,293	58,778	4,393	3,412	3,169	3,603	614	144,262

Table 15. (Continued)

State	Market segment	Prepaid	Current	Delinquent	In default	In foreclosure process	Completed foreclosure process	Unknown	Total
Pacific	Subprime	1,381,211	241,631	60,941	74,854	69,687	257,591	22,744	2,108,659
	Alt-A	840,067	600,888	66,272	83,016	76,816	110,767	8,269	1,786,095
United States	Subprime	5,317,205	1,525,932	417,012	401,612	372,829	1,272,681	83,674	9,390,945
	Alt-A	2,184,688	1,877,989	191,354	192,673	240,287	316,965	25,350	5,029,306
	Total Nonprime	7,501,893	3,403,921	608,366	594,285	613,116	1,589,646	109,024	14,420,251

Source: GAO analysis of LP data.

Note: For some loans, the data were insufficient to classify into a status category. These "unknown" loans are included in the total column. This table does not include data for Guam, Puerto Rico, and the Virgin Islands.

ENCLOSURE VI. STATUS OF NONPRIME LOANS ORIGINATED FROM 2000 THROUGH 2007 BY CONGRESSIONAL DISTRICT AS OF MARCH 31, 2009

This enclosure contains the results of our analysis of Loan Performance (LP) data on the status of nonprime mortgages by congressional district. The analysis covers mortgages originated from 2000 through 2007, as of March 31, 2009. All figures reported are estimated.

Table 16. Estimated Percentage of 2000-2007 Active Nonprime Loans Seriously Delinquent by Congressional District as of March 31, 2009.

State	Congressional district	Estimated number of active loans	Estimated number of seriously delinquent loans	Estimated percentage of seriously delinquent loans
Alabama	01	8,367	1,734	20.72%
	02	4,524	740	16.35%
	03	5,628	953	16.94%
	04	3,964	553	13.96%
	05	5,574	752	13.49%
	06	9,457	1,595	16.86%
	07	7,691	1,582	20.56%
Alaska	00	4,670	596	12.76%
Arizona	01	12,891	2,474	19.19%
	02	32,646	8,472	25.95%
	03	23,809	5,430	22.81%
	04	22,956	7,916	34.48%
	05	19,344	3,523	18.21%
	06	31,421	7,638	24.31%
	07	24,909	6,669	26.77%

Table 16. (Continued)

State	Congressional district	Estimated number of active loans	Estimated number of seriously delinquent loans	Estimated percentage of seriously delinquent loans
	08	13,671	2,032	14.86%
Arkansas	01	4,120	610	14.80%
	02	7,471	1,134	15.18%
	03	6,273	916	14.60%
	04	4,055	576	14.21%
California	01	16,356	2,862	17.50%
	02	17,818	3,931	22.06%
	03	27,505	7,581	27.56%
	04	24,450	4,872	19.93%
	05	20,660	6,171	29.87%
	06	19,568	2,844	14.53%
	07	23,011	6,714	29.18%
	08	9,323	943	10.11%
	09	14,626	3,325	22.73%
	10	26,103	6,659	25.51%
	11	31,137	8,889	28.55%
	12	14,667	2,153	14.68%
	13	16,658	4,230	25.39%
	14	13,966	1,711	12.25%
	15	11,997	2,075	17.30%
	16	18,700	4,850	25.94%
	17	15,290	4,091	26.75%
	18	18,044	6,602	36.59%
	19	22,336	6,443	28.84%
	20	12,913	3,402	26.34%

Table 16. (Continued)

State	Congressional district	Estimated number of active loans	Estimated number of seriously delinquent loans	Estimated percentage of seriously delinquent loans
California	21	21,783	5,251	24.11%
	22	29,435	8,355	28.38%
	23	12,095	2,524	20.87%
	24	25,447	5,033	19.78%
	25	36,255	12,686	34.99%
	26	21,200	4,782	22.56%
	27	19,602	5,607	28.60%
	28	15,676	4,274	27.26%
	29	13,626	2,369	17.39%
	30	15,796	2,242	14.20%
	31	9,282	2,237	24.10%
	32	13,972	3,624	25.94%
	33	13,452	3,193	23.74%
	34	10,804	3,012	27.88%
	35	17,473	4,860	27.81%
	36	13,844	1,842	13.30%
	37	18,406	5,346	29.04%
	38	17,539	5,144	29.33%
	39	16,028	4,536	28.30%
	40	15,680	3,841	24.49%
	41	35,210	11,458	32.54%
	42	22,547	4,957	21.99%
	43	25,205	9,484	37.63%
	44	32,885	10,704	32.55%
	45	38,044	12,526	32.93%

Table 16. (Continued)

State	Congressional district	Estimated number of active loans	Estimated number of seriously delinquent loans	Estimated percentage of seriously delinquent loans
California	46	18,151	3,200	17.63%
	47	12,117	4,093	33.77%
	48	20,978	3,738	17.82%
	49	30,461	9,358	30.72%
	50	20,962	3,579	17.07%
	51	24,279	7,412	30.53%
	52	19,513	3,918	20.08%
	53	15,425	2,838	18.40%
Colorado	01	16,233	2,359	14.53%
	02	16,549	1,859	11.23%
	03	12,852	1,419	11.04%
	04	14,775	1,909	12.92%
	05	15,318	2,003	13.08%
	06	21,362	2,860	13.39%
	07	16,790	2,665	15.87%
Connecticut	01	10,304	2,022	19.62%
	02	9,488	1,885	19.87%
	03	12,358	2,842	22.99%
	04	13,751	2,859	20.79%
	05	11,250	2,513	22.34%
Delaware	00	14,349	2,976	20.74%
District of Columbia	98	10,935	1,887	17.25%
Florida	01	13,098	3,090	23.59%
	02	12,460	3,169	25.43%
	03	21,417	7,332	34.24%

Table 16. (Continued)

State	Congressional district	Estimated number of active loans	Estimated number of seriously delinquent loans	Estimated percentage of seriously delinquent loans
Florida	04	17,258	4,406	25.53%
	05	23,869	8,064	33.78%
	06	16,795	4,945	29.44%
	07	24,034	7,874	32.76%
	08	29,026	11,119	38.31%
	09	23,329	7,702	33.02%
	10	19,003	5,878	30.93%
	11	22,936	8,523	37.16%
	12	23,967	8,476	35.37%
	13	22,404	8,552	38.17%
	14	36,735	17,596	47.90%
	15	30,652	12,338	40.25%
	16	24,874	10,471	42.10%
	17	28,296	11,748	41.52%
	18	26,230	11,279	43.00%
	19	28,875	12,142	42.05%
	20	31,603	12,476	39.48%
	21	25,895	10,602	40.94%
	22	28,409	11,063	38.94%
	23	31,435	13,738	43.70%
	24	26,958	9,396	34.86%•
	25	34,801	15,924	45.76%
Georgia	01	6,076	944	15.54%
	02	4,061	692	17.03%
	03	17,662	3,561	20.16%

Table 16. (Continued)

State	Congressional district	Estimated number of active loans	Estimated number of seriously delinquent loans	Estimated percentage of seriously delinquent loans
Georgia	04	18,611	4,008	21.54%
	05	15,359	3,013	19.62%
	06	14,440	2,003	13.87%
	07	21,907	4,102	18.73%
	08	9,016	1,770	19.64%
	09	11,905	1,993	16.74%
	10	7,396	1,097	14.83%
	11	15,467	2,778	17.96%
	12	6,597	1,117	16.94%
	13	22,406	4,939	22.04%
Hawaii	01	9,483	1,283	13.53%
	02	17,315	3,485	20.12%
Idaho	01	17,686	3,277	18.53%
	02	9,073	1,170	12.90%
Illinois	01	13,612	4,150	30.49%
	02	21,197	6,484	30.59%
	03	11,283	3,421	30.32%
	04	9,039	2,830	31.31%
	05	8,970	2,625	29.26%
	06	9,539	2,453	25.72%
	07	12,361	3,632	29.38%
	08	11,944	2,844	23.81%
	09	7,119	1,875	26.33%
	10	7,989	1,803	22.56%
	11	8,939	2,188	24.48%

Table 16. (Continued)

State	Congressional district	Estimated number of active loans	Estimated number of seriously delinquent loans	Estimated percentage of seriously delinquent loans
Illinois	12	5,723	1,279	22.35%
	13	11,309	2,777	24.56%
	14	12,691	3,643	28.71%
	15	3,749	632	16.87%
	16	8,727	1,958	22.44%
	17	3,817	699	18.30%
	18	4,095	744	18.17%
	19	3,815	734	19.25%
Indiana	01	12,258	3,027	24.69%
	02	9,193	1,998	21.74%
	03	8,244	1,744	21.16%
	04	8,696	1,752	20.15%
	05	10,409	2,082	20.01%
	06	8,361	1,667	19.93%
	07	12,689	3,177	25.04%
	08	6,283	1,305	20.76%
	09	6,335	1,353	21.36%
Iowa	01	3,718	651	17.50%
	02	3,360	624	18.57%
	03	6,014	1,223	20.34%
	04	3,608	608	16.84%
	05	3,873	648	16.74%
Kansas	01	3,048	369	12.10%
	02	5,577	819	14.69%
	03	8,862	1,357	15.32%

Table 16. (Continued)

State	Congressional district	Estimated number of active loans	Estimated number of seriously delinquent loans	Estimated percentage of seriously delinquent loans
Kansas	04	6,284	741	11.80%
Kentucky	01	3,373	552	16.35%
	02	5,704	1,008	17.68%
	03	9,120	1,943	21.31%
	04	6,907	1,299	18.81%
	05	2,789	431	15.46%
	06	6,982	1,185	16.98%
Louisiana	01	7,513	1,400	18.63%
	02	7,596	1,676	22.07%
	03	5,707	1,047	18.35%
	04	5,860	1,106	18.88%
	05	4,130	782	18.94%
	06	10,026	1,840	18.35%
	07	4,573	641	14.02%
Maine	01	8,314	1,918	23.07%
	02	6,665	1,528	22.93%
Maryland	01	12,430	2,349	18.90%
	02	12,252	2,568	20.96%
	03	14,397	2,736	19.00%
	04	22,254	6,462	29.04%
	05	24,167	6,566	27.17%
	06	12,321	2,645	21.47%
	07	13,249	2,771	20.91%
	08	13,580	2,984	21.97%
Massachusetts	01	6,878	1,749	25.44%

Table 16. (Continued)

State	Congressional district	Estimated number of active loans	Estimated number of seriously delinquent loans	Estimated percentage of seriously delinquent loans
Massachusetts	02	9,489	2,577	27.15%
	03	8,504	2,269	26.68%
	04	7,506	1,740	23.18%
	05	8,748	2,248	25.70%
	06	7,650	1,887	24.67%
	07	7,190	1,758	24.46%
	08	6,456	1,491	23.09%
	09	10,443	2,832	27.12%
	10	10,370	2,427	23.40%
Michigan	01	5,296	751	14.18%
	02	6,836	1,194	17.46%
	03	7,862	1,441	18.32%
	04	6,363	1,089	17.11%
	05	8,810	1,905	21.62%
	06	7,818	1,217	15.56%
	07	8,675	1,693	19.52%
	08	10,022	1,743	17.39%
	09	10,264	1,949	18.99%
	10	8,998	1,633	18.15%
	11	10,934	2,171	19.86%
	12	13,307	2,792	20.98%
	13	13,412	3,619	26.98%
	14	16,734	4,749	28.38%
	15	10,579	2,293	21.68%
Minnesota	01	4,569	706	15.45%

Table 16. (Continued)

State	Congressional district	Estimated number of active loans	Estimated number of seriously delinquent loans	Estimated percentage of seriously delinquent loans
Minnesota	02	11,674	2,121	18.17%
	03	10,514	2,036	19.36%
	04	8,264	1,747	21.15%
	05	9,615	2,003	20.83%
	06	11,823	2,391	20.22%
	07	4,434	698	15.74%
	08	7,766	1,439	18.53%
Mississippi	01	8,106	1,783	21.99%
	02	7,266	1,768	24.33%
	03	5,213	993	19.04%
	04	6,485	1,168	18.01%
Missouri	01	14,888	3,191	21.43%
	02	6,904	979	14.18%
	03	8,552	1,381	16.15%
	04	5,133	732	14.26%
	05	13,148	2,285	17.38%
	06	7,865	1,092	13.89%
	07	6,791	946	13.93%
	08	3,539	440	12.44%
	09	4,899	639	13.05%
Montana	00	7,701	1,046	13.58%
Nebraska	01	4,342	646	14.89%
	02	6,699	1,032	15.40%
	03	2,861	353	12.34%
Nevada	01	38,333	12,115	31.60%

Table 16. (Continued)

State	Congressional district	Estimated number of active loans	Estimated number of seriously delinquent loans	Estimated percentage of seriously delinquent loans
Nevada	02	23,034	5,213	22.63%
	03	54,884	16,040	29.23%
New Hampshire	01	9,890	1,641	16.59%
	02	8,627	1,479	17.14%
New Jersey	01	10,062	2,803	27.86%
	02	12,509	3,397	27.15%
	03	11,487	3,021	26.30%
	04	11,284	2,911	25.79%
	05	9,355	2,108	22.53%
	06	8,952	2,586	28.89%
	07	7,940	1,955	24.62%
	08	10,106	3,381	33.45%
	09	8,965	2,460	27.44%
	10	11,301	4,766	42.17%
	11	7,763	1,700	21.90%
	12	9,340	2,184	23.38%
	13	9,978	3,443	34.51%
New Mexico	01	9,376	1,402	14.95%
	02	5,125	687	13.40%
	03	7,338	1,066	14.52%
New York	01	18,727	5,201	27.77%
	02	16,540	5,482	33.14%
	03	12,470	3,110	24.94%
	04	14,778	4,511	30.52%
	05	7,139	1,268	17.76%

Table 16. (Continued)

State	Congressional district	Estimated number of active loans	Estimated number of seriously delinquent loans	Estimated percentage of seriously delinquent loans
New York	06	15,363	5,313	34.58%
	07	6,888	1,758	25.52%
	08	3,453	421	12.18%
	09	7,808	1,809	23.16%
	10	9,920	3,490	35.18%
	11	5,371	1,477	27.51%
	12	4,838	1,375	28.42%
	13	9,060	1,951	21.54%
	14	3,219	234	7.28%
	15	985	180	18.25%
	16	1,950	618	31.68%
	17	8,573	2,154	25.13%
	18	8,835	1,539	17.42%
	19	12,330	2,643	21.44%
	20	8,407	1,838	21.86%
	21	6,651	1,453	21.85%
	22	7,582	1,848	24.38%
	23	3,547	622	17.54%
	24	4,539	736	16.21%
	25	4,950	832	16.81%
	26	4,680	709	15.14%
	27	4,642	690	14.86%
	28	5,926	1,013	17.09%
	29	4,256	660	15.50%
North Carolina	01	4,239	717	16.91%

Table 16. (Continued)

State	Congressional district	Estimated number of active loans	Estimated number of seriously delinquent loans	Estimated percentage of seriously delinquent loans
North Carolina	02	7,425	1,248	16.80%
	03	7,881	1,065	13.51%
	04	8,815	1,138	12.91%
	05	5,634	830	14.73%
	06	7,976	1,245	15.61%
	07	7,973	1,119	14.03%
	08	7,607	1,197	15.74%
	09	14,259	2,139	15.00%
	10	6,922	1,117	16.14%
	11	6,196	816	13.17%
	12	11,330	1,901	16.77%
	13	8,447	1,315	15.57%
North Dakota	00	2,481	290	11.69%
Ohio	01	9,532	2,085	21.87%
	02	6,999	1,312	18.74%
	03	8,958	2,218	24.76%
	04	6,735	1,409	20.92%
	05	5,328	1,055	19.81%
	06	5,041	1,119	22.20%
	07	8,565	1,884	21.99%
	08	7,822	1,685	21.55%
	09	9,034	2,088	23.11%
	10	9,930	2,324	23.40%
	11	13,342	4,109	30.79%
	12	10,983	2,386	21.72%

Table 16. (Continued)

State	Congressional district	Estimated number of active loans	Estimated number of seriously delinquent loans	Estimated percentage of seriously delinquent loans
Ohio	13	9,804	2,384	24.32%
	14	8,263	1,693	20.49%
	15	8,502	1,854	21.80%
	16	7,789	1,661	21.33%
	17	8,974	2,418	26.94%
	18	5,500	1,109	20.16%
Oklahoma	01	9,529	1,472	15.45%
	02	5,062	774	15.29%
	03	5,446	727	13.35%
	04	7,708	1,001	12.99%
	05	9,651	1,496	15.51%
Oregon	01	13,437	1,991	14.81%
	02	14,031	2,496	17.79%
	03	16,537	2,574	15.57%
	04	11,041	1,540	13.95%
	05	12,880	1,995	15.49%
Pennsylvania	01	12,226	2,255	18.44%
	02	11,155	2,038	18.27%
	03	5,052	874	17.30%
	04	7,401	1,289	17.42%
	05	3,580	595	16.61%
	06	8,070	1,315	16.29%
	07	8,034	1,387	17.26%
	08	8,129	1,491	18.34%
	09	5,079	863	16.99%

Table 16. (Continued)

State	Congressional district	Estimated number of active loans	Estimated number of seriously delinquent loans	Estimated percentage of seriously delinquent loans
Pennsylvania	10	6,834	1,330	19.47%
	11	11,295	2,571	22.76%
	12	5,125	919	17.94%
	13	8,836	1,501	16.99%
	14	8,259	1,520	18.41%
	15	9,816	1,894	19.29%
	16	5,987	977	16.32%
	17	6,963	1,121	16.10%
	18	8,376	1,447	17.28%
	19	7,703	1,363	17.69%
Rhode Island	01	7,267	1,498	20.61%
	02	9,067	2,126	23.45%
South Carolina	01	16,401	2,892	17.63%•
	02	12,169	2,080	17.09%
	03	5,860	847	14.46%
	04	8,321	1,401	16.83%
	05	7,294	1,220	16.73%
	06	6,968	1,234	17.71%
South Dakota	00	3,505	503	14.35%
Tennessee	01	5,972	870	14.56%
	02	8,734	1,392	15.93%
	03	8,693	1,574	18.11%
	04	6,106	1,010	16.54%
	05	12,653	2,042	16.14%
	06	10,089	1,723	17.07%

Table 16. (Continued)

State	Congressional district	Estimated number of active loans	Estimated number of seriously delinquent loans	Estimated percentage of seriously delinquent loans
Tennessee	07	11,883	2,094	17.62%
	08	8,122	1,732	21.33%
	09	15,837	3,923	24.77%
Texas	01	5,318	565	10.63%
	02	15,268	2,259	14.80%
	03	13,982	1,594	11.40%
	04	11,611	1,383	11.91%
	05	11,169	1,494	13.37%
	06	14,352	1,983	13.82%
	07	13,066	1,521	11.64%
	08	10,785	1,348	12.50%
	09	15,203	2,094	13.77%
	10	18,637	2,504	13.43%
	11	5,472	450	8.22%
	12	13,779	1,672	12.13%
	13	4,554	468	10.29%
	14	11,070	1,537	13.88%
	15	8,246	1,002	12.16%
	16	8,392	785	9.35%
	17	8,071	855	10.59%
	18	14,554	2,175	14.95%
	19	5,106	463	9.06%
	20	10,036	1,205	12.00%
	21	13,993	1,480	10.57%
	22	18,852	2,743	14.55%

Table 16. (Continued)

State	Congressional district	Estimated number of active loans	Estimated number of seriously delinquent loans	Estimated percentage of seriously delinquent loans
Texas	23	11,230	1,367	12.18%
	24	14,862	2,029	13.65%
	25	10,872	1,015	9.33%
	26	17,265	2,109	12.21%
	27	9,244	1,039	11.24%
	28	9,775	1,232	12.60%
	29	11,207	1,472	13.14%
	30	14,193	2,326	16.39%
	31	10,650	1,064	9.99%
	32	8,257	894	10.82%
Utah	01	12,831	1,733	13.51%
	02	14,794	2,493	16.85%
	03	14,745	2,406	16.32%
Vermont	00	4,721	878	18.60%
Virginia	01	14,898	2,941	19.74%
	02	11,582	1,535	13.25%
	03	12,125	2,023	16.68%
	04	11,878	1,985	16.71%
	05	6,234	764	12.26%
	06	5,922	788	13.30%
	07	11,408	1,838	16.11%
	08	12,230	1,869	15.28%
	09	3,058	358	11.69%
	10	21,147	4,282	20.25%
	11	19,809	4,351	21.96%

Table 16. (Continued)

State	Congressional district	Estimated number of active loans	Estimated number of seriously delinquent loans	Estimated percentage of seriously delinquent loans
Washington	01	13,812	2,017	14.61%
	02	15,324	2,467	16.10%
	03	15,426	2,811	18.22%
	04	8,885	953	10.72%
	05	8,316	1,014	12.20%
	06	15,119	2,594	17.16%
	07	11,318	1,372	12.12%
	08	17,651	2,966	16.80%
	09	16,478	3,101	18.82%
West Virginia	01	2,310	343	14.86%
	02	4,329	899	20.77%
	03	2,286	345	15.09%
Wisconsin	01	7,233	1,758	24.30%
	02	4,740	1,046	22.07%
	03	4,097	958	23.39%
	04	11,517	3,299	28.65%
	05	5,498	1,245	22.65%
	06	4,459	1,010	22.64%
	07	4,024	863	21.46%
	08	4,375	984	22.48%
Wyoming	00	4,823	432	8.96%

Source: GAO analysis of LP data.

ENCLOSURE VII. GAO CONTACT AND STAFF ACKNOWLEDGMENTS

GAO Contact: William B. Shear, (202) 512-8678 or shearw@gao.gov

Staff Acknowledgments: In addition to the individual named above, Steve Westley (Assistant Director), William Bates, Emily Chalmers, DuEwa Kamara, Jamila Kennedy, John McGrail, John Mingus, Colleen Moffatt, Marc Molino, and Bob Pollard made key contributions to this report.

End Notes

[1] Although the categories are not rigidly defined, subprime loans feature higher interest rates and fees and are generally made to borrowers who have tarnished credit histories. Alt-A loans are generally for borrowers whose credit histories are close to prime, but the loans have one or more high-risk features such as limited documentation of income or assets.

[2] See Inside Mortgage Finance, *The 2009 Mortgage Market Statistical Annual* (Bethesda, Md., 2009), 4.

[3] See GAO, *Information on Recent Default and Foreclosure Trends for Home Mortgages and Associated Economic and Market Developments*, GAO-08-78R (Washington, D.C.: Oct. 16, 2007).

[4] LP is a unit of First American CoreLogic, Incorporated.

[5] Nonagency mortgage-backed securities (MBS), also known as private-label MBS, are backed by nonconforming conventional mortgages securitized primarily by investment banks. Nonconforming mortgages are those that do not meet the purchase requirements of Fannie Mae or Freddie Mac because they are too large or do not meet their underwriting criteria.

[6] The LP database has a loan-level indicator for loan class (i.e., subprime or Alt-A), but it is not well populated. We therefore used the pool-level classification. According to mortgage researchers, some of the loans in subprime pools may not be subprime loans, and some of the loans in Alt-A pools may not be Alt-A loans.

[7] Unless noted otherwise, we treat delinquent loans, loans in default, and loans in the foreclosure process as mutually exclusive categories. We considered a loan to have completed the foreclosure process if it was in real estate-owned status as of March 31, 2009, or was paid off after being 90 or more days delinquent, in the foreclosure process, or in real estate-owned status.

[8] A loan cohort is a group of loans originated in the same year.

[9] The LP data provide the state and ZIP code of the property associated with each loan.

[10] The DTI ratio is the borrower's total monthly debt service payments divided by monthly gross income.

[11] In comparison, as of the first quarter of 2007, active nonprime loans originated from 2000 through 2005 had a serious delinquency rate of 7.4 percent.

[12] There is no uniform definition of default across the lending industry. For purposes of this report, we use the definition provided.

[13] For more information about some of these products, see GAO, *Alternative Mortgage Products: Impacts on Defaults Remains Unclear, but Disclosure of Risks to Borrowers Could Be Improved*, GAO-06-1021 (Washington, D.C.: Sept. 16, 2006). As we reported in 2007, of the top 25 originators of nonprime loans in 2006—which accounted for over 90 percent of the dollar volume of all such originations—21 were nonbank lenders, including 14 independent lenders and 7 nonbank subsidiaries of banks, thrifts, or holding companies. See GAO-08-78R.

[14] Percentage is from FHFA's purchase-only house price index.

[15] As previously noted, the data we used for our analysis do not cover the entire nonprime market but do cover the large majority of nonagency securitized mortgages within that market.

[16] See GAO-08-78R.

[17] LTV ratio is the amount of the loan divided by the value of the home at origination.

[18] The CLTV field in the LP data was frequently not populated, but the LTV field almost always was. In some cases, the CLTV field likely was blank because there was no piggyback loan associated with the mortgage, but in other cases there likely was a piggyback loan that was not captured in the data. We determined average CLTV ratios by using the CLTV field when it was populated and the LTV field when the CLTV field was blank. As a result, it is likely that the average CLTV ratios we present are somewhat lower than the actual averages.

[19] The figures presented are for the 61 percent of nonprime loans for which the data contained DTI information. Twenty-nine percent of the subprime loans and 56 percent of the Alt-A loans in the LP database did not contain DTI information.

[20] Our analysis of ARMs excluded balloon mortgages, which can have a fixed or adjustable interest rate. A balloon mortgage does not fully amortize over the term of the loan, leaving a balance due at maturity. The final payment is called a balloon payment because it is generally much larger than the other payments.

[21] See, for example, Shane Sherlund, "The Past, Present, and Future of Subprime Mortgages," Finance and Economics Discussion Series 2008-63, Federal Reserve Board (November 2008). See also, Christopher Foote, Kristopher Gerardi, Lorenz Goette, and Paul Willen, "Subprime Facts: What (We Think) We Know about the Subprime Crisis and What We Don't," Working Papers No. 08-2, Federal Reserve Board (May 2008).

[22] See GAO-06-1021.

[23] See, for example, Roberto Quercia, Michael Stegman, and Walter Davis, "The Impact of Predatory Loan Terms on Subprime Foreclosures: The Special Case of Prepayment Penalties and Balloon Payments," *Housing Policy Debate*, vol. 18, no. 2 (2007), 311-346. However, other research has found that prepayment penalties are not associated with higher default rates. See, for example, Sherlund, "The Past, Present, and Future of Subprime Mortgages."

[24] Although typically associated with the Alt-A market, loans with low or no documentation of borrower income or assets were also offered in the subprime market, which serves borrowers with lower credit scores.

[25] According to the LP data, the overwhelming majority of nonprime mortgages with less than full documentation had low documentation rather than no documentation.

[26] In comparison, as of the first quarter of 2007, active nonprime loans originated from 2000 through 2005 had a serious delinquency rate of 7.4 percent.

[27] Three-year foreclosure rates for the 2007 cohort will not be available until 2010. However, as of March 31, 2009, the subprime and Alt-A cumulative foreclosure rates for the 2007 cohort were 10 percent and 7 percent, respectively.

[28] The nine Census divisions include Pacific (Hawaii, Alaska, Washington, Oregon, and California); Mountain (Montana, Idaho, Wyoming, Nevada, Utah, Colorado, Arizona, and New Mexico); West North Central (North Dakota, South Dakota, Minnesota, Nebraska, Iowa, Kansas, and Missouri); West South Central (Oklahoma, Arkansas, Texas, and Louisiana); East North Central (Michigan, Wisconsin, Illinois, Indiana, and Ohio); East South Central (Kentucky, Tennessee, Mississippi, and Alabama); New England (Maine, New Hampshire, Vermont, Massachusetts, Rhode Island, and Connecticut); Mid Atlantic (New York, New Jersey, and Pennsylvania); and South Atlantic (Delaware, Maryland, District of Columbia, Virginia, West Virginia, North Carolina, South Carolina, Georgia, and Florida).

[29] According to data from the 2000 Census, the United States has 435 congressional districts. Each congressional district elects a member to the United States House of Representatives. California has the most districts with 53, and seven states (Alaska, Delaware, Montana, North Dakota, South Dakota, Vermont, and Wyoming) have just one district.

[30] As previously discussed, we defined subprime loans as loans in subprime pools and Alt-A loans as loans in Alt-A pools.

In: Mortgage Markets and the Role of Nonprime Loans   ISBN: 978-1-61122-918-9
Editor: Eric J. Carlson   © 2011 Nova Science Publishers, Inc.

Chapter 2

LOAN PERFORMANCE AND NEGATIVE HOME EQUITY IN THE NONPRIME MORTGAGE MARKET

United States Government Accountability Office

December 16, 2009

The Honorable Carolyn B. Maloney
Chair
Joint Economic Committee
House of Representatives

The Honorable Charles E. Schumer
Vice Chairman
Joint Economic Committee
United States Senate

Subject: *Loan Performance and Negative Home Equity in the Nonprime Mortgage Market*

As we reported to you in July 2009, the number of nonprime mortgage originations (including subprime and Alt-A loans) grew rapidly from 2000 through 2006, a period during which average house prices appreciated dramatically.[1] In dollar terms, the nonprime share of mortgage originations rose from about 12 percent ($125 billion) in 2000 to approximately 34 percent ($1 trillion) in 2006. These mortgages have been associated with what was subsequently recognized as a speculative housing bubble. As house prices subsequently fell, the subprime and Alt-A market segments contracted sharply, and very few nonprime originations were made after mid-2007. Borrowers who had obtained nonprime mortgages earlier in the decade increasingly fell behind on their mortgage payments, helping to push default and foreclosure rates to historical highs.

Economic conditions and a weak housing market have contributed to the increase in troubled loans. In particular, falling house prices have left many borrowers in a negative equity position—that is, their mortgage balances exceed the current value of their homes. Negative equity makes borrowers more vulnerable to foreclosure by, among other factors, limiting their ability to sell or refinance their homes in the event they cannot stay current on their mortgage payments.

To inform congressional decision making about efforts to address problems in the mortgage market, you requested that we examine the evolution and condition of the market for nonprime loans. On July 28, 2009, we provided you with an interim report on certain characteristics of nonprime loans and borrowers, and the performance of nonprime mortgages originated from 2000 through 2007 (the last year in which substantial numbers of nonprime mortgages were made) as of March 31, 2009. This report (1) provides information on the performance of these nonprime loans as of June 30, 2009, and describes forecasts made by others of future loan performance; and (2) examines the extent of negative home equity among nonprime borrowers in selected metropolitan areas and nationwide. In addition, enclosure VI describes the preliminary results of our analysis of the demographic characteristics of nonprime borrowers—including race and ethnicity—whose loans originated in 2005.[2] We identified these characteristics by merging loan-level records from two data sources. This report also provides supplemental information on the performance of nonprime mortgages by annual loan cohort, product type, Census division, state, and congressional district. This supplemental information is presented in enclosures I through IV.

As agreed with your offices, in a final report we will provide information on the influence of nonprime loan and borrower characteristics and economic conditions on the likelihood of mortgage default and foreclosure. We will also describe the features and limitations of primary sources of data on nonprime mortgage performance and borrower characteristics. In addition, the final report will update information on the performance of nonprime mortgages and provide additional analysis of the characteristics of nonprime borrowers.

To conduct our work, we analyzed data from LoanPerformance's (LP) Asset-backed Securities database for nonprime loans originated from 2000 through 2007.[3] The database contains loan-level data on the majority of nonagency securitized mortgages in subprime and Alt-A pools.[4] For example, for the period 2001 through July 2007 the LP database contains information covering, in dollar terms, an estimated 87 percent of securitized subprime loans and 98 percent of securitized Alt-A loans. Research has found that nonprime mortgages that were not securitized (i.e., mortgages that lenders held in their portfolios) may have different characteristics and performance histories than those that were securitized. For purposes of our analysis, we defined a subprime loan as a loan in a subprime pool and an Alt-A loan as a loan in an Alt-A pool.[5] We focused our analysis on first-lien purchase and refinance mortgages for one- to four-family residential units. For certain analyses, we supplemented the LP data with data on house prices from the Federal Housing Finance Agency (FHFA) and Standard & Poor's (S&P)/Case-Shiller indexes, and data on borrower characteristics from the Home Mortgage Disclosure Act (HMDA) data set.

To examine the recent and expected performance of nonprime mortgages, we calculated the number and percentage of mortgages that were in different performance categories—for example, current (up-to-date on payments), delinquent (30 to 89 days behind), in default (90 or more days behind), in the foreclosure process, or having completed the foreclosure process as of June 30, 2009.[6] We classified mortgages in default or in the foreclosure process as "seriously delinquent." We also examined mortgage performance by loan cohort, loan type, and geographic area, including Census divisions, states, and congressional districts.[7] For detailed information on the performance of nonprime loans by these geographic areas, see enclosures III and IV. We also reviewed select studies containing forecasts of the performance of the mortgage market and interviewed the authors of those studies. We focused on four nonproprietary forecasts conducted in 2008 or 2009 that we identified through literature searches and discussions with industry researchers.

To examine the extent of negative equity among nonprime borrowers, we used the LP data and house price indexes from FHFA and S&P/Case-Shiller. More specifically, we used the indexes to adjust the appraised value of each home at loan origination to an estimated value as of June 30, 2009. We then subtracted the unpaid mortgage balance as of that date from the house value to estimate the borrower's home equity. We used two different indexes for these calculations because they offer different advantages. To estimate negative equity nationwide, we used the FHFA All-Transactions House Price Index (FHFA index) because it provides the broadest geographic coverage.[8] Because the FHFA index likely understates average house price declines experienced by nonprime borrowers from 2005 through 2008, our estimates of negative equity using this index are also likely to be understated. For estimates of negative equity in specific metropolitan areas, we used the S&P/Case-Shiller Tiered Price Indices (S&P/Case-Shiller index) because it uses data from a broader range of properties than the FHFA index and includes separate indexes for homes in different price ranges within a metropolitan area.[9] See enclosure V for a detailed description of the methodology we used to estimate negative equity and key differences between the two sets of house price indexes.

We tested the reliability of the data used in this report by reviewing documentation on the process the data providers use to collect and ensure the reliability and integrity of their data, and by conducting reasonableness checks on data elements to identify any missing, erroneous, or outlying data. We also interviewed LP representatives to discuss the interpretation of various data fields. We concluded that the data we used were sufficiently reliable for our purposes. We conducted this engagement in Washington, D.C., from August 2009 through November 2009 in accordance with all sections of GAO's Quality Assurance Framework that are relevant to our objectives. The framework requires that we plan and perform the engagement to obtain sufficient and appropriate evidence to meet our stated objectives and to discuss any limitations in our work. We believe that the evidence obtained provides a reasonable basis for our findings based on our audit objectives.

RESULTS IN BRIEF

The performance of mortgages in the nonprime market segment worsened during the second quarter of 2009 (April 1 through June 30, 2009), as the number of loans that completed the foreclosure process or became seriously delinquent increased from the previous quarter. For example, 147,000 loans completed the foreclosure process in the second quarter, an increase of 9 percent from the first quarter, and the number of seriously delinquent loans grew by about 48,000, a 4 percent increase. The growth in serious delinquencies, coupled with a decline in the total number of active loans due to prepayments and completed foreclosures, increased the serious delinquency rate from 23 percent to 26 percent during the second quarter. Although serious delinquencies were most prevalent among subprime borrowers and for adjustable-rate products, serious delinquencies in the second quarter of 2009 were growing most rapidly for Alt-A borrowers and fixed-rate mortgages. The number of nonprime loans that were seriously delinquent rose by approximately 2 percent (16,000) in the subprime market, compared with 7 percent (32,000) in the Alt-A market. For fixed-rate Alt-A loans, the corresponding increase was 11 percent (13,000). Forecasts made by others suggest that weaknesses in the nonprime mortgage market will persist, primarily due to expected declines in home prices.

Our analysis of borrowers with active nonprime mortgages originated from 2000 through 2007 indicates that a substantial proportion had negative equity in their homes as of June 30, 2009. Our estimates using the S&P/Case-Shiller index for 16 metropolitan areas showed that the percentage of borrowers with negative equity ranged from about 9 percent (Denver, Colorado) to more than 90 percent (Las Vegas, Nevada). Our estimates also indicate that in the 16 metropolitan areas we reviewed, nonprime borrowers who obtained their mortgages to purchase a home were more likely to have negative home equity than those who refinanced their mortgages. Using the FHFA index, we estimated that one-quarter of nonprime borrowers with active loans nationwide had negative equity in their homes as of June 30, 2009. We also found that the incidence of negative equity was highest among borrowers who obtained their mortgages in 2005, 2006, and 2007.

BACKGROUND

The nonprime mortgage market has two segments:

- *Subprime*—Generally serves borrowers with blemished credit histories, and the loans feature higher interest rates and fees than prime loans.
- *Alt-A*—Generally serves borrowers whose credit histories are close to prime, but the loans have one or more high-risk features such as limited documentation of income or assets or the option of making monthly payments that are lower than would be required for a fully amortizing loan.

In both of these categories, two types of loans are common: fixed-rate mortgages, which have unchanging interest rates, and adjustable-rate mortgages (ARM), which have interest rates that can adjust periodically based on changes in a specified index. Specific types of ARMs are prevalent in each market segment. "Short-term hybrid ARMs" accounted for most subprime mortgage originations in recent years.[10] These loans have a fixed interest rate for an initial period but then "reset" to an adjustable rate for the remaining term of the loan. In the Alt-A segment, "payment-option ARMs" are a common adjustable-rate product.[11] For an initial period of typically 5 years, or when the loan balance reaches a specified cap, this product provides the borrower with multiple payment options each month, including minimum payments that are lower than what would be needed to cover any of the principal or all of the accrued interest. After the initial period, payments are "recast" to include an amount that will fully amortize the outstanding balance over the remaining loan term.

Nonprime mortgages, like all mortgages, can fall into any one of several payment categories:

- *Current*—The borrower is meeting scheduled payments.
- *Delinquent*—The borrower has missed one or more scheduled monthly payments.
- *Default*—The borrower is 90 or more days delinquent.[12] At this point, foreclosure proceedings against the borrower become a strong possibility.
- *Foreclosure*—The borrower has been delinquent for more than 90 days, and the lender has elected to foreclose in what is an often lengthy process with several possible outcomes. For instance, the borrower may sell the property or the lender may repossess the home.
- *Prepaid*—The borrower has paid off the entire loan balance before it is due. Prepayment often occurs as a result of the borrower selling the home or refinancing into a new mortgage.

In this report, we describe mortgages in default or in the foreclosure process as "seriously delinquent."

The amount of equity a homeowner has in a mortgaged property may influence how well the mortgage performs. In general, higher levels of home equity are associated with lower probabilities of default and foreclosure. Equity is a homeowner's financial interest in a property, or the difference between the value of a property and the amount still owed on the mortgage. Typically, home equity increases over time as the mortgage balance is paid down and home values appreciate. However, if the home value falls below the amount owed on the mortgage, the borrower will be in a position of negative equity. Borrowers with nonprime loans may be especially vulnerable to negative equity because they typically make small down payments and, as previously discussed, may have loans with payment options that defer payment of accrued interest, thereby increasing the outstanding loan balance.

House price appreciation or depreciation in a geographic area is commonly measured by changes in a house price index. Such indexes are based on the sales prices or appraised values for the same housing units over time. FHFA and S&P/Case-Shiller produce two widely used house price indexes that use this method.

THE PERFORMANCE OF NONPRIME MORTGAGES DETERIORATED INTO MID-2009, AND CONTINUING DETERIORATION APPEARS LIKELY

The performance of mortgages in the nonprime market segment worsened during the second quarter of 2009 (April 1 through June 30, 2009), as the number of loans that completed the foreclosure process or became seriously delinquent grew from the previous quarter.[13] Although serious delinquencies were most prevalent among subprime borrowers and for adjustable-rate products, serious delinquencies in the second quarter of 2009 were growing most rapidly for Alt-A borrowers and fixed-rate mortgages. Forecasts made by others suggest that weaknesses in the nonprime mortgage market will persist, primarily due to expected declines in home prices.

Foreclosures and Serious Delinquencies Increased across Market Segments and Product Types

As of June 30, 2009, approximately 1.7 million of the 14.4 million nonprime loans (12 percent) originated from 2000 through 2007 had completed the foreclosure process (see figure 1). Of that 1.7 million, about 147,000 loans completed foreclosure in the second quarter of 2009, an increase of 9 percent from the first quarter. Subprime mortgages accounted for about 89,000, or about 61 percent, of the completed foreclosures in the second quarter. Although foreclosures and serious delinquencies increased, the number of mortgage prepayments also grew. As of June 30, 2009, more than half of nonprime mortgages (54 percent or 7.8 million) were prepaid as of June 30, 2009.[14] Of that 7.8 million, approximately 154,000 mortgages were prepaid in the second quarter of 2009, an increase of about 2 percent from the previous quarter.

Other measures of the performance of nonprime mortgages have also weakened since the first quarter of 2009. Of the 4.9 million nonprime loans still active as of the second quarter of 2009, approximately 3.1 million (63 percent) were current (i.e., borrowers were meeting scheduled payments), down by about 328,000 (10 percent) from the previous quarter. During the second quarter, the number of seriously delinquent loans—loans either in default or in the foreclosure process—grew from 1,208,000 to 1,256,000 (4 percent). This growth, coupled with a decline in the total number of active nonprime loans due to prepayments and completed foreclosures, increased the serious delinquency rate from 23 percent to 26 percent during the second quarter.[15]

Although the absolute number of seriously delinquent loans was higher in the subprime market than in the Alt-A market, the rate of growth in serious delinquencies in the second quarter was higher for Alt-A loans. At the end of the second quarter of 2009, about 791,000 subprime loans (31 percent) and 466,000 Alt-A loans (20 percent) were seriously delinquent. In that quarter, serious delinquencies grew by approximately 16,000 loans (2 percent) in the subprime market and 32,000 loans (7 percent) in the Alt-A market.

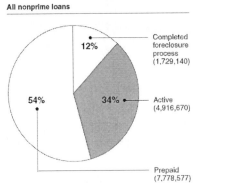 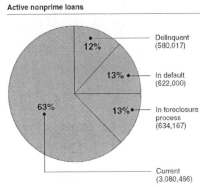

Source: GAO analysis of LP data.

Note: We considered loans to be delinquent if borrowers were 30 to 89 days late on their mortgage payments. We considered loans to be in default if borrowers were 90 or more days late. Percentages in graphs may not add to 100 percent due to rounding.

Figure 1. Percentage of All Nonprime Loans and All Active Nonprime Loans Originated from 2000 through 2007 by Performance Status, as of June 30, 2009.

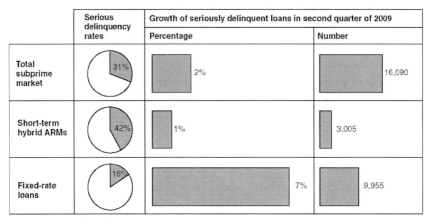

Source: GAO analysis of LP data.

Note: We considered loans to be seriously delinquent if borrowers were 90 days or more late on their mortgage payments or in the foreclosure process.

Figure 2. Subprime Serious Delinquency Rates as of June 30, 2009, and Growth of Seriously Delinquent Subprime Loans in the Second Quarter of 2009.

Additionally, while certain ARM products had the highest serious delinquency rates as of the end of the second quarter, the rate of growth in serious delinquencies was higher for fixed-rate mortgages in that quarter. For example, in the subprime market, 42 percent of short-term hybrid ARMs were seriously delinquent as of the end of the second quarter, compared with 16 percent of fixed-rate mortgages (see figure 2). However, while the number of short-term hybrid ARMs that were seriously delinquent increased by 1 percent (from about 584,000 to 587,000) over the quarter, the corresponding increase for subprime fixed-rate loans was 7 percent (from about 142,000 to 152,000).

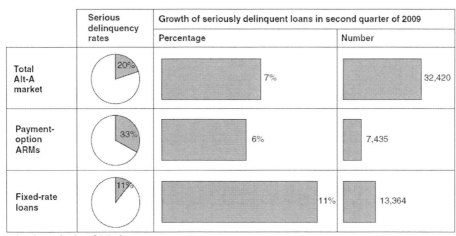

Source: GAO analysis of LP data.

Note: We considered loans to be seriously delinquent if borrowers were 90 days or more late on their mortgage payments or in the foreclosure process.

Figure 3. Alt-A Serious Delinquency Rates as of June 30, 2009, and Growth of Seriously Delinquent Alt-A Loans in the Second Quarter of 2009.

In the Alt-A market, 33 percent of payment-option ARMs were seriously delinquent as of June 30, 2009, compared with 11 percent of fixed-rate loans (see figure 3). But while the number of payment-option ARMs that were seriously delinquent grew by 6 percent (from somewhat over 122,000 to about 130,000), the corresponding increase for fixed-rate loans was 11 percent (from about 118,000 to about 131,000).

Enclosures I and II provide more detailed information about the performance of nonprime loans by cohort year and product type. For detailed data on the performance of nonprime loans by Census division, state, and congressional district see enclosures III and IV.

Forecasters Predict That the Weak Performance of Nonprime Loans Will Persist, Largely Due to Declining Home Prices

The four studies we reviewed that sought to forecast the performance of the U.S. mortgage market generally predicted that elevated levels of default and foreclosure will persist.[16] The studies differed in the methods they used to predict future performance, and none focused specifically on the nonprime market, although 3 included forecasts of the subprime segment of the nonprime market.[17]

Two studies of the subprime market segment estimated that the number of these loans entering foreclosure annually would gradually decline after peaking in 2008 but would likely remain in the hundreds of thousands per year. For example, a Credit Suisse study estimated that 1.9 million subprime loans would enter foreclosure between the third quarter of 2008 and the end of 2012.[18] (The study estimated that about 1.1 million of these foreclosures would occur from 2010 through 2012.) While none of the four studies we reviewed addressed the Alt-A market specifically, the authors told us that default and foreclosure rates in that market segment have yet to peak. One author explained this phenomenon by noting that Alt-A borrowers often had higher levels of initial equity compared with subprime borrowers, which provided a larger cushion against falling home prices.

Among the factors contributing to future defaults and foreclosures, forecasters identified declining home prices as the most important. Additionally, forecasters indicated that factors affecting the affordability of mortgages—such as unemployment, loan recasts, and mortgage modifications—would also affect loan performance in coming years.

House Price Depreciation

We and others have reported on the strong statistical relationship between changes in house prices and the likelihood of mortgage defaults and foreclosures.[19] Falling house prices can result in negative home equity—that is, a mortgage balance that exceeds the current value of the property. Homeowners with negative equity may find it difficult to sell or refinance the property to avoid foreclosure. They may also have incentives to stop making mortgage payments to minimize their financial losses. Prior research suggests that negative equity is a necessary, but not sufficient, condition for foreclosure.[20] Besides having negative equity, borrowers who end up in foreclosure often experience a "trigger event," such as job loss or divorce that reduces their ability to make mortgage payments.

Three of the four forecasts we reviewed included the assumption that average house prices would continue to fall appreciably into 2010, resulting in a higher incidence and severity of negative equity among nonprime borrowers.[21] For example, one forecast assumed cumulative house price depreciation of 8.5 percent over the 3 year period ending in the last quarter of 2010, while another assumed a cumulative 15 percent decline over the 2 year period ending in mid-2010. On the basis of data from home purchases, S&P/Case-Shiller and FHFA have both reported that average house prices at the national level increased in the third quarter of 2009. However, several recent forecasts have projected house price declines in 2010.[22]

All of the forecasters indicated that house price changes will play a key role in future mortgage performance. For example, a study that simulated subprime mortgage performance found that the number of subprime defaults was more sensitive to house price trends than other explanatory variables. Similarly, the authors of a study addressing the entire mortgage market told us that anticipated house price declines accounted for about 80 percent of the defaults they were forecasting.

Factors Affecting Mortgage Affordability

Forecasters we spoke with noted several factors affecting the affordability of mortgage payments will influence the number of nonprime loans that will end in foreclosure over the next few years. These factors include job loss, mortgage recasts, and federal loan modification efforts.

- *Job loss*—Loss of employment is a common event that can lead to foreclosure because of its direct impact on a borrower's ability to make mortgage payments. All of the forecasts we reviewed acknowledged job loss as a contributor to mortgage defaults and foreclosures. However, three forecasts noted that the impacts of unemployment may be difficult to capture for several reasons, including the fact that unemployment data are aggregated and do not capture the effects of job losses on individual households. Further, the forecasts used older projections of unemployment in their analysis, many of which had predicted lower peaks, such as 8 percent unemployment by the end of 2009. Some more recent estimates suggest that unemployment rates will peak at around 10 percent in 2010, a level that one of the forecasts included in its worst-case scenario. As of November 2009, the unemployment rate was 10 percent.
- *Mortgage recasts*—Payment-option ARMs, a common Alt-A product, allow borrowers to make minimum payments for an initial period that are lower than needed to cover any of the principal or all of the accrued interest. After the initial period, payments are "recast" to include an amount that will fully amortize the outstanding balance over the remaining loan term. Consequently, payment-option ARMs can result in payment shock, especially if the borrower was making only the minimum payment. Although none of the forecasts we reviewed specifically attempted to model the impact of payment-option ARM recasts, the authors told us that recasts would likely lead to additional foreclosures for many Alt-A borrowers who may not be able to afford the higher payments. Large numbers of payment-option ARMs are scheduled to recast beginning in 2010.
- *Federal loan modification efforts*—Loan modifications involve making temporary or permanent changes to the term of the existing loan agreement and can include

reducing the interest rate charged, extending the loan term, or implementing forbearance plans.[23] Loan modifications may prevent or delay foreclosures on nonprime mortgages by making mortgage payments more affordable. Under the Home Affordable Modification Program (HAMP), the Department of the Treasury (Treasury), Fannie Mae, and Freddie Mac will use up to $75 billion to encourage loan modifications. The authors of the studies we reviewed agreed that loan modifications had the potential to reduce future nonprime foreclosures, but some noted the difficulty of predicting an exact number. Treasury has estimated that up to 3 to 4 million borrowers who were at risk of default and foreclosure could be offered a loan modification under HAMP. However, as we reported in July 2009, Treasury's estimate reflects uncertainty created by data gaps and the need to make numerous assumptions, and therefore may be overstated.[24]

A SUBSTANTIAL PROPORTION OF NONPRIME MORTGAGE BORROWERS HAVE NEGATIVE HOME EQUITY

Our analysis of borrowers with active nonprime mortgages originated from 2000 through 2007 indicates that a substantial proportion had negative equity in their homes as of June 30, 2009. Our estimates using the S&P/Case-Shiller Tiered Price Indices (S&P Case-Shiller index) for 16 metropolitan areas showed that the percentage of borrowers with negative equity ranged from about 9 percent to more than 90 percent. Using the FHFA All-Transactions Index (FHFA index), we estimated that about one-quarter of nonprime borrowers with active loans nationwide had negative equity in their homes as of June 30, 2009.[25]

Estimates of Negative Equity in 16 Metropolitan Areas

To estimate the extent of negative equity among nonprime borrowers, we compared borrowers' outstanding balances on first-lien loans with the estimated values of their homes as of June 30, 2009.[26] Because of data limitations, we could not identify borrowers with multiple mortgaged properties. To the extent that some borrowers had more than one mortgaged property, our results may overstate the actual number of individual borrowers with negative home equity. For our estimates of negative equity for specific metropolitan areas, we used the S&P/Case-Shiller index—which includes separate indexes for homes in low, middle, and high price ranges within a metropolitan area—to adjust the appraised value of each home to an updated market value. The S&P/Case-Shiller index is available for 17 metropolitan areas.

We estimated the extent of negative home equity for nonprime borrowers with active loans in 16 of the 17 metropolitan areas covered by the S&P/Case-Shiller index.[27] As shown in table 1, we estimate that the metropolitan areas with the highest percentage of nonprime borrowers with negative home equity as of June 30, 2009, were Las Vegas, Nevada (94.3 percent); Phoenix, Arizona (89.4 percent); Miami, Florida (85.8 percent); and Minneapolis, Minnesota (80.6 percent). The metropolitan areas with the lowest percentages included

Denver, Colorado (9.3 percent) and Portland, Oregon (12.7 percent). It is important to note that the 17 metropolitan areas covered by the S&P/Case-Shiller index may represent areas with higher proportions of negative equity than is generally found across the country. Seven of the 17 metropolitan areas are in states (California, Florida, Nevada, and Arizona) that in recent years experienced the most dramatic declines in house prices.

Estimates of Negative Equity by Loan and Borrower Type

For the same 16 metropolitan areas examined above, we estimated the extent of negative home equity by loan class (subprime or Alt-A), loan purpose, loan product, and borrower type (owner occupant or nonowner occupant) using the S&P/Case-Shiller index. Our estimates of negative equity are as of June 30, 2009, and are for nonprime borrowers in the 16 metropolitan areas whose loans were active as of that date. We found that:

- Subprime borrowers were more likely than Alt-A borrowers to be in a negative equity position. We estimate that about 63 percent of subprime borrowers had negative home equity, compared with 57 percent of Alt-A borrowers.
- Borrowers who obtained a mortgage to purchase a home were more likely to have negative equity than those who refinanced an existing loan. Additionally, borrowers who refinanced their mortgages to convert their home equity into money for personal use (cash-out refinancing) were more likely to have negative equity than borrowers who refinanced without taking cash out. More specifically, we estimate that 68 percent of borrowers with purchase loans had negative home equity, compared with 55 percent of borrowers with cash-out refinance loans, and 50 percent of borrowers with no-cash-out refinance loans.
- Borrowers with adjustable-rate loans were more likely to have negative equity than borrowers with fixed-rate loans. For example, we estimate that 80 percent of borrowers with payment-option ARMs and 75 percent of borrowers with short-term hybrid ARMs were in a negative equity position. By comparison, an estimated 39 percent of borrowers with fixed-rate mortgages had negative home equity.
- Borrowers who were owner-occupants were somewhat more likely to have negative home equity than borrowers who were not owner-occupants (e.g., investors). More specifically, we estimate that 60 percent of owner-occupants were in a negative equity position, compared with 56 percent of non-owner-occupants.

Estimates of Negative Equity Nationwide

To estimate the extent of negative home equity nationwide, we used the FHFA index because it comprises separate indexes for 384 metropolitan areas covering approximately 84 percent of the U.S. population.[28] The FHFA index does not include data for homes with certain types of financing, including subprime mortgages. Partly for this reason, the FHFA index shows more modest declines in average house prices from 2005 through 2008, compared with the S&P/Case-Shiller index. As a result, our estimates using the FHFA index likely understate the extent of negative equity among nonprime borrowers.[29] See enclosure V for additional information about the major differences between the FHFA and S&P/Case-Shiller indexes and how using different indexes can affect estimates of negative equity.

Nationwide, we estimate that 25 percent of the borrowers who obtained nonprime mortgages from 2000 through 2007 and whose loans were active as of June 30, 2009, had negative home equity as of that date. The estimated proportion of nonprime borrowers in a negative equity position varied by location. We estimated that this proportion ranged from no negative equity in 20 metropolitan areas to more than 80 percent in 5 (see figure 4).[30] The 35 metropolitan areas with proportions greater than 50 percent were located in five states: Arizona, California, Florida, Michigan, and Nevada.

Additionally, we estimate that 5.5 percent of borrowers with active nonprime loans had "near negative equity"—that is, home equity of 0 to 5 percent. Borrowers with near negative equity face similar challenges to borrowers with negative equity when selling or refinancing their homes because mortgage closing costs (e.g., lender fees and title charges) are generally between 3 to 5 percent of the value of the home.

Table 1. Estimates of Negative Equity in Selected Metropolitan Areas Using the S&P/Case-Shiller Index, as of June 30, 2009.

Metropolitan area	Number of nonprime borrowers with active loans	Estimated number with negative equity	Estimated percentage with negative equity
Las Vegas, NV	92,949	87,685	94.3
Phoenix, AZ	131,069	117,185	89.4
Miami, FL	225,355	193,360	85.8
Minneapolis, MN	49,435	39,841	80.6
Tampa, FL	85,641	67,343	78.6
San Diego, CA	86,499	62,160	71.9
Chicago, IL	128,929	86,523	67.1
Washington, DC	130,760	83,682	64.0
Los Angeles, CA	315,289	201,009	63.8
Atlanta, GA	122,302	73,001	59.7
San Francisco, CA	103,369	61,652	59.6
New York, NY	295,932	76,204	25.8
Seattle, WA	69,353	17,327	25.0
Boston, MA	54,844	12,670	23.1
Portland, OR	42,014	5,323	12.7
Denver, CO	60,280	5,583	9.3
Total	**1,994,020**	**1,190,548**	**59.7**

Source: GAO analysis of LP data and S&P/Case-Shiller index.

Note: As of November 2009, the S&P/Case-Shiller index did not include 2009 data for the Cleveland, Ohio metropolitan area. As a result, we did not estimate negative equity for that area.

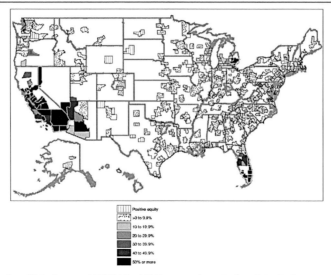

Source: GAO analysis of LP data and FHFA's All-Transactions Index; MapInfo.

Figure 4. Estimated Percentage of Nonprime Borrowers with Negative Home Equity by Metropolitan Area Using the FHFA Index as of June 30, 2009.

Nationwide, we estimate that the total amount of negative equity (i.e., the difference between mortgage balances and estimated property values) was about $54.8 billion. Among borrowers in a negative equity position, the median borrower had negative equity of approximately $36,274. We estimate that 75 percent of borrowers in a negative equity position had negative home equity of more than $15,615 and 25 percent had negative home equity of more than $67,335. Another measure of negative equity is the ratio of the current loan balance to the current value of the property (current loan-to-value ratio). A current loan-to-value (LTV) ratio of more than 100 percent indicates negative equity in the property, with a higher ratio representing greater negative equity as a percentage of the property value.[31] As of June 30, 2009, we estimate nearly 63 percent of nonprime borrowers with negative home equity had current LTV ratios of 101 to 119 percent, while about 5 percent had current LTV ratios of 150 percent or higher (see figure 5).

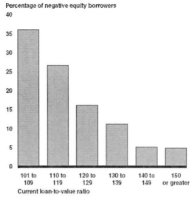

Source: GAO analysis of LP data and FHFA All-Transactions Index.

Figure 5. Estimated Current LTV Ratios of Nonprime Borrowers with Active Loans Who Had Negative Home Equity as of June 30, 2009.

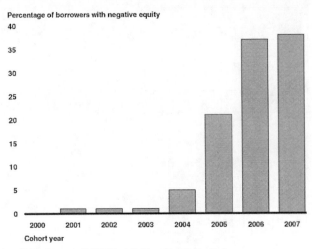

Source: GAO analysis of LP data and FHFA All-Transactions Index.

Figure 6. Estimated Percentage of Nonprime Borrowers with Active Loans Who Had Negative Home Equity as of June 30, 2009, by Loan Origination Year.

We also found that borrowers who obtained their loans later in the decade were more likely to have negative home equity than borrowers who obtained their loans earlier. This pattern reflects the greater home equity that earlier borrowers accumulated by paying down their loan balances and experiencing the home price appreciation that occurred in most of the country during the first half of the decade. We estimate that no more than 1 percent of borrowers with loans that originated from 2000 through 2003 and whose loans were still active as of June 30, 2009, were in a negative equity position as of that date (see figure 6). In contrast, we estimate that 37 percent of borrowers with active loans that originated in 2007 had negative home equity as of that date.

As agreed with your offices, unless you publicly announce its contents earlier, we plan no further distribution of this report until 30 days from the report date. At that time, we will send copies of this report to interested congressional parties and other interested parties. In addition, the report will be available at no charge on GAO's Web site at http://www.gao.gov.

If you or your staff have any questions about this report, please contact me at (202) 512-8678 or shearw@gao.gov. Contact points for our Offices of Congressional Relations and Public Affairs may be found on the last page of this report. Key contributors to this report are listed in enclosure VIII.

William B. Shear Director, Financial Markets and Community Investment
Enclosures

ENCLOSURE I. STATUS OF NONPRIME LOANS ORIGINATED FROM 2000 THROUGH 2007 BY COHORT YEAR AND PRODUCT TYPE, AS OF JUNE 30, 2009

This enclosure contains the results of our analysis of LoanPerformance (LP) data on the status of nonprime mortgages originated from 2000 through 2007, as of June 30, 2009. Tables 2 and 3 provide information in percentages and total numbers, respectively.

Table 2. Percentage of Nonprime Loans in Different Status Categories by Cohort Year as of June 30, 2009.

Subprime — ARM

Cohort year	Prepaid	Current	Delinquent	In default	In foreclosure process	Completed foreclosure process	Total
2000	80%	3%	1%	1%	0%	15%	100%
2001	83%	3%	1%	1%	0%	11%	100%
2002	83%	5%	2%	1%	1%	9%	100%
2003	82%	8%	1%	1%	1%	7%	100%
2004	73%	14%	3%	2%	2%	7%	100%
2005	47%	28%	5%	4%	5%	11%	100%
2006	23%	32%	8%	10%	10%	16%	100%
2007	16%	37%	11%	16%	11%	10%	100%
Total	**58%**	**19%**	**4%**	**4%**	**4%**	**11%**	**100%**

Subprime — Short-term hybrid ARM

Cohort year	Prepaid	Current	Delinquent	In default	In foreclosure process	Completed foreclosure process	Total
2000	77%	2%	1%	0%	0%	21%	100%
2001	78%	2%	1%	1%	0%	18%	100%
2002	82%	2%	1%	1%	0%	14%	100%
2003	84%	3%	1%	1%	1%	11%	100%
2004	78%	5%	2%	2%	1%	12%	100%
2005	57%	10%	4%	5%	5%	19%	100%

Subprime — Fixed rate

Cohort year	Prepaid	Current	Delinquent	In default	In foreclosure process	Completed foreclosure process	Total
2000	72%	6%	2%	1%	0%	18%	100%
2001	72%	9%	2%	1%	1%	14%	100%
2002	73%	13%	3%	1%	1%	9%	100%
2003	66%	22%	3%	1%	1%	6%	100%
2004	53%	32%	5%	3%	2%	6%	100%
2005	35%	40%	8%	5%	4%	7%	100%
2006	22%	43%	11%	9%	6%	8%	100%
2007	14%	46%	14%	12%	7%	6%	100%
Total	**51%**	**29%**	**6%**	**4%**	**3%**	**8%**	**100%**

Subprime — Other

Cohort year	Prepaid	Current	Delinquent	In default	In foreclosure process	Completed foreclosure process	Total
2000	66%	6%	2%	1%	1%	25%	100%
2001	71%	7%	2%	1%	1%	19%	100%
2002	70%	12%	2%	1%	1%	13%	100%
2003	66%	18%	4%	2%	1%	9%	100%
2004	54%	33%	4%	2%	2%	5%	100%
2005	33%	33%	8%	6%	7%	13%	100%

Table 2. (Continued)

Subprime

Cohort year	Prepaid	Current	Delinquent	In default	In foreclosure process	Completed foreclosure process	Total
2006	30%	18%	8%	11%	11%	23%	100%
2007	18%	27%	11%	15%	14%	15%	100%
Total	62%	9%	4%	5%	4%	17%	100%

ARM

Cohort year	Prepaid	Current	Delinquent	In default	In foreclosure process	Completed foreclosure process	Total
2000	90%	6%	1%	0%	0%	3%	100%
2001	94%	2%	0%	0%	0%	3%	100%
2002	92%	4%	0%	0%	0%	3%	100%
2003	85%	11%	1%	1%	0%	3%	100%
2004	72%	18%	2%	1%	2%	5%	100%
2005	46%	31%	3%	4%	5%	11%	100%
2006	24%	36%	5%	7%	11%	16%	100%
2007	13%	47%	7%	10%	12%	12%	100%
Total	48%	28%	3%	4%	6%	10%	100%

Payment-option ARM

Cohort year	Prepaid	Current	Delinquent	In default	In foreclosure process	Completed foreclosure process	Total
2000	97%	2%	0%	0%	0%	1%	100%
2001	94%	4%	0%	0%	0%	1%	100%
2002	92%	7%	0%	0%	0%	0%	100%
2003	85%	11%	1%	1%	1%	1%	100%
2004	77%	15%	2%	2%	2%	2%	100%
2005	54%	23%	3%	7%	6%	8%	100%
2006	26%	34%	6%	11%	11%	12%	100%
2007	12%	47%	8%	12%	13%	9%	100%
Total	44%	28%	4%	8%	8%	8%	100%

Alt-A

Cohort year	Prepaid	Current	Delinquent	In default	In foreclosure process	Completed foreclosure process	Total
2006	19%	34%	11%	10%	11%	16%	100%
2007	11%	38%	14%	12%	13%	11%	100%
Total	40%	24%	7%	6%	6%	16%	100%

Fixed rate

Cohort year	Prepaid	Current	Delinquent	In default	In foreclosure process	Completed foreclosure process	Total
2000	92%	2%	0%	0%	0%	6%	100%
2001	90%	4%	0%	0%	0%	5%	100%
2002	81%	13%	1%	0%	0%	4%	100%
2003	60%	36%	1%	1%	1%	2%	100%
2004	49%	44%	2%	1%	1%	2%	100%
2005	33%	53%	4%	3%	4%	5%	100%
2006	24%	50%	6%	5%	7%	8%	100%
2007	14%	61%	6%	6%	7%	6%	100%
Total	44%	42%	3%	2%	3%	5%	100%

Other

Cohort year	Prepaid	Current	Delinquent	In default	In foreclosure process	Completed foreclosure process	Total
2000	85%	5%	1%	0%	0%	9%	100%
2001	84%	4%	1%	0%	0%	10%	100%
2002	84%	6%	1%	0%	0%	8%	100%
2003	75%	20%	1%	1%	1%	3%	100%
2004	67%	27%	1%	1%	1%	3%	100%
2005	37%	31%	4%	4%	8%	16%	100%
2006	19%	36%	7%	9%	14%	15%	100%
2007	9%	49%	8%	8%	15%	11%	100%
Total	42%	29%	5%	5%	8%	10%	100%

Source: GAO analysis of LP data.

Note: Percentages for ARMs and fixed-rate mortgages do not include balloon mortgages, which account for most of the "other" category. Balloon mortgages can have fixed or adjustable interest rates.

Table 3. Number of Nonprime Loans in Different Status Categories by Cohort Year as of June 30, 2009.

Subprime — ARM

Cohort year	Prepaid	Current	Delinquent	In default	In foreclosure process	Completed foreclosure process	Total
2000	10,204	384	137	80	29	1,968	12,802
2001	7,048	268	89	69	30	975	8,479
2002	17,446	979	320	182	137	1,947	21,011
2003	35,223	3,283	596	439	339	3,001	42,881
2004	38,236	7,258	1,344	1,084	967	3,699	52,588
2005	26,324	15,416	2,651	2,352	2,922	6,322	55,987
2006	11,210	15,398	3,937	4,643	5,001	7,909	48,098
2007	2,412	5,665	1,647	2,509	1,699	1,500	15,432
Total	148,103	48,651	10,721	11,358	11,124	27,321	257,278

Subprime — Fixed rate

Cohort year	Prepaid	Current	Delinquent	In default	In foreclosure process	Completed foreclosure process	Total
2000	112,149	10,036	2,611	1,545	709	27,717	154,767
2001	130,408	16,662	4,201	2,337	1,219	25,358	180,185
2002	167,995	29,867	5,859	2,983	1,734	20,331	228,769
2003	284,032	95,924	13,674	6,410	4,527	25,538	430,105
2004	242,520	146,996	23,207	12,807	8,112	27,578	461,220
2005	150,195	171,157	34,222	23,063	15,199	30,453	424,289
2006	78,450	153,669	39,451	32,834	21,238	29,495	355,137
2007	13,081	42,108	12,997	10,686	6,535	5,291	90,698
Total	1,178,830	666,419	136,222	92,665	59,273	191,761	2,325,170

Short-term hybrid ARM

Cohort year	Prepaid	Current	Delinquent	In default	In foreclosure process	Completed foreclosure process	Total
2000	189,826	3,875	1,413	1,015	530	51,185	247,844
2001	246,485	6,769	2,881	2,097	1,114	56,315	315,661
2002	424,943	11,512	4,533	3,520	2,015	70,103	516,626
2003	670,733	21,929	8,664	6,973	5,079	84,379	797,757
2004	1,114,037	66,817	27,042	30,669	20,504	168,972	1,428,041
2005	1,012,637	182,424	73,282	90,087	89,013	339,339	1,786,782
2006	381,560	232,563	98,227	136,406	142,140	298,959	1,289,855
2007	35,251	54,504	22,359	29,260	27,054	29,811	198,239
Total	4,075,472	580,393	238,401	300,027	287,449	1,099,063	6,580,805

Other

Cohort year	Prepaid	Current	Delinquent	In default	In foreclosure process	Completed foreclosure process	Total
2000	25,216	2,359	609	350	266	9,685	38,485
2001	22,559	2,131	550	317	200	6,092	31,849
2002	12,825	2,246	431	267	173	2,356	18,298
2003	6,874	1,921	391	171	142	953	10,452
2004	1,896	1,134	131	83	65	176	3,485
2005	5,250	5,281	1,255	1,026	1,039	1,986	15,837
2006	16,412	30,012	9,454	8,729	9,327	14,247	88,181
2007	2,928	10,056	3,704	3,130	3,467	2,859	26,144
Total	93,960	55,140	16,525	14,073	14,679	38,354	232,731

Alt-A — ARM

Cohort year	Prepaid	Current	Delinquent	In default	In foreclosure process	Completed foreclosure process	Total
2000	5,277	329	42	15	12	177	5,852
2001	22,618	587	61	45	49	817	24,177
2002	44,496	2,020	129	111	91	1,287	48,134
2003	93,110	11,780	692	655	540	2,837	109,614

Alt-A — Fixed rate

Cohort year	Prepaid	Current	Delinquent	In default	In foreclosure process	Completed foreclosure process	Total
2000	61,367	1,182	119	52	53	3,819	66,592
2001	99,110	4,840	455	262	149	5,479	110,295
2002	141,852	23,042	1,442	735	610	7,121	174,802
2003	183,627	110,535	4,041	1,991	1,798	6,521	308,513

Table 3. (Continued)

Cohort year	Prepaid	Current	Delinquent	In default	In foreclosure process	Completed foreclosure process	Total
2004	332,729	84,957	7,026	5,810	7,706	21,448	459,676
2005	268,556	179,972	19,317	20,503	31,858	61,709	581,915
2006	116,993	171,781	25,047	35,300	53,030	77,850	480,001
2007	23,799	88,062	12,767	17,827	22,553	22,223	187,211
Total	907,578	539,488	65,081	80,266	115,819	188,348	1,896,580
Payment-option ARM							
2000	4,086	90	5	6	2	28	4,217
2001	643	28	1	1	2	7	682
2002	4,216	308	11	4	9	22	4,570
2003	6,430	823	96	42	87	93	7,571
2004	94,931	18,188	2,067	2,662	2,356	2,997	123,201
2005	167,253	71,096	10,100	20,243	17,707	23,727	310,126
2006	83,870	111,633	19,723	35,713	36,487	38,833	326,259
2007	7,472	28,351	4,799	6,977	7,598	5,322	60,519
Total	368,901	230,517	36,802	65,648	64,248	71,029	837,145

Cohort year	Prepaid	Current	Delinquent	In default	In foreclosure process	Completed foreclosure process	Total
2004	169,022	152,619	7,754	4,515	4,515	8,652	347,077
2005	180,648	292,614	20,616	13,862	19,612	25,762	553,114
2006	119,449	248,495	27,959	23,214	36,519	39,972	495,608
2007	25,576	109,407	11,188	10,081	13,299	9,927	179,478
Total	980,651	942,734	73,574	54,712	76,555	107,253	2,235,479
Other							
2000	1,228	74	12	4	2	133	1,453
2001	2,903	141	28	8	7	349	3,436
2002	3,242	225	36	19	17	301	3,840
2003	7,391	1,938	111	72	79	295	9,886
2004	4,132	1,650	74	64	63	158	6,141
2005	488	405	56	59	99	210	1,317
2006	5,058	9,296	1,795	2,464	3,693	3,828	26,134
2007	640	3,415	579	561	1,060	737	6,992
Total	25,082	17,144	2,691	3,251	5,020	6,011	59,199

Source: GAO analysis of LP data.

Note: Numbers for ARMs and fixed-rate mortgages do not include balloon mortgages, which account for most of the "other" category. Balloon mortgages can have fixed or adjustable interest rates.

ENCLOSURE II. STATUS OF NONPRIME LOANS ORIGINATED FROM 2004 THROUGH 2007 BY YEAR AND QUARTER, AS OF JUNE 30, 2009

This enclosure contains the results of our analysis of LoanPerformance (LP) data on the annual and quarterly status of nonprime mortgages originated from 2004 through 2007, as of June 30, 2009. Tables 4 and 5 provide information in percentages and total numbers, respectively.

Table 4. Percentage of Nonprime Loans Originated in 2004 through 2007 in Different Status Categories as of June 30, 2009.

Status date	Subprime							Alt-A						
	Prepaid (cumulative)	Current	Delinquent	In default	In foreclosure process	Completed foreclosure process (cumulative)	Total	Prepaid (cumulative)	Current	Delinquent	In default	In foreclosure process	Completed foreclosure process (cumulative)	Total
2007 Cohort														
December 31, 2007	5%	71%	15%	4%	4%	1%	100%	5%	87%	5%	1%	2%	0%	100%
December 31, 2008	13%	41%	16%	11%	10%	8%	100%	11%	63%	8%	6%	7%	5%	100%
June 30, 2009	16%	34%	12%	14%	12%	12%	100%	13%	53%	7%	8%	10%	9%	100%
2006 Cohort														
December 31, 2006	7%	78%	11%	2%	2%	0%	100%	6%	90%	3%	0%	0%	0%	100%
December 31, 2007	18%	50%	13%	6%	7%	6%	100%	17%	70%	6%	2%	3%	2%	100%
December 31, 2008	25%	28%	11%	9%	10%	16%	100%	22%	48%	7%	6%	8%	8%	100%
June 30, 2009	27%	24%	9%	10%	10%	20%	100%	24%	41%	6%	7%	10%	12%	100%
2005 Cohort														
December 31, 2005	7%	83%	8%	1%	1%	0%	100%	6%	92%	2%	0%	0%	0%	100%
December 31, 2006	28%	54%	9%	3%	3%	3%	100%	23%	72%	3%	0%	1%	0%	100%
December 31, 2007	46%	28%	8%	4%	5%	8%	100%	36%	55%	4%	1%	2%	2%	100%
December 31, 2008	51%	19%	6%	5%	5%	15%	100%	40%	43%	4%	3%	4%	6%	100%
June 30, 2009	52%	17%	5%	5%	5%	17%	100%	42%	38%	3%	4%	5%	8%	100%
2004 Cohort														
December 31, 2004	6%	86%	6%	1%	1%	0%	100%	5%	93%	2%	0%	0%	0%	100%
December 31, 2005	34%	52%	7%	2%	2%	2%	100%	28%	69%	2%	0%	0%	0%	100%
December 31, 2006	60%	26%	5%	2%	2%	5%	100%	47%	50%	2%	0%	0%	1%	100%
December 31, 2007	69%	16%	4%	2%	2%	8%	100%	58%	37%	2%	1%	1%	2%	100%
December 31, 2008	71%	12%	3%	2%	1%	10%	100%	62%	30%	2%	1%	1%	3%	100%
June 30, 2009	72%	12%	3%	2%	2%	10%	100%	64%	28%	2%	1%	2%	4%	100%

Source: GAO analysis of LP data.

Table 5. Number of Nonprime Loans Originated in 2004 through 2007 in Different Status Categories as of June 30, 2009.

2007 Cohort

Status date	Subprime							Alt-A						
	Prepaid (cumulative)	Current	Delinquent	In default	In foreclosure process	Completed foreclosure process (cumulative)	Total	Prepaid (cumulative)	Current	Delinquent	In default	In foreclosure process	Completed foreclosure process (cumulative)	Total
December 31, 2007	16,702	231,732	48,916	14,677	13,944	2,575	328,546	20,524	375,033	21,007	6,470	7,883	1,179	432,096
December 31, 2008	44,058	135,117	51,296	37,274	32,844	27,904	328,493	46,120	272,870	35,102	24,909	31,796	22,279	433,076
June 30, 2009	51,459	112,333	40,707	45,585	38,755	39,654	328,493	56,164	229,235	29,333	35,446	44,490	38,408	433,076

2006 Cohort

Status date	Subprime							Alt-A						
	Prepaid (cumulative)	Current	Delinquent	In default	In foreclosure process	Completed foreclosure process (cumulative)	Total	Prepaid (cumulative)	Current	Delinquent	In default	In foreclosure process	Completed foreclosure process (cumulative)	Total
December 31, 2006	91,519	1,048,577	152,186	27,941	24,897	5,257	1,350,377	58,154	944,997	35,953	3,871	4,530	1,045	1,048,550
December 31, 2007	3 08,751	882,179	234,132	109,507	132,283	97,330	1,764,182	222,312	919,887	78,744	30,693	42,114	26,350	1,320,100
December 31, 2008	445,971	499,686	198,891	165,708	167,881	285,050	1,763,187	292,837	639,616	97,616	80,028	99,716	110,668	1,320,481
June 30, 2009	468,037	431,642	151,069	182,612	177,706	352,118	1,763,184	3 17,435	541,205	74,524	96,691	129,729	161,215	1,320,799

2005 Cohort

Status date	Subprime							Alt-A						
	Prepaid (cumulative)	Current	Delinquent	In default	In foreclosure process	Completed foreclosure process (cumulative)	Total	Prepaid (cumulative)	Current	Delinquent	In default	In foreclosure process	Completed foreclosure process (cumulative)	Total
December 31, 2005	122,100	1,438,784	140,860	22,174	14,074	2,925	1,740,917	69,322	1,073,961	25,836	2,592	862	177	1,172,750
December 31, 2006	627,777	1,210,898	210,942	63,499	70,422	59,164	2,242,702	332,527	1,035,468	40,766	7,148	10,283	7,125	1,433,317
December 31, 2007	1,051,031	642,437	180,324	99,140	112,349	176,696	2,261,977	513,236	795,044	51,339	20,826	27,123	32,340	1,439,908

Table 5. (Continued)

Status date	Subprime							Alt-A						
	Prepaid (cumulative)	Current	Delinquent	In default	In foreclosure process	Completed foreclosure process (cumulative)	Total	Prepaid (cumulative)	Current	Delinquent	In default	In foreclosure process	Completed foreclosure process (cumulative)	Total
December 31, 2008	1,149,945	417,846	138,511	108,054	104,623	332,522	2,251,501	580,024	611,185	59,857	44,656	52,863	84,010	1,432,595
June 30, 2009	1,171,815	374,278	111,410	116,528	108,173	379,118	2,261,322	610,719	544,087	50,089	54,667	69,276	111,674	1,440,512
2004 Cohort														
December 31, 2004	93,670	1,294,270	97,242	11,653	8,467	1,282	1,506,584	37,168	667,091	12,295	968	548	133	718,203
December 31, 2005	661,253	1,002,040	142,526	46,016	36,363	32,192	1,920,390	260,603	631,707	19,096	4,375	2,663	2,756	921,200
December 31, 2006	1,144,949	502,979	100,780	41,053	40,637	91,913	1,922,311	432,908	459,054	16,964	3,830	4,430	8,832	926,018
December 31, 2007	1,329,079	305,661	69,054	40,021	36,249	149,349	1,929,413	540,156	344,039	16,852	5,921	6,110	16,885	929,963
December 31, 2008	1,368,911	239,764	59,388	41,398	27,984	189,626	1,927,071	576,516	281,900	18,657	10,129	10,637	28,001	925,840
June 30, 2009	1,377,506	222,205	51,724	44,643	29,648	200,565	1,926,291	594,846	257,414	16,921	13,051	14,640	33,266	930,138

Source: GAO analysis of LP data.

ENCLOSURE III. STATUS OF NONPRIME LOANS ORIGINATED FROM 2000 THROUGH 2007 BY CENSUS DIVISION AND STATE AS OF JUNE 30, 2009

This enclosure contains the results of our analysis of LoanPerformance (LP) data on the status of nonprime mortgages by Census division and state. The analysis covers mortgages originated from 2000 through 2007, as of June 30, 2009. Tables 6 and 7 provide information in percentages and total numbers, respectively.

Table 6. Percentage of 2000 through 2007 Nonprime Loans in Different Status Categories by State and Census Division, as of June 30, 2009.

State	Market segment	Prepaid	Current	Delinquent	In default	In foreclosure process	Completed foreclosure process	Unknown	Total
Connecticut	Subprime	62.93%	14.67%	4.56%	3.91%	4.16%	9.69%	0.09%	123,038
	Alt-A	48.26%	36.79%	4.05%	2.86%	4.21%	3.78%	0.06%	44,726
Maine	Subprime	64.01%	14.71%	4.39%	3.00%	4.84%	8.96%	0.09%	36,309
	Alt-A	48.98%	36.40%	3.54%	2.07%	5.05%	3.90%	0.05%	9,697
Massachusetts	Subprime	67.19%	10.66%	3.49%	4.92%	3.13%	10.45%	0.16%	202,214
	Alt-A	52.89%	31.27%	3.52%	3.42%	3.82%	4.96%	0.12%	85,212
New Hampshire	Subprime	62.24%	14.69%	5.11%	4.33%	2.06%	11.51%	0.07%	41,429
	Alt-A	48.73%	36.28%	3.93%	2.81%	1.87%	6.29%	0.10%	15586
Rhode Island	Subprime	70.42%	9.43%	3.10%	2.85%	2.40%	11.61%	0.18%	52814
	Alt-A	51.74%	30.08%	3.92%	2.92%	3.56%	7.67%	0.10%	15,746
Vermont	Subprime	65.86%	15.93%	4.15%	2.99%	4.31%	6.64%	0.11%	9,754
	Alt-A	51.93%	37.26%	3.35%	1.79%	3.37%	2.25%	0.05%	3,913
New England	**Subprime**	**65.71%**	**12.37%**	**3.96%**	**4.18%**	**3.38%**	**10.28%**	**0.13%**	**465,558**
	Alt-A	**50.99%**	**33.44%**	**3.72%**	**3.06%**	**3.78%**	**4.90%**	**0.09%**	**174,880**
New Jersey	Subprime	69.61%	10.20%	3.44%	3.92%	5.55%	7.15%	0.13%	264,675
	Alt-A	52.84%	30.14%	3.57%	3.22%	6.78%	3.35%	0.10%	143,696
New York	Subprime	59.26%	16.95%	4.71%	5.06%	5.94%	7.99%	0.09%	384,847
	Alt-A	43.17%	39.45%	4.16%	4.67%	5.52%	2.99%	0.04%	165,959
Pennsylvania	Subprime	53.01%	21.94%	6.21%	5.25%	3.63%	9.90%	0.07%	262,666
	Alt-A	44.81%	42.87%	3.73%	2.54%	2.74%	3.25%	0.07%	81,596
Mid Atlantic	**Subprime**	**60.46%**	**16.43%**	**4.77%**	**4.78%**	**5.16%**	**8.30%**	**0.10%**	**912,188**
	Alt-A	**47.06%**	**36.74%**	**3.86%**	**3.69%**	**5.40%**	**3.18%**	**0.07%**	**391,251**

Table 6. (Continued)

State	Market segment	Prepaid	Current	Delinquent	In default	In foreclosure process	Completed foreclosure process	Unknown	Total
Illinois	Subprime	63.36%	11.30%	3.84%	4.15%	3.95%	13.26%	0.14%	450,107
	Alt-A	52.31%	29.94%	3.34%	3.41%	4.91%	6.02%	0.06%	147,516
Indiana	Subprime	43.63%	18.32%	5.35%	4.59%	4.12%	23.87%	0.12%	176,207
	Alt-A	39.56%	39.43%	3.60%	2.78%	4.09%	10.52%	0.02%	38,356
Michigan	Subprime	48.97%	12.56%	4.73%	4.82%	1.82%	26.97%	0.13%	373,287
	Alt-A	37.59%	37.48%	4.33%	3.41%	2.59%	14.57%	0.03%	94,666
Ohio	Subprime	45.49%	17.64%	5.02%	4.58%	4.31%	22.84%	0.12%	319,380
	Alt-A	36.65%	43.20%	3.76%	2.87%	4.29%	9.19%	0.04%	73,562
Wisconsin	Subprime	63.70%	11.45%	3.81%	3.34%	3.92%	13.67%	0.10%	131,059
	Alt-A	48.35%	36.45%	3.41%	2.28%	3.88%	5.59%	0.04%	29,600
East North Central	**Subprime**	**53.35%**	**13.89%**	**4.51%**	**4.40%**	**3.50%**	**20.22%**	**0.13%**	**1,450,040**
	Alt-A	**44.10%**	**35.79%**	**3.70%**	**3.16%**	**4.06%**	**9.15%**	**0.05%**	**383,700**
Iowa	Subprime	57.25%	15.49%	4.32%	2.86%	3.31%	16.68%	0.08%	52,626
	Alt-A	44.39%	43.21%	3.13%	1.45%	2.46%	5.34%	0.02%	10,534
Kansas	Subprime	56.27%	16.81%	4.66%	3.38%	2.11%	16.68%	0.09%	49,747
	Alt-A	44.44%	44.50%	2.72%	1.51%	1.60%	5.22%	0.01%	16,847
Minnesota	Subprime	60.75%	10.67%	3.28%	3.20%	2.57%	19.41%	0.13%	162,899
	Alt-A	38.59%	37.84%	3.79%	3.14%	3.77%	12.83%	0.05%	67,315
Missouri	Subprime	55.18%	14.14%	4.89%	4.10%	1.47%	20.11%	0.11%	180,297
	Alt-A	45.60%	38.83%	3.21%	2.23%	1.45%	8.64%	0.05%	48,821
Nebraska	Subprime	51.68%	19.84%	5.09%	3.90%	2.33%	17.10%	0.07%	29,599
	Alt-A	41.88%	45.53%	3.08%	2.12%	1.66%	5.74%	0.00%	6,987
North Dakota	Subprime	60.04%	19.78%	4.79%	3.07%	2.40%	9.90%	0.02%	4,464
	Alt-A	44.63%	46.37%	2.55%	1.19%	1.79%	3.42%	0.05%	1,844

Table 6. (Continued)

State	Market segment	Prepaid	Current	Delinquent	In default	In foreclosure process	Completed foreclosure process	Unknown	Total
South Dakota	Subprime	57.63%	17.35%	4.71%	2.81%	3.06%	14.42%	0.01%	7,321
	Alt-A	45.04%	42.85%	2.65%	2.03%	2.32%	5.09%	0.04%	2,418
West North Central	**Subprime**	**57.25%**	**13.84%**	**4.27%**	**3.55%**	**2.19%**	**18.79%**	**0.10%**	**486,953**
	Alt-A	**42.15%**	**39.77%**	**3.38%**	**2.47%**	**2.57%**	**9.61%**	**0.04%**	**154,766**
Delaware	Subprime	60.20%	16.92%	5.41%	4.72%	5.06%	7.62%	0.06%	24,643
	Alt-A	47.55%	38.96%	3.67%	2.64%	3.81%	3.31%	0.06%	11,752
District of Columbia	Subprime	71.05%	10.51%	3.30%	3.89%	2.53%	8.56%	0.17%	17,369
	Alt-A	51.62%	35.67%	3.28%	2.75%	2.40%	4.23%	0.05%	15,458
Florida	Subprime	56.24%	13.03%	4.07%	4.83%	10.45%	11.31%	0.08%	935,137
	Alt-A	37.31%	32.21%	3.93%	5.04%	14.99%	6.45%	0.07%	528,148
Georgia	Subprime	48.93%	15.31%	5.85%	6.31%	2.73%	20.77%	0.10%	267,324
	Alt-A	38.79%	40.27%	4.57%	3.36%	2.73%	10.22%	0.06%	157,912
Maryland	Subprime	70.19%	11.05%	3.86%	4.43%	3.06%	7.30%	0.11%	255,100
	Alt-A	49.36%	33.73%	3.94%	4.11%	4.40%	4.37%	0.10%	135,828
North Carolina	Subprime	53.79%	17.56%	6.22%	5.12%	2.04%	15.17%	0.10%	179,429
	Alt-A	45.86%	40.80%	3.66%	2.53%	1.81%	5.29%	0.04%	86,516
South Carolina	Subprime	51.05%	18.18%	5.95%	4.19%	3.69%	16.84%	0.11%	94,131
	Alt-A	46.33%	38.42%	3.47%	2.29%	3.73%	5.70%	0.06%	48,869
Virginia	Subprime	65.27%	13.10%	4.21%	4.19%	1.99%	11.15%	0.09%	213,173
	Alt-A	44.66%	35.19%	3.44%	3.50%	2.93%	10.18%	0.09%	162,456
West Virginia	Subprime	53.22%	19.87%	6.48%	4.90%	2.39%	12.97%	0.18%	16,904
	Alt-A	40.10%	40.22%	5.11%	2.89%	3.14%	8.41%	0.12%	4,813
South Atlantic	**Subprime**	**57.69%**	**13.82%**	**4.61%**	**4.89%**	**6.30%**	**12.59%**	**0.09%**	**2,003,210**
	Alt-A	**41.30%**	**34.97%**	**3.90%**	**4.12%**	**8.56%**	**7.08%**	**0.07%**	**1,151,752**

Table 6. (Continued)

State	Market segment	Prepaid	Current	Delinquent	In default	In foreclosure process	Completed foreclosure process	Unknown	Total
Alabama	Subprime	50.02%	19.34%	6.65%	6.39%	1.88%	15.68%	0.04%	84,277
	Alt-A	43.98%	41.21%	3.84%	2.53%	1.66%	6.75%	0.03%	27,191
Kentucky	Subprime	49.53%	18.94%	5.39%	3.96%	3.64%	18.44%	0.10%	71,582
	Alt-A	41.80%	43.09%	3.43%	2.14%	2.96%	6.57%	0.02%	18,423
Mississippi	Subprime	43.35%	20.94%	7.62%	7.62%	2.34%	18.05%	0.08%	52,116
	Alt-A	41.74%	41.89%	4.42%	2.79%	1.94%	7.18%	0.03%	9,374
Tennessee	Subprime	46.71%	19.50%	6.36%	6.93%	1.77%	18.65%	0.07%	168,260
	Alt-A	42.00%	43.41%	3.70%	2.54%	1.39%	6.94%	0.02%	46,029
East South Central	**Subprime**	**47.52%**	**19.56%**	**6.41%**	**6.34%**	**2.23%**	**17.86%**	**0.07%**	**376,235**
	Alt-A	**42.47%**	**42.62%**	**3.75%**	**2.49%**	**1.80%**	**6.84%**	**0.02%**	**101,017**
Arkansas	Subprime	47.12%	23.65%	6.53%	5.31%	2.05%	15.31%	0.03%	37,683
	Alt-A	38.59%	47.16%	3.30%	2.39%	1.68%	6.89%	0.00%	11,341
Louisiana	Subprime	52.49%	21.54%	6.42%	5.08%	3.25%	11.12%	0.10%	89,804
	Alt-A	47.34%	40.58%	3.55%	2.09%	2.50%	3.91%	0.03%	19,371
Oklahoma	Subprime	45.32%	23.79%	5.69%	3.76%	3.54%	17.85%	0.05%	66,156
	Alt-A	37.99%	49.96%	2.95%	1.46%	2.39%	5.23%	0.01%	18,229
Texas	Subprime	41.67%	28.45%	7.27%	5.05%	2.18%	15.35%	0.04%	569,956
	Alt-A	37.42%	48.73%	3.30%	2.01%	1.35%	7.18%	0.02%	185,902
West South Central	**Subprime**	**43.53%**	**26.99%**	**6.99%**	**4.95%**	**2.41%**	**15.07%**	**0.05%**	**763,599**
	Alt-A	**38.34%**	**48.08%**	**3.29%**	**1.99%**	**1.54%**	**6.74%**	**0.02%**	**234,843**
Arizona	Subprime	61.22%	11.28%	3.48%	4.78%	3.76%	15.39%	0.08%	300,651
	Alt-A	46.70%	30.78%	3.39%	3.73%	3.12%	10.84%	0.06%	233,384
Colorado	Subprime	55.20%	14.03%	3.44%	3.12%	2.34%	21.78%	0.09%	188,746
	Alt-A	46.48%	38.85%	2.63%	1.90%	2.26%	7.84%	0.04%	138,461

Table 6. (Continued)

State	Market segment	Prepaid	Current	Delinquent	In default	In foreclosure process	Completed foreclosure process	Unknown	Total
Idaho	Subprime	61.54%	14.77%	4.20%	4.02%	3.40%	12.01%	0.04%	38,244
	Alt-A	47.94%	37.41%	3.09%	2.61%	3.90%	5.03%	0.03%	31,987
Montana	Subprime	64.48%	15.06%	3.91%	3.71%	2.69%	10.13%	0.02%	12,971
	Alt-A	53.74%	37.09%	2.58%	1.86%	2.02%	2.70%	0.00%	8,848
Nevada	Subprime	57.90%	10.47%	3.19%	5.41%	4.60%	18.36%	0.07%	152,571
	Alt-A	37.47%	30.49%	4.17%	6.30%	7.16%	14.36%	0.05%	152,067
New Mexico	Subprime	64.51%	15.09%	4.12%	2.81%	2.74%	10.60%	0.12%	40,487
	Alt-A	50.82%	38.34%	2.69%	1.66%	3.30%	3.13%	0.06%	22,322
Utah	Subprime	66.35%	11.77%	3.46%	3.15%	2.40%	12.80%	0.07%	80,321
	Alt-A	55.47%	31.60%	2.59%	2.08%	2.88%	5.34%	0.04%	56,951
Wyoming	Subprime	65.73%	17.40%	4.25%	2.96%	1.44%	8.21%	0.02%	9,745
	Alt-A	55.57%	38.10%	2.13%	1.24%	0.75%	2.21%	0.00%	4,517
Mountain	**Subprime**	**60.01%**	**12.29%**	**3.49%**	**4.19%**	**3.35%**	**16.59%**	**0.08%**	**823,736**
	Alt-A	**45.62%**	**33.23%**	**3.28%**	**3.63%**	**4.37%**	**9.82%**	**0.05%**	**648,537**
Alaska	Subprime	63.45%	16.79%	4.54%	3.73%	2.24%	9.23%	0.02%	9,433
	Alt-A	47.68%	41.99%	2.90%	1.73%	1.70%	4.01%	0.00%	3,937
California	Subprime	67.39%	9.34%	2.40%	3.78%	3.21%	13.76%	0.12%	1,745,440
	Alt-A	48.43%	29.68%	3.37%	5.46%	4.85%	8.18%	0.03%	1,530,336
Hawaii	Subprime	65.82%	17.60%	3.35%	3.66%	4.59%	4.91%	0.07%	42,053
	Alt-A	48.67%	38.89%	3.12%	2.90%	4.42%	1.97%	0.04%	28,459
Oregon	Subprime	63.72%	15.09%	3.67%	3.77%	3.17%	10.51%	0.06%	106,917
	Alt-A	49.73%	38.12%	2.79%	2.50%	2.80%	4.03%	0.03%	78,473
Washington	Subprime	65.58%	13.79%	3.62%	3.85%	2.96%	10.15%	0.05%	204,684
	Alt-A	50.95%	37.49%	2.99%	2.47%	2.86%	3.22%	0.03%	144,133

Table 6. (Continued)

State	Market segment	Prepaid	Current	Delinquent	In default	In foreclosure process	Completed foreclosure process	Unknown	Total
Pacific	**Subprime**	**66.98%**	**10.26%**	**2.61%**	**3.78%**	**3.21%**	**13.05%**	**0.11%**	**2,108,527**
	Alt-A	**48.69%**	**30.85%**	**3.31%**	**5.04%**	**4.59%**	**7.49%**	**0.03%**	**1,785,338**
United States	**Subprime**	58.39%	14.38%	4.28%	4.45%	3.97%	14.43%	0.10%	9,390,046
	Alt-A	45.39%	34.34%	3.54%	4.05%	5.20%	7.41%	0.05%	5,026,084
	Total Nonprime	53.86%	21.34%	4.02%	4.31%	4.40%	11.98%	0.08%	14,416,130

Source: GAO analysis of LP data.

Note: Some data were insufficient to classify loans into a status category but these "unknown" loans are included in the total number of loans. This table does not include data for Guam, Puerto Rico, and the Virgin Islands.

Table 7. Number of 2000 through 2007 Nonprime Loans in Different Status Categories by Census Division and State, as of June 30, 2009.

State	Market segment	Prepaid	Current	Delinquent	In default	In foreclosure process	Completed foreclosure process	Unknown	Total
Connecticut	Subprime	77,422	18,054	5,608	4,806	5,124	11,918	106	123,038
	Alt-A	21,585	16,455	1,811	1,278	1,881	1,690	26	44,726
Maine	Subprime	23,243	5,341	1,593	1,089	1,758	3,253	32	36,309
	Alt-A	4,750	3,530	343	201	490	378	5	9,697
Massachusetts	Subprime	135,866	21,560	7,065	9,953	6,325	21,128	317	202,214
	Alt-A	45,071	26,645	2,996	2,912	3,259	4,229	100	85,212
New Hampshire	Subprime	25,785	6,085	2,115	1,793	855	4,769	27	41,429
	Alt-A	7,595	5,654	613	438	291	980	15	15,586
Rhode Island	Subprime	37,192	4,979	1,639	1,507	1,269	6,134	94	52,814
	Alt-A	8,147	4,737	618	460	561	1,207	16	15,746

Table 7. (Continued)

State	Market segment	Prepaid	Current	Delinquent	In default	In foreclosure process	Completed foreclosure process	Unknown	Total
Vermont	Subprime	6,424	1,554	405	292	420	648	11	9,754
	Alt-A	2,032	1,458	131	70	132	88	2	3,913
New England	Subprime	305,932	57,573	18,425	19,440	15,751	47,850	587	465,558
	Alt-A	89,180	58,479	6,512	5,359	6,614	8,572	164	174,880
New Jersey	Subprime	184,231	27,004	9,100	10,376	14,702	18,912	350	264,675
	Alt-A	75,925	43,311	5,134	4,634	9,737	4,818	137	143,696
New York	Subprime	228,070	65,232	18,120	19,475	22,856	30,752	342	384,847
	Alt-A	71,643	65,464	6,910	7,745	9,163	4,963	71	165,959
Pennsylvania	Subprime	139,227	57,617	16,311	13,780	9,522	26,015	194	262,666
	Alt-A	36,561	34,977	3,047	2,070	2,239	2,648	54	81,596
Mid Atlantic	Subprime	551,528	149,853	43,531	43,631	47,080	75,679	886	912,188
	Alt-A	184,129	143,752	15,091	14,449	21,139	12,429	262	391,251
Illinois	Subprime	285,197	50,873	17,279	18,687	17,767	59,676	628	450,107
	Alt-A	77,168	44,165	4,929	5,035	7,245	8,885	89	147,516
Indiana	Subprime	76,880	32,273	9,431	8,089	7,260	42,066	208	176,207
	Alt-A	15,175	15,122	1,380	1,065	1,570	4,035	9	38,356
Michigan	Subprime	182,786	46,901	17,668	17,989	6,799	100,669	475	373,287
	Alt-A	35,589	35,478	4,096	3,229	2,448	13,793	33	94,666
Ohio	Subprime	145,272	56,344	16,025	14,626	13,781	72,944	388	319,380
	Alt-A	26,962	31,776	2,769	2,114	3,154	6,757	30	73,562
Wisconsin	Subprime	83,480	15,012	4,992	4,383	5,143	17,913	136	131,059
	Alt-A	14,311	10,790	1,010	674	1,149	1,654	12	29,600
East North	Subprime	773,615	201,403	65,395	63,774	50,750	293,268	1,835	1,450,040
Central	Alt-A	169,205	137,331	14,184	12,117	15,566	35,124	173	383,700

Table 7. (Continued)

State	Market segment	Prepaid	Current	Delinquent	In default	In foreclosure process	Completed foreclosure process	Unknown	Total
Iowa	Subprime	30,130	8,151	2,275	1,505	1,742	8,780	43	52,626
	Alt-A	4,676	4,552	330	153	259	562	2	10,534
Kansas	Subprime	27,994	8,361	2,320	1,680	1,051	8,298	43	49,747
	Alt-A	7,487	7,497	459	254	269	879	2	16,847
Minnesota	Subprime	98,957	17,374	5,337	5,218	4,185	31,622	206	162,899
	Alt-A	25,976	25,470	2,548	2,115	2,540	8,634	32	67,315
Missouri	Subprime	99,485	25,495	8,814	7,399	2,654	36,259	191	180,297
	Alt-A	22,260	18,959	1,568	1,089	706	4,217	22	48,821
Nebraska	Subprime	15,298	5,873	1,506	1,153	689	5,060	20	29,599
	Alt-A	2,926	3,181	215	148	116	401	0	6,987
North Dakota	Subprime	2,680	883	214	137	107	442	1	4,464
	Alt-A	823	855	47	22	33	63	1	1,844
South Dakota	Subprime	4,219	1,270	345	206	224	1,056	1	7,321
	Alt-A	1,089	1,036	64	49	56	123	1	2,418
West North Central	**Subprime**	**278,763**	**67,407**	**20,811**	**17,298**	**10,652**	**91,517**	**505**	**486,953**
	Alt-A	**65,237**	**61,550**	**5,231**	**3,830**	**3,979**	**14,879**	**60**	**154,766**
Delaware	Subprime	14,836	4,170	1,333	1,163	1,246	1,879	16	24,643
	Alt-A	5,588	4,579	431	310	448	389	7	11,752
District of Columbia	Subprime	12,340	1,826	573	676	439	1,486	29	17,369
	Alt-A	7,979	5,514	507	425	371	654	8	15,458
Florida	Subprime	525,935	121,841	38,065	45,142	97,683	105,722	749	935,137
	Alt-A	197,050	170,109	20,746	26,634	79,149	34,088	372	528,148
Georgia	Subprime	130,795	40,930	15,643	16,876	7,285	55,516	279	267,324
	Alt-A	61,260	63,589	7,219	5,308	4,312	16,134	90	157,912

Table 7. (Continued)

State	Market segment	Prepaid	Current	Delinquent	In default	In foreclosure process	Completed foreclosure process	Unknown	Total
Maryland	Subprime	179,054	28,200	9,846	11,301	7,802	18,613	284	255,100
	Alt-A	67,038	45,811	5,357	5,583	5,979	5,930	130	135,828
North Carolina	Subprime	96,509	31,510	11,162	9,181	3,658	27,228	181	179,429
	Alt-A	39,678	35,302	3,169	2,191	1,565	4,575	36	86,516
South Carolina	Subprime	48,052	17,109	5,598	3,941	3,478	15,854	99	94,131
	Alt-A	22,642	18,777	1,694	1,119	1,821	2,786	30	48,869
Virginia	Subprime	139,146	27,922	8,973	8,931	4,252	23,764	185	213,173
	Alt-A	72,554	57,166	5,594	5,690	4,765	16,542	145	162,456
West Virginia	Subprime	8,997	3,358	1,095	828	404	2,192	30	16,904
	Alt-A	1,930	1,936	246	139	151	405	6	4,813
South Atlantic	**Subprime**	**1,155,664**	**276,866**	**92,288**	**98,039**	**126,247**	**252,254**	**1,852**	**2,003,210**
	Alt-A	**475,719**	**402,783**	**44,963**	**47,399**	**98,561**	**81,503**	**824**	**1,151,752**
Alabama	Subprime	42,155	16,296	5,601	5,388	1,587	13,216	34	84,277
	Alt-A	11,959	11,206	1,043	689	451	1,836	7	27,191
Kentucky	Subprime	35,454	13,555	3,858	2,836	2,604	13,200	75	71,582
	Alt-A	7,701	7,938	632	394	545	1,210	3	18,423
Mississippi	Subprime	22,594	10,914	3,970	3,972	1,217	9,409	40	52,116
	Alt-A	3,913	3,927	414	262	182	673	3	9,374
Tennessee	Subprime	78,602	32,810	10,704	11,659	2,985	31,378	122	168,260
	Alt-A	19,332	19,983	1,704	1,168	641	3,193	8	46,029
Louisiana	Subprime	47,141	19,344	5,761	4,563	2,916	9,988	91	89,804
	Alt-A	9,171	7,861	687	404	485	758	5	19,371
Oklahoma	Subprime	29,984	15,739	3,767	2,487	2,343	11,806	30	66,156
	Alt-A	6,925	9,108	538	267	435	954	2	18,229
Texas	Subprime	237,490	162,136	41,418	28,779	12,401	87,504	228	569,956
	Alt-A	69,560	90,589	6,134	3,728	2,517	13,341	33	185,902

Table 7. (Continued)

State	Market segment	Prepaid	Current	Delinquent	In default	In foreclosure process	Completed foreclosure process	Unknown	Total
West South Central	**Subprime**	**332,370**	**206,130**	**53,407**	**37,831**	**18,434**	**115,066**	**361**	**763,599**
	Alt-A	**90,033**	**112,906**	**7,733**	**4,670**	**3,627**	**15,834**	**40**	**234,843**
Arizona	Subprime	184,070	33,918	10,453	14,385	11,318	46,259	248	300,651
	Alt-A	108,995	71,847	7,914	8,710	10,489	25,289	140	233,384
Colorado	Subprime	104,186	26,477	6,495	5,886	4,415	41,115	172	188,746
	Alt-A	64,355	53,790	3,645	2,629	3,129	10,862	51	138,461
Idaho	Subprime	23,536	5,648	1,608	1,539	1,302	4,595	16	38,244
	Alt-A	15,335	11,966	988	834	1,246	1,609	9	31,987
Montana	Subprime	8,364	1,954	507	481	349	1,314	2	12,971
	Alt-A	4,755	3,282	228	165	179	239	0	8,848
Nevada	Subprime	88,344	15,973	4,861	8,253	7,014	28,016	110	152,571
	Alt-A	56,985	46,361	6,344	9,573	10,881	21,843	80	152,067
New Mexico	Subprime	26,117	6,111	1,670	1,137	1,111	4,292	49	40,487
	Alt-A	11,345	8,558	600	371	737	698	13	22,322
Utah	Subprime	53,294	9,456	2,778	2,528	1,928	10,280	57	80,321
	Alt-A	31,593	17,997	1,477	1,184	1,638	3,040	22	56,951
Wyoming	Subprime	6,405	1,696	414	288	140	800	2	9,745
	Alt-A	2,510	1,721	96	56	34	100	0	4,517
Mountain	**Subprime**	**494,316**	**101,233**	**28,786**	**34,497**	**27,577**	**136,671**	**656**	**823,736**
	Alt-A	**295,873**	**215,522**	**21,292**	**23,522**	**28,333**	**63,680**	**315**	**648,537**
Alaska	Subprime	5,985	1,584	428	352	211	871	2	9,433
	Alt-A	1,877	1,653	114	68	67	158	0	3,937
California	Subprime	1,176,213	163,064	41,897	65,942	56,041	240,228	2,055	1,745,440
	Alt-A	741,079	454,170	51,601	83,496	74,288	125,175	527	1,530,336
Hawaii	Subprime	27,679	7,403	1,407	1,541	1,929	2,063	31	42,053
	Alt-A	13,850	11,067	889	825	1,257	560	11	28,459

Table 7. (Continued)

State	Market segment	Prepaid	Current	Delinquent	In default	In foreclosure process	Completed foreclosure process	Unknown	Total
Oregon	Subprime	68,127	16,133	3,924	4,036	3,393	11,235	69	106,917
	Alt-A	39,021	29,910	2,192	1,963	2,194	3,166	27	78,473
Washington	Subprime	134,225	28,227	7,411	7,874	6,058	20,784	105	204,684
	Alt-A	73,434	54,031	4,304	3,567	4,116	4,639	42	144,133
Pacific	**Subprime**	**1,412,229**	**216,411**	**55,067**	**79,745**	**67,632**	**275,181**	**2,262**	**2,108,527**
	Alt-A	**869,261**	**550,831**	**59,100**	**89,919**	**81,922**	**133,698**	**607**	**1,785,338**
United States	Subprime	5,483,222	1,350,451	401,843	418,110	372,516	1,354,689	9,215	9,390,046
	Alt-A	2,281,542	1,726,208	177,899	203,778	261,560	372,631	2,466	5,026,084
	Total Nonprime	**7,764,764**	**3,076,659**	**579,742**	**621,888**	**634,076**	**1,727,320**	**11,681**	**14,416,130**

Source: GAO analysis of LP data.
Note: Some data were insufficient to classify loans into a status category but these "unknown" loans are included in the total number of loans. This table does not include data for Guam, Puerto Rico, and the Virgin Islands.

ENCLOSURE IV. STATUS OF NONPRIME LOANS ORIGINATED FROM 2000 THROUGH 2007 BY CONGRESSIONAL DISTRICT AS OF JUNE 30, 2009

This enclosure contains the results of our analysis of LoanPerformance (LP) data on the status of nonprime mortgages by congressional district. The analysis covers mortgages originated from 2000 through 2007, as of June 30, 2009. All figures reported are estimated.

Table 8. Estimated Percentage of 2000 through 2007 Active Nonprime Loans in Default and in the Foreclosure Process by Congressional District as of June 30, 2009.

State	Congressional district	Estimated number of active loans	Estimated percentage of active loans in default	Estimated percentage of active loans in the foreclosure process	Estimated percentage of active loans that are seriously delinquent
Alabama	01	7,831	16.62	5.73	22.35
	02	4,168	13.60	4.63	18.23
	03	5,231	14.47	4.29	18.77
	04	3,667	11.87	4.03	15.90
	05	5,177	10.87	4.15	15.03
	06	8,902	13.75	4.91	18.66
	07	7,228	16.86	5.12	21.97
Alaska	00	4,478	9.38	6.16	15.54
Arizona	01	11,932	11.30	10.01	21.30
	02	30,366	14.33	13.76	28.09
	03	22,150	12.90	12.56	25.46
	04	20,464	19.66	17.15	36.80
	05	18,041	9.88	10.59	20.47
	06	28,325	13.40	13.69	27.09
	07	24,793	14.76	14.05	28.81
	08	12,915	9.96	6.70	16.66
Arkansas	01	3,801	10.69	4.65	15.34
	02	6,882	11.72	4.49	16.22
	03	5,781	10.25	5.66	15.90
	04	3,620	12.00	3.55	15.55
California	01	15,556	10.65	8.80	19.45
	02	16,851	12.71	11.48	24.19
	03	25,868	16.48	13.52	30.00
	04	23,109	12.55	10.05	22.60

Table 8. (Continued)

State	Congressional district	Estimated number of active loans	Estimated percentage of active loans in default	Estimated percentage of active loans in the foreclosure process	Estimated percentage of active loans that are seriously delinquent
California	05	19,357	16.79	15.52	32.32
	06	18,354	9.08	7.77	16.85
	07	21,675	16.89	15.20	32.08
	08	8,840	6.85	5.35	12.19
	09	13,814	13.60	11.96	25.56
	10	24,462	15.02	12.98	28.01
	11	28,949	16.65	14.75	31.41
	12	13,918	9.66	7.67	17.34
	13	15,745	15.42	13.14	28.56
	14	13,071	8.17	6.47	14.64
	15	11,195	11.21	9.40	20.62
	16	17,392	16.25	13.83	30.08
	17	14,356	15.43	13.67	29.10
	18	16,536	19.42	18.86	38.29
	19	20,940	16.51	14.10	30.62
	20	12,236	15.57	13.30	28.88
	21	20,715	14.69	11.86	26.56
	22	27,674	16.12	14.36	30.48
	23	11,541	12.45	10.71	23.16
	24	24,176	12.45	10.18	22.63
	25	33,661	19.55	17.65	37.20
	26	20,024	13.63	11.39	25.01
	27	18,883	16.98	14.87	31.84
	28	14,886	16.01	14.51	30.52
	29	12,886	10.80	9.42	20.22
	30	14,869	9.28	7.71	17.00

Table 8. (Continued)

State	Congressional district	Estimated number of active loans	Estimated percentage of active loans in default	Estimated percentage of active loans in the foreclosure process	Estimated percentage of active loans that are seriously delinquent
California	31	8,865	14.69	12.75	27.43
	32	13,389	15.61	12.87	28.49
	33	12,868	15.27	11.66	26.94
	34	10,377	16.26	14.87	31.13
	35	16,775	16.73	13.96	30.69
	36	13,236	9.14	6.55	15.69
	37	17,640	17.87	14.28	32.14
	38	16,850	17.89	14.63	32.52
	39	15,393	17.08	14.28	31.36
	40	14,890	14.50	13.21	27.71
	41	33,190	18.08	16.70	34.77
	42	21,402	13.67	11.49	25.16
	43	23,925	21.06	19.14	40.20
	44	31,125	18.71	16.73	35.44
	45	35,348	18.34	17.03	35.37
	46	17,217	11.25	9.24	20.50
	47	11,421	18.23	18.51	36.73
	48	19,767	11.05	9.49	20.53
	49	28,438	17.38	16.22	33.60
	50	19,724	10.33	9.32	19.65
	51	22,934	17.65	15.61	33.26
	52	18,357	12.75	10.12	22.86
	53	14,590	10.49	9.99	20.49
Colorado	01	15,106	8.41	7.81	16.23
	02	15,481	6.78	6.22	13.00
	03	11,910	7.15	6.17	13.32

Table 8. (Continued)

State	Congressional district	Estimated number of active loans	Estimated percentage of active loans in default	Estimated percentage of active loans in the foreclosure process	Estimated percentage of active loans that are seriously delinquent
Colorado	04	13,854	7.65	7.13	14.78
	05	14,313	7.93	7.06	14.99
	06	19,896	8.32	6.82	15.14
	07	15,777	9.34	8.29	17.63
Connecticut	01	9,775	10.38	11.54	21.91
	02	9,075	11.53	10.73	22.26
	03	11,924	12.03	13.21	25.24
	04	13,212	10.38	14.00	24.38
	05	10,716	11.13	13.51	24.65
Delaware	00	13,657	10.75	12.40	23.15
District of Columbia	00	10,337	10.65	7.86	18.50
Florida	01	12,552	9.37	16.62	25.99
	02	11,918	8.64	18.86	27.50
	03	20,242	14.12	23.10	37.22
	04	16,513	10.94	16.88	27.82
	05	22,857	11.13	25.20	36.33
	06	16,000	11.62	20.60	32.22
	07	23,017	11.32	24.77	36.09
	08	27,549	12.34	29.15	41.49
	09	22,471	10.17	25.90	36.08
	10	18,603	9.60	24.38	33.98
	11	22,273	11.37	28.83	40.20
	12	22,899	12.15	26.21	38.37
	13	21,706	10.65	31.85	42.50
	14	33,953	12.25	37.64	49.90

Table 8. (Continued)

State	Congressional district	Estimated number of active loans	Estimated percentage of active loans in default	Estimated percentage of active loans in the foreclosure process	Estimated percentage of active loans that are seriously delinquent
Florida	15	29,211	12.11	31.48	43.59
	16	23,576	11.90	33.15	45.05
	17	27,306	14.34	31.41	45.74
	18	25,541	11.36	35.86	47.22
	19	27,851	12.03	33.99	46.02
	20	30,355	12.87	30.79	43.66
	21	25,063	13.22	32.23	45.44
	22	27,338	11.06	31.85	42.90
	23	30,197	13.29	34.42	47.71
	24	25,800	12.45	25.44	37.88
	25	33,658	13.63	36.39	50.01
Georgia	01	5,711	12.09	5.79	17.88
	02	3,708	13.01	5.15	18.15
	03	16,681	14.82	7.52	22.34
	04	17,514	15.70	8.29	23.99
	05	14,276	12.65	8.86	21.50
	06	13,611	9.95	5.99	15.94
	07	20,814	14.10	7.81	21.90
	08	8,367	15.51	5.67	21.19
	09	11,119	12.54	6.55	19.09
	10	6,953	11.04	5.45	16.50
	11	14,635	13.30	6.89	20.18
	12	6,158	12.83	5.45	18.29
	13	21,236	16.25	8.09	24.34
Hawaii	01	9,511	7.80	8.75	16.55
	02	16,781	9.67	14.02	23.69

Table 8. (Continued)

State	Congressional district	Estimated number of active loans	Estimated percentage of active loans in default	Estimated percentage of active loans in the foreclosure process	Estimated percentage of active loans that are seriously delinquent
Idaho	01	16,613	10.15	11.35	21.51
	02	8,469	7.97	7.81	15.78
Illinois	01	12,712	16.06	16.42	32.48
	02	20,061	17.59	15.25	32.84
	03	10,727	16.39	17.61	34.00
	04	8,583	15.06	20.38	35.43
	05	8,510	14.10	19.07	33.17
	06	9,018	13.66	15.21	28.86
	07	11,835	14.46	17.31	31.77
	08	11,347	13.22	13.60	26.83
	09	6,843	12.88	17.83	30.70
	10	7,524	11.67	14.15	25.82
	11	8,308	14.18	12.96	27.14
	12	5,223	14.31	8.63	22.94
	13	10,720	13.76	13.91	27.67
	14	12,057	14.32	17.63	31.95
	15	3,470	9.48	8.17	17.67
	16	8,164	12.91	12.46	25.37
	17	3,458	10.22	8.21	18.42
	18	3,747	10.78	8.45	19.24
	19	3,493	11.77	7.81	19.58
Indiana	01	11,537	15.13	12.53	27.65
	02	8,475	12.02	11.03	23.06
	03	7,584	11.18	11.77	22.94
	04	8,077	9.98	12.12	22.10
	05	9,630	10.04	11.52	21.56

Table 8. (Continued)

State	Congressional district	Estimated number of active loans	Estimated percentage of active loans in default	Estimated percentage of active loans in the foreclosure process	Estimated percentage of active loans that are seriously delinquent
Indiana	06	7,679	10.28	10.58	20.85
	07	11,521	13.36	12.98	26.33
	08	5,698	12.39	9.46	21.85
	09	5,852	12.30	10.41	22.71
Iowa	01	3,400	8.48	9.82	18.29
	02	3,066	8.26	10.97	19.21
	03	5,589	9.21	11.88	21.10
	04	3,302	8.60	10.58	19.17
	05	3,585	8.77	8.74	17.52
Kansas	01	2,738	7.58	5.51	13.08
	02	5,173	9.50	6.40	15.89
	03	8,200	9.91	6.33	16.24
	04	5,763	7.27	5.54	12.81
Kentucky	01	3,062	9.61	7.48	17.08
	02	5,267	10.22	8.52	18.74
	03	8,485	10.29	12.40	22.69
	04	6,421	10.74	9.43	20.17
	05	2,602	8.65	8.12	16.76
	06	6,481	9.32	9.30	18.62
Louisiana	01	6,985	10.69	9.02	19.71
	02	7,056	13.32	10.05	23.37
	03	5,331	11.96	7.68	19.62
	04	5,355	12.79	7.29	20.09
	05	3,779	13.01	6.62	19.63
	06	9,295	11.39	8.09	19.48
	07	4,194	9.48	6.17	15.67

Table 8. (Continued)

State	Congressional district	Estimated number of active loans	Estimated percentage of active loans in default	Estimated percentage of active loans in the foreclosure process	Estimated percentage of active loans that are seriously delinquent
Maine	01	7,935	9.68	15.35	25.03
	02	6,304	8.22	16.06	24.27
Maryland	01	11,931	11.65	9.26	20.91
	02	11,909	14.06	9.34	23.39
	03	13,801	11.94	9.50	21.44
	04	21,336	16.63	14.65	31.29
	05	23,694	16.50	12.68	29.18
	06	11,692	12.86	11.06	23.91
	07	12,561	12.87	9.92	22.79
	08	12,869	12.28	12.22	24.50
Massachusetts	01	6,624	16.71	11.42	28.14
	02	9,127	17.30	12.39	29.69
	03	8,176	16.72	13.03	29.75
	04	7,230	14.90	10.51	25.42
	05	8,340	16.38	11.86	28.24
	06	7,338	15.84	11.80	27.64
	07	6,878	14.27	12.95	27.22
	08	6,183	13.51	11.67	25.18
	09	10,073	17.63	12.08	29.71
	10	10,048	14.83	10.96	25.79
Michigan	01	4,963	10.45	5.63	16.08
	02	6,353	12.44	6.82	19.27
	03	7,337	12.72	7.06	19.78
	04	5,933	11.45	6.41	17.85
	05	8,059	17.44	6.07	23.50
	06	7,274	10.99	6.34	17.34

Table 8. (Continued)

State	Congressional district	Estimated number of active loans	Estimated percentage of active loans in default	Estimated percentage of active loans in the foreclosure process	Estimated percentage of active loans that are seriously delinquent
Michigan	07	8,075	13.29	7.80	21.09
	08	9,397	12.31	7.03	19.34
	09	9,571	13.66	7.54	21.19
	10	8,465	13.04	7.72	20.74
	11	10,298	14.50	7.28	21.78
	12	12,351	16.34	7.58	23.92
	13	11,742	23.28	5.80	29.08
	14	14,642	24.28	6.25	30.54
	15	9,916	16.25	7.30	23.56
Minnesota	01	4,290	9.95	7.96	17.93
	02	11,090	10.96	9.84	20.80
	03	9,928	11.14	10.53	21.67
	04	7,739	11.35	12.16	23.50
	05	9,025	11.65	11.42	23.07
	06	11,206	12.51	10.53	23.04
	07	4,130	10.56	7.96	18.52
	08	7,303	11.09	10.40	21.48
Mississippi	01	7,587	18.82	5.38	24.20
	02	6,569	19.64	5.85	25.48
	03	4,756	14.77	5.46	20.25
	04	5,921	13.74	5.86	19.59
Missouri	01	13,869	17.47	5.64	23.12
	02	6,476	11.07	4.95	16.03
	03	8,002	12.17	5.19	17.36
	04	4,770	10.87	4.44	15.30
	05	12,089	13.26	5.08	18.34

Table 8. (Continued)

State	Congressional district	Estimated number of active loans	Estimated percentage of active loans in default	Estimated percentage of active loans in the foreclosure process	Estimated percentage of active loans that are seriously delinquent
Missouri	06	7,316	11.01	4.47	15.49
	07	6,261	9.89	5.31	15.19
	08	3,262	10.46	4.34	14.81
	09	4,540	10.56	4.55	15.09
Montana	00	7,134	9.03	7.40	16.43
Nebraska	01	4,019	10.08	6.40	16.47
	02	6,228	10.84	6.32	17.15
	03	2,606	8.28	5.73	14.01
Nevada	01	35,911	17.91	17.60	35.51
	02	21,702	12.89	13.17	26.06
	03	51,500	16.64	16.89	33.53
New Hampshire	01	9,398	11.85	6.56	18.42
	02	8,186	13.25	5.83	19.07
New Jersey	01	9,631	14.67	16.15	30.82
	02	12,037	12.91	17.39	30.30
	03	10,992	12.69	16.35	29.04
	04	10,748	11.36	16.98	28.34
	05	8,911	10.26	15.81	26.07
	06	8,655	11.81	19.99	31.80
	07	7,509	10.70	17.56	28.25
	08	9,645	12.82	24.37	37.18
	09	8,605	11.13	20.56	31.69
	10	10,818	14.88	30.84	45.72
	11	7,338	9.39	15.85	25.24
	12	8,956	10.67	16.08	26.75
	13	9,692	12.41	26.58	38.99

Table 8. (Continued)

State	Congressional district	Estimated number of active loans	Estimated percentage of active loans in default	Estimated percentage of active loans in the foreclosure process	Estimated percentage of active loans that are seriously delinquent
New Mexico	01	8,687	7.70	9.42	17.13
	02	4,707	6.85	8.39	15.23
	03	6,902	7.51	9.16	16.66
New York	01	18,203	13.42	17.36	30.78
	02	16,002	15.31	21.19	36.51
	03	12,120	13.40	14.86	28.26
	04	14,296	15.06	18.88	33.95
	05	6,853	9.93	11.00	20.93
	06	14,939	16.69	21.26	37.95
	07	6,712	13.29	16.06	29.35
	08	3,286	5.80	8.86	14.67
	09	7,536	11.43	15.15	26.57
	10	9,659	12.84	25.94	38.79
	11	5,188	11.64	19.43	31.07
	12	4,679	11.35	20.50	31.84
	13	8,777	12.07	12.61	24.68
	14	3,021	4.28	4.90	9.17
	15	935	8.14	13.11	21.28
	16	1,899	13.95	21.75	35.70
	17	8,309	13.52	15.25	28.78
	18	8,445	10.55	9.84	20.39
	19	11,854	12.93	11.33	24.26
	20	7,986	13.05	10.77	23.82
	21	6,263	12.48	11.90	24.37
	22	7,233	13.90	12.93	26.82
	23	3,348	10.69	8.33	19.03

Table 8. (Continued)

State	Congressional district	Estimated number of active loans	Estimated percentage of active loans in default	Estimated percentage of active loans in the foreclosure process	Estimated percentage of active loans that are seriously delinquent
New York	24	4,302	10.90	7.45	18.36
	25	4,617	9.92	8.90	18.82
	26	4,398	9.78	6.77	16.55
	27	4,324	10.33	5.98	16.33
	28	5,488	9.98	8.25	18.24
	29	3,977	10.70	6.46	17.15
North Carolina	01	3,899	13.63	5.48	19.11
	02	6,916	12.99	5.75	18.74
	03	7,454	10.05	5.43	15.48
	04	8,166	10.95	3.98	14.93
	05	5,222	11.89	4.67	16.56
	06	7,469	12.42	4.96	17.37
	07	7,357	10.69	5.13	15.81
	08	7,100	12.04	5.35	17.39
	09	13,339	11.03	5.95	16.99
	10	6,362	12.30	5.58	17.89
	11	5,751	9.87	5.15	15.01
	12	10,609	12.23	6.18	18.42
	13	7,888	12.30	5.03	17.34
North Dakota	00	2,287	6.84	6.10	12.99
Ohio	01	8,848	12.40	10.47	22.88
	02	6,525	10.09	10.36	20.44
	03	8,154	13.25	12.03	25.28
	04	6,223	11.40	10.80	22.21
	05	4,986	10.27	11.19	21.46
	06	4,728	11.38	11.86	23.24

Table 8. (Continued)

State	Congressional district	Estimated number of active loans	Estimated percentage of active loans in default	Estimated percentage of active loans in the foreclosure process	Estimated percentage of active loans that are seriously delinquent
Ohio	07	8,002	11.95	11.13	23.07
	08	7,281	11.49	11.25	22.74
	09	8,364	11.85	12.80	24.65
	10	9,289	11.90	12.15	24.06
	11	12,105	16.81	13.37	30.18
	12	10,220	11.14	11.21	22.35
	13	9,136	11.32	13.94	25.26
	14	7,862	9.63	12.62	22.25
	15	7,938	10.80	11.65	22.46
	16	7,246	10.52	11.22	21.74
	17	8,343	12.36	16.08	28.43
	18	5,139	11.89	9.94	21.83
Oklahoma	01	8,842	8.40	8.36	16.75
	02	4,676	8.39	8.11	16.49
	03	4,987	7.68	7.44	15.12
	04	7,163	7.28	7.13	14.41
	05	8,981	7.93	8.65	16.58
Oregon	01	12,656	9.34	8.66	17.99
	02	13,122	10.16	10.27	20.42
	03	15,537	9.43	8.70	18.13
	04	10,364	8.70	7.22	15.92
	05	11,992	9.28	8.66	17.94
Pennsylvania	01	11,475	10.78	8.97	19.76
	02	10,438	10.87	9.37	20.22
	03	4,726	11.19	7.39	18.58
	04	6,934	11.50	7.36	18.86

Table 8. (Continued)

State	Congressional district	Estimated number of active loans	Estimated percentage of active loans in default	Estimated percentage of active loans in the foreclosure process	Estimated percentage of active loans that are seriously delinquent
Pennsylvania	05	3,349	10.81	7.12	17.95
	06	7,613	9.50	8.18	17.68
	07	7,625	10.96	8.07	19.03
	08	7,726	12.08	8.35	20.42
	09	4,808	11.65	6.85	18.49
	10	6,471	12.30	9.92	22.22
	11	10,732	12.80	12.31	25.12
	12	4,821	11.88	7.04	18.94
	13	8,419	11.04	7.98	19.02
	14	7,660	12.25	7.02	19.27
	15	9,350	11.98	8.82	20.80
	16	5,656	9.85	8.34	18.19
	17	6,484	10.26	6.98	17.24
	18	7,839	11.81	6.95	18.77
	19	7,248	11.75	8.59	20.35
Rhode Island	01	6,979	11.61	11.00	22.61
	02	8,648	13.25	12.16	25.42
South Carolina	01	15,607	8.73	11.80	20.53
	02	11,431	9.67	9.93	19.60
	03	5,407	8.18	7.61	15.78
	04	7,773	9.39	10.06	19.45
	05	6,737	10.49	8.13	18.61
	06	6,535	10.81	8.86	19.66
South Dakota	00	3,254	7.81	8.60	16.41
Tennessee	01	5,522	10.99	4.81	15.81
	02	8,019	13.46	4.78	18.23

Table 8. (Continued)

State	Congressional district	Estimated number of active loans	Estimated percentage of active loans in default	Estimated percentage of active loans in the foreclosure process	Estimated percentage of active loans that are seriously delinquent
Tennessee	03	8,050	14.98	4.35	19.33
	04	5,596	13.87	4.58	18.44
	05	11,735	13.47	4.13	17.59
	06	9,347	14.51	4.38	18.88
	07	11,088	15.24	4.24	19.49
	08	7,488	18.91	4.07	22.97
	09	14,673	21.08	4.76	25.84
Texas	01	4,894	8.20	3.89	12.08
	02	14,442	11.24	4.61	15.84
	03	13,167	8.46	4.37	12.84
	04	10,816	8.71	4.78	13.49
	05	10,516	9.68	4.82	14.50
	06	13,575	10.40	4.73	15.13
	07	12,313	8.48	4.09	12.56
	08	10,085	9.17	3.99	13.16
	09	14,495	10.41	4.40	14.81
	10	17,656	10.10	4.65	14.75
	11	4,896	7.17	2.87	10.03
	12	12,459	8.93	4.38	13.32
	13	4,143	8.28	3.61	11.88
	14	10,494	10.14	4.07	14.21
	15	7,560	9.89	4.28	14.17
	16	7,915	7.84	3.01	10.85
	17	7,499	7.72	3.85	11.57
	18	13,765	10.96	4.53	15.49
	19	4,701	6.41	3.51	9.91

Table 8. (Continued)

State	Congressional district	Estimated number of active loans	Estimated percentage of active loans in default	Estimated percentage of active loans in the foreclosure process	Estimated percentage of active loans that are seriously delinquent
Texas	20	9,454	8.51	4.22	12.74
	21	13,235	7.73	3.91	11.64
	22	17,942	11.21	4.13	15.34
	23	10,512	9.31	4.33	13.63
	24	14,037	10.12	4.84	14.95
	25	10,172	6.76	3.64	10.40
	26	16,691	8.82	4.52	13.35
	27	8,693	8.90	3.69	12.58
	28	9,207	10.27	4.59	14.86
	29	10,642	9.75	3.76	13.51
	30	13,337	11.84	5.56	17.40
	31	9,983	7.30	3.80	11.10
	32	7,731	7.69	4.68	12.37
Utah	01	11,718	8.28	7.63	15.92
	02	13,591	9.63	10.06	19.69
	03	13,593	10.51	9.60	20.10
Vermont	00	4,423	8.19	12.39	20.57
Virginia	01	14,151	13.51	7.67	21.18
	02	11,045	9.87	5.31	15.17
	03	11,481	12.87	5.46	18.33
	04	11,269	12.95	5.64	18.59
	05	5,834	10.09	4.15	14.24
	06	5,580	10.55	4.57	15.13
	07	10,766	12.51	6.26	18.77
	08	11,487	8.91	7.64	16.56
	09	2,865	9.84	4.56	14.42

Table 8. (Continued)

State	Congressional district	Estimated number of active loans	Estimated percentage of active loans in default	Estimated percentage of active loans in the foreclosure process	Estimated percentage of active loans that are seriously delinquent
Virginia	10	19,925	12.07	9.70	21.77
	11	18,653	12.99	10.46	23.45
Washington	01	13,058	8.77	8.75	17.52
	02	14,488	10.46	8.95	19.42
	03	14,531	10.60	10.38	20.99
	04	8,286	7.16	5.15	12.30
	05	7,793	7.81	6.43	14.24
	06	14,290	10.57	9.30	19.87
	07	10,761	7.50	6.97	14.48
	08	16,603	10.91	9.68	20.59
	09	15,634	12.13	10.30	22.44
West Virginia	01	2,099	9.85	5.80	15.67
	02	4,001	13.36	8.36	21.72
	03	2,059	10.87	4.81	15.69
Wisconsin	01	6,822	11.26	15.20	26.46
	02	4,437	10.02	13.41	23.44
	03	3,843	10.33	15.61	25.94
	04	10,824	14.73	15.48	30.20
	05	5,165	11.99	13.23	25.21
	06	4,185	10.92	13.29	24.21
	07	3,720	9.24	14.77	24.03
	08	4,101	10.33	14.36	24.70
Wyoming	00	4,442	7.72	3.92	11.64

Source: GAO analysis of LP data.

ENCLOSURE V. ESTIMATING NEGATIVE HOME EQUITY

To estimate the extent of negative home equity among nonprime borrowers in major metropolitan areas, we used loan-level information from LoanPerformance's (LP) Asset-backed Securities database and house price indexes from the Federal Housing Finance Agency (FHFA) and S&P/Case-Shiller as of June 30, 2009. We also reviewed industry and academic literature concerning estimates of negative home equity and the methodologies and data used to generate house price indexes.

Comparison of House Price Indexes

FHFA and S&P/Case-Shiller publish a number of house price indexes covering different levels of geography. For the negative equity analysis in this report, we used the following indexes:

- *FHFA All-Transactions Index (FHFA index)*—Calculated using sales data from home purchases and appraisal information from mortgage refinancings. FHFA publishes both a national version and separate indexes for 384 metropolitan areas.
- *S&P/Case-Shiller Tiered Price Indices (S&P/Case-Shiller index)*—Calculated using sales data from home purchases and available for 17 metropolitan areas.[32] The indexes for each metropolitan area provide separate house price trends for low-, middle-, and high-priced homes within each metropolitan area. S&P/Case-Shiller also publishes a national house price index.

The FHFA and S&P/Case-Shiller indexes use the same basic methodology. The methodology measures average price changes for single-family homes (excluding new construction, condominiums, and cooperatives) based on sales (or for FHFA, sales and refinancings) of the same properties at different points in time. This approach requires that each property included in the index be sold or refinanced at least twice to form a pair of house values (valuation pairs) from which appreciation or depreciation can be measured. The use of repeat transactions on the same homes helps to control for differences in the quality of the houses in the data.

Although they use a similar methodology, the FHFA and S&P/Case-Shiller indexes use different data sources and weighting schemes, which contribute to differences in the rates of house price appreciation or depreciation that they show. [33]

- *Data*—The FHFA indexes are based on data for homes with conventional, conforming mortgages—that is, mortgages purchased or securitized by Fannie Mae or Freddie Mac that meet the underwriting guidelines of those agencies. As a result, the FHFA indexes do not reflect homes with other types of financing. In contrast, the S&P/Case-Shiller indexes are based on data for properties with a wider range of financing—including subprime loans, jumbo mortgages, and mortgages guaranteed by the Federal Housing Administration or Department of Veterans Affairs—as well as mortgages purchased or securitized by Fannie Mae and Freddie Mac. Also, as previously noted, the FHFA indexes used in this report use both sales and appraisal data, while the S&P/Case-Shiller indexes use sales data only.[34]

- *Weights*—To limit the influence of atypical changes in the value of individual homes, the FHFA and S&P/Case-Shiller indexes assign weights to each valuation pair. However, they use different weighting schemes. For example, FHFA assigns lower weights than S&P/Case-Shiller to data for homes with lengthy periods between valuations. Additionally, the S&P/Case-Shiller indexes are value-weighted, meaning that price trends for more expensive homes have greater influence on estimated price changes than other homes. In contrast, FHFA's index is unit-weighted and therefore assigns each valuation pair the same weight, all other things being equal.

Because of these and other differences between the FHFA and S&P/Case-Shiller indexes, they historically have shown different appreciation and depreciation rates. Figure 7 illustrates the differences in the FHFA and S&P/Case-Shiller national indexes from the first quarter of 2000 through the second quarter of 2009. Particularly in recent years, the S&P/Case-Shiller index shows steeper increases and declines in home prices than the FHFA index.

To illustrate the impact of different house price indexes on estimates of negative home equity as of June 30, 2009, we compared estimates we made using the FHFA index and the S&P/Case-Shiller index. We limited the comparison to nonprime borrowers with active loans in 15 of the 16 metropolitan areas for which both indexes had identical geographic coverage.[35] Across all 15 metropolitan areas, the estimated percentages of nonprime borrowers with negative equity were lower using the FHFA index compared with the estimates we made using the S&P/Case-Shiller index (see figure 8). The difference ranged from 8.4 percentage points in the Denver, Colorado metropolitan area to 73.1 percentage points in the Minneapolis, Minnesota metropolitan area.

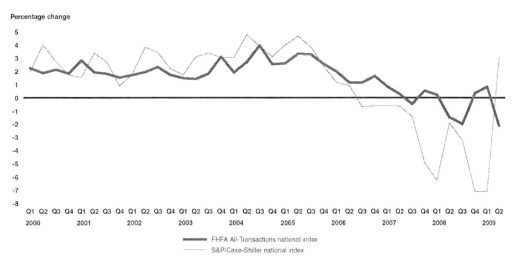

Source: GAO analysis of FHFA All-Transactions Index (national version) and S&P/Case-Shiller U.S. National Home Price Index.

Figure 7. Quarterly Changes in House Price Appreciation Rates, First Quarter 2000 to Second Quarter 2009.

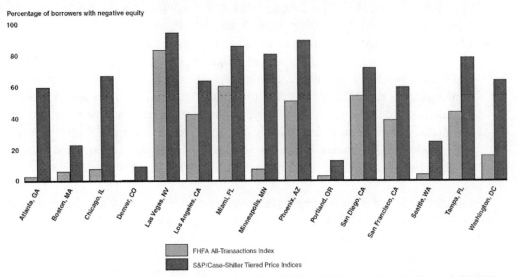

Source: GAO analysis of LP data and data from the FHFA All-Transactions Index and S&P/Case-Shiller Tiered Price Indices.

Figure 8. Estimates of Negative Equity in Selected Metropolitan Areas Using the FHFA and S&P/Case-Shiller Indexes.

Methodology for Estimating Negative Equity

To estimate negative equity nationwide and across metropolitan areas, and for certain loan and borrower characteristics, we analyzed LP data and house price data from the FHFA index and the S&P/Case-Shiller index. We used LP variables for property state and ZIP code, loan origination date, loan origination amount, appraised property value at loan origination, and current loan balance. We also used LP variables indicating the loan class (subprime or Alt-A), loan purpose, loan product, and whether the loan was made to an owner-occupant to disaggregate our estimates by loan and borrower characteristic.

Our overall methodology was as follows. First, using the LP data, we identified first-lien loans originated from 2000 through 2007 that were still active (i.e., had not prepaid or completed the foreclosure process) as of the end of the second quarter of 2009 (June 30). Due to data limitations, our analysis did not account for any second liens that the borrowers had on their properties. To the extent that borrowers had second liens, our analysis may understate the extent of negative home equity. Second, we used Census data files and mapping software to associate the records for those loans (which contain the state and ZIP code of the mortgaged property) with house price index data (which are available by metropolitan statistical area or county). We excluded from our analysis loans for properties outside of the geographic areas covered by the house price indexes.[36] Third, we estimated the extent to which the home associated with each loan had changed in value. To do so, we calculated the percentage change in the value of the corresponding house price index from the quarter the loan was originated through the second quarter of 2009. We then estimated the home's value at the end of the second quarter of 2009 by adjusting the appraised home value at loan origination by the percentage change in the house price index. Finally, we estimated the borrower's home equity by subtracting the loan balance at the end of the second quarter of 2009 from our estimate of the updated home value. When the loan balance exceeded the updated home value, we considered the borrower to be in a negative equity position. Because of data limitations, we could not identify borrowers with multiple mortgaged properties. To the extent that some borrowers had more than one mortgaged property, our results may overstate the actual number of individual borrowers with negative home equity.

To examine the extent of negative equity by loan origination year and nationally, we used the FHFA index and LP loan-level data for the 384 metropolitan statistical areas (MSA) that the FHFA index covered.[37] For each loan that was active as of the end of the second quarter of 2009, we estimated the borrower's home equity as of that date using the methodology described above. We then aggregated these loan-level estimates to calculate the number and percentage of borrowers with negative equity by annual loan cohort and for MSAs nationwide.[38] For borrowers with negative home equity, we calculated the total and median dollar amount of negative equity, as well as the distribution of borrowers across different ranges of negative equity (in terms of both dollars and a percentage of the current home value). Additionally, we used our loan-level estimates of home equity to calculate the number and percentage of borrowers nationwide with near negative equity—that is, home equity of 0 to 5 percent.

To estimate the extent of negative home equity in specific MSAs and by loan and borrower characteristic, we used the S&P/Case-Shiller index and LP data for 16 of the 17 MSAs that the indexes covered. As of November 2009, the S&P/Case-Shiller index did not include 2009 data for the Cleveland, Ohio MSA. As a result, we did not estimate negative home equity for that MSA. The S&P/Case-Shiller index includes separate indexes for homes in different price ranges—low, middle, and high. Accordingly, for each loan record, we used the home's appraised value at loan origination to determine the appropriate tiered index with which to update the home value. Using the methodology described previously, we estimated the borrower's home equity for each loan that was active as of the end of the second quarter of 2009. We then aggregated these loan-level estimates to calculate the number and percentage of borrowers in each of the 16 MSAs that had negative home equity at the end of the second quarter of 2009. We also aggregated the loan-level estimates by loan class (subprime or Alt-A), loan purpose (purchase, cash-out refinance, or no-cash-out refinance), loan product (fixed-rate mortgage, short-term hybrid adjustable-rate mortgage (ARM), payment-option ARM, long-term ARM, and other ARM), and borrower type (owner-occupant or nonowner occupant).

ENCLOSURE VI. DEMOGRAPHIC CHARACTERISTICS OF NONPRIME BORROWERS IN 2005

Data limitations have complicated efforts to analyze the demographic characteristics of nonprime borrowers, such as race and ethnicity. Existing data sets either provide detailed information about nonprime loans but limited information about the borrowers (e.g., LoanPerformance data) or have more extensive information about borrowers but do not specify which loans are nonprime (e.g., Home Mortgage Disclosure Act data). To examine the demographic characteristics of nonprime borrowers with loans originated in 2005 (the peak year for nonprime originations), we extracted a 2 percent random sample of records in the LoanPerformance (LP) database and matched them to Home Mortgage Disclosure Act (HMDA) records. We achieved a match rate of approximately 74 percent, representing about 55,000 records. Of these, about 35,200 were for subprime loans and about 19,800 were for Alt-A loans. (See enclosure VII for a detailed discussion of our methodology.)

From our analysis of the matched loan records, we estimate that about 67 percent of the nonprime borrowers with loans originated in 2005 were White, while 14 percent were Black or African-American, and 4 percent were Asian.[39] Approximately 2 percent of the borrowers were American Indian, Alaska Native, Native Hawaiian, or Other Pacific Islander.[40] For about 14 percent of the borrowers, the HMDA data did not contain information about race. In addition, we estimate that 18 percent of nonprime borrowers identified their ethnicity as Hispanic or Latino.[41]

White borrowers accounted for a smaller estimated proportion of the nonprime mortgage market than they did of the mortgage market as a whole, while Black or African-American borrowers and Hispanic or Latino borrowers accounted for larger proportions. HMDA data for first-lien mortgages originated in 2005 for one- to four-unit properties indicate that approximately 74 percent of the borrowers were White and 8 percent were Black or African-American. Slightly more than 12 percent did not provide information on race. About 11 percent of borrowers in the HMDA data identified their ethnicities as Hispanic or Latino.

As shown in table 9, White borrowers accounted for a higher estimated proportion of Alt-A loans (73 percent) than subprime loans (63 percent). The same pattern was true for Asian borrowers. In contrast, we estimate that Black or African-American borrowers accounted for a higher proportion of subprime loans (17 percent) than Alt-A loans (7 percent). Hispanic or Latino borrowers also accounted for a higher estimated percentage of subprime loans (19 percent) than Alt-A loans (15 percent), while the reverse was true for non-Hispanic or -Latino borrowers, who obtained 66 percent of the subprime loans and 73 percent of the Alt-A loans.

Table 9. Estimated Percentage of Nonprime Borrowers with Subprime and Alt-A Loans, by Race and Ethnicity.

Borrower category	Number of borrowers	Percent Subprime	Alt-A
Race			
White	36,721	63	73
Black or African- American	7,423	17	7
Asian	2,223	3	6
Other	924	2	2
Not reported	7,636	15	12
Ethnicity			
Hispanic or Latino	9,691	19	15
Non-Hispanic or -Latino	37,797	66	73
Not reported	7,538	14	13

Source: GAO analysis of LP and HMDA data.

Note: Figures in table are from our analysis of the approximately 55,000 loans for which we were able to match LP records with HMDA records. All percentage estimates in this table have 95 percent confidence intervals that are within plus or minus 0.7 percentage points of the estimate itself.

Across all races and ethnicities, most nonprime borrowers obtained a short-term hybrid adjustable-rate mortgage (ARM), the most common subprime mortgage product. However, higher estimated proportions of Black or African-American borrowers and Hispanic or Latino borrowers received short-term hybrid ARMs compared with other racial and ethnic groups (see table 10). For example, we estimate that about 69 percent of Black or African-American borrowers obtained a short-term hybrid ARM, compared with about 52 percent of White borrowers. The proportion of borrowers who obtained a payment-option ARM varied considerably by racial and ethnic category, ranging from about 3 percent of Black or African-American borrowers to 18 percent of Asian borrowers. Across all racial and ethnic groups, the estimated proportion of fixed-rate mortgages was more even, ranging from 18 percent for Hispanic or Latino borrowers to roughly one-quarter or more for White and non-Hispanic or - Latino borrowers.

In a follow-on study to this report, we will expand on this analysis by analyzing a larger pool of nonprime borrowers and examining the demographic characteristics of borrowers with troubled loans and negative home equity.

Table 10. Estimated Percentage of Borrowers that Obtained Different Nonprime Loan Products, by Race and Ethnicity.

Borrower category	Number of borrowers	Percent				
		Fixed-rate loans	Short-term hybrid ARM	Payment-option ARM	Longer-term ARM[a]	Other ARM
Race						
White	36,721	26	52	9	10	3
Black or African-American	7,423	21	69	3	5	1
Asain	2.322	21	44	18	13	4
Other	924	22	55	10	10	3
Not reported	7,636	27	54	8	9	2
Ethnicity						
Hispanic or Latino	9,691	18	63	9	7	2
Non- Hispanic or - Latino	37,797	27	52	8	10	2
Not reported	7,538	27	54	8	9	2

Source: GAO analysis of LP and HMDA data.

Note: Figures in table are from our analysis of the approximately 55,000 loans for which we were able to match LP records with HMDA records. Percentage estimates by race in this table have 95 percent confidence intervals that are within plus or minus 3.2 percentage points of the estimate itself. For ethnicity categories, the percentage estimates have 95 percent confidence intervals that are within plus or minus 1.1 percentage points of the estimate itself.

[a] Longer-term ARMs have interest rates that are fixed for 5, 7, or 10 years before adjusting.

ENCLOSURE VII. MATCHING LOANPERFORMANCE AND HOME MORTGAGE DISCLOSURE ACT RECORDS

Data Sources

To describe the race and ethnicity of nonprime borrowers, we matched loan-level records from two primary data sources, LoanPerformance's (LP) Asset-backed Securities database and Home Mortgage Disclosure Act (HMDA) data compiled by the Federal Financial Institutions Examination Council. The LP database provides extensive information about the characteristics and performance of securitized nonprime mortgages. However, it contains relatively little information about borrowers, providing only credit scores and debt-service-to-income ratios.[42] In contrast, HMDA data contain limited information about loan characteristics and nothing about performance, but do provide information on borrowers' race, ethnicity, and income. HMDA data are estimated to capture about 80 percent of the mortgages funded each year and cover all major market segments, including nonprime loans. HMDA data should therefore capture most of the loans in the LP database.

While the LP and HMDA data emphasize different kinds of loan and borrower information, they do have some information in common. These common data items—including loan amount, loan purpose, loan origination date, property location, and loan originator—allow the two data sets to be matched on a loan-by-loan basis. We will discuss in more detail issues related to data compatibility and completeness that affected the matching process we developed.

To conduct our analysis, we extracted from the LP database a 2 percent random sample of loans originated in 2005 for a total of 74,079 loans.[43] We selected 2005 originations because the LP database showed the highest number of nonprime originations in that year. Our sample included conventional first-lien purchase and refinance loans to owner-occupants, investors, and owners of second homes. We excluded loans for units in multifamily structures and for manufactured housing, loans in Puerto Rico and the Virgin Islands, and loans with terms other than 15, 30, or 40 years.

We used the HMDA data file for 2005. As with the LP data, we focused on first lien purchase and refinance loans originated in 2005. We excluded loans in which the property type was something other than one- to four-family residential units. Because the LP database contained only conventional loans in private label securitizations, we also excluded loans that involved government programs—such as mortgages guaranteed by the Federal Housing Administration or the Department of Veterans Affairs—and conventional loans that were indicated as sold to Fannie Mae, Freddie Mac, Ginnie Mae, or Farmer Mac. This process resulted in 8,781,084 HMDA loan records.

Steps Taken to Make the Data Sets Compatible

Matching the loan records from the two data sources required us to make the common data items compatible. We were able to use a straightforward process for the loan amount and purpose that required only rounding the LP loan amount to the nearest $1,000 and aggregating the three LP refinance categories into one. However, the process was more complicated for origination date and property location.[44] We determined that the name of the loan originator was not particularly useful for making initial matches of loan records because this information was missing for a substantial percentage of the LP records. However,the originator's name was useful in assessing the quality of the matches that we made using other data elements.

Loan Origination Dates

We found two issues with the origination date field in the LP data. First, almost 18 percent of loans in our LP sample had an origination date that was the first day of a month.[45] This distribution pattern was inconsistent with the distribution of origination days in HMDA, which showed a much more even pattern throughout the month, with an increase in originations toward the end rather than the beginning of each month (see figuer 9). Because of this inconsistency, we relied on origination month rather than origination day to match loan records.

Second, the LP data showed that the first mortgage payment month was generally 2 months after the origination month but could also be 1 month—mostly for loans that originated early in a month—or 3 months—mostly for loans that originated later in a month (see figure 10).

To address these issues, we matched some LP loan records twice, once using the origination month provided in the LP data and a second time using a replicated LP loan record (e.g., same loan amount and purpose) with an adjusted origination month. For the replicated records, we moved the origination month back a month if the first payment was due the next month and forward if the first payment was not due for 3 months. For instance, if a loan originated in April and the first payment month was due in May, we adjusted the origination month to March. But if a loan originated in April and had a first payment month of July, we adjusted the origination month to May.

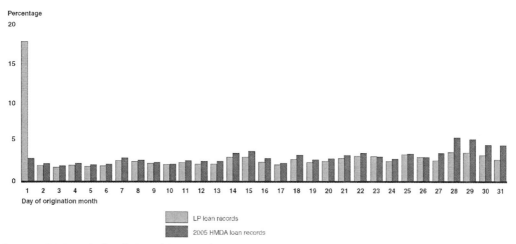

Source: GAO analysis of LP and HMDA data.

Figure 9. Distribution of Origination Days in the LP and HMDA Data.

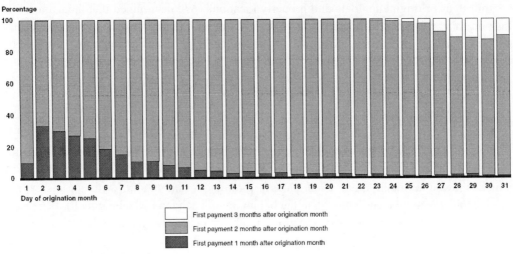

Source: GAO analysis of LP data.

Figure 10. Relationship Between Origination Month and First Payment Month in the LP Data.

Property Location

The LP and HMDA data provided different geographic identifiers for loans, with the LP data providing the ZIP code and the HMDA data the census tract. To facilitate record matching based on property location, we related the census tract information in the HMDA data to a corresponding ZIP code or ZIP codes in the LP data using 2000 Census files and ZIP code boundary files from Pitney Bowes Business Insight. Using mapping software, we overlaid census tract boundaries on ZIP code boundaries to determine the proportion of each census tract's area that fell within a given ZIP code area. For each census tract, we kept all ZIP codes that accounted for at least 5 percent of that tract's area. About 60 percent of census tracts were associated with only one ZIP code (meeting the 5 percent threshold), and almost all census tracts (97.5 percent) included no more than four ZIP codes. When a census tract was associated with only one ZIP code, all HMDA records in that census tract were candidates to match LP records in that ZIP code. All HMDA records in tracts with more than one ZIP code were candidates to match LP records in those ZIP codes.

Matching Methodology

We matched loan records in the LP and HMDA data sets as follows. First, we made initial matches by identifying LP and HMDA loans with the same property ZIP code (based on the ZIP code-census tract combinations discussed previously), origination month, loan amount, and loan purpose. After finding all possible HMDA matches for each LP record, we classified these initial matches as either one-to-one matches (LP records with one corresponding HMDA record), one-to-many matches (LP records with more than one corresponding HMDA record), or nonmatches (LP records with no corresponding HMDA record). One-to-one matches accounted for 54.7 percent of our LP data set, one-to-many matches accounted for 30.9 percent, and nonmatches accounted for 14.3 percent.

We believe that the LP records that we were unable to match to HMDA records were similar in important respects to LP records that we could match. For instance, loans in subprime pools represented 61 percent of the overall LP sample and 61.5 percent of matched loans. Purchase loans represented 46.6 percent of the overall LP sample and 47.9 percent of matched loans. In terms of geography, state shares of unmatched and matched loans were similar. Loans in California represented 22.8 percent of the full LP sample and 22.5 percent of matched records. Further, subprime borrowers with unmatched records had a median credit score of 615, compared with 621 for matched records. Likewise, Alt-A borrowers with unmatched LP records and Alt-A borrowers with matched records had identical median credit scores of 709. Unmatched LP records in general had slightly higher loan amounts, with the differences between matched and unmatched Alt-A loan values being a little more pronounced. For instance, the median loan amount for unmatched Alt-A records was $259,000, compared with $227,250 for matched Alt- A records. This could be related to the somewhat greater representation in the set of unmatched LP records of loans in California, where house prices and loan amounts were high.

Quality Checks

We performed three types of quality checks on our initial one-to-one and one-to-many matches. First, we used information about the loan originator—information that was included in both the LP and HMDA data. The HMDA data clearly identified loan originators—referred to as "HMDA respondents"—using a series of codes that corresponded to a list of standardized originator names. But in more than 40 percent of the LP records in our sample, the originator name was marked as not available. In other cases, the originator was listed by a generic term such as "conduit," or was an entity that appeared to be involved in the securitization process but was not necessarily the originator. Originators that were listed were often referred to in a number of ways—for example, "Taylor Bean;" "Taylor Bean Whitaker;" "Taylor, Bean & Whitaker;" "TaylorBean;" "TBW;" and "TBW Mortgage Corp." all referred to HMDA respondent "Taylor, Bean & Whitaker." For LP loans with originator information, we standardized the originator names in the LP data, and we used these same originator names for the HMDA data. We compared the standardized originator names in matched records. If the standardized names matched, we classified the match as a robust match, and deleted any other HMDA records that might have matched to that LP record.

Table 11. Results of the Matching Process, LP to HMDA Loan Records.

Market segment	Number of LP records	Initial matches to HMDA records		Robust matches to HMDA records	
		Number	Percentage	Number	Percentage
Subprime	45,175	39,040	86.4	35,196	77.9
Alt-A	28,904	24,413	84.5	19,830	68.6
Total	**74,079**	**63,453**	**85.7**	**55,026**	**74.3**

Source: GAO analysis of LP and HMDA data.

Second, for LP loans with no originator name, we examined the relationship between the HMDA loan originator and the issuer of the securities associated with the loan. Many institutions, such as Countrywide and Ameriquest, originated and securitized large numbers of nonprime loans. While some of these institutions identified themselves as the originator of a loan, some typically did not make the originator information available. In these cases, if the LP securitizer matched the HMDA originator, we classified an initial match as a robust match. If the issuer did not originate substantial numbers of nonprime loans, or also relied on other originators to provide loans for its securitizations, we developed criteria to check for evidence of business relationships between the issuer and various originating institutions. This check had two components. First, if within the LP data set we identified an originator-issuer combination, we defined that combination as a business relationship. Second, we considered combinations of originators from the HMDA data and issuers from the LP data. For an originator-issuer combination to be a business relationship, a combination had to appear at least five times in our set of initial one-to-one matches and meet one of two criteria. Specifically, either the originator must have made 5 percent of the issuer's securitized loans or the issuer had to have securitized 5 percent of the loans made by the originator. We classified initial matches for which such business relationships existed as robust matches.

Additionally, if none of these tests resulted in a robust match, we examined the loan origination day in the LP and HMDA data sets. If the days matched exactly, we classified an initial match as a robust match. Finally, for some one-to-many matches that shared originator, issuer, or business relationship characteristics, we examined the LP and HMDA characterizations of whether the borrower was an owner-occupant or not. In some cases, we were able to classify an initial match as a robust match if LP and HMDA owner-occupant characteristics matched. Overall, we produced robust matches for about 74 percent of the records in our LP data set, including about 78 percent of the loans in subprime pools and 69 percent of the loans in Alt-A pools (see table 11).

ENCLOSURE VIII. GAO CONTACT AND STAFF ACKNOWLEDGMENTS

GAO Contact: William B. Shear, (202) 512-8678 or shearw@gao.gov

Staff Acknowledgments: In addition to the individual named above, Steve Westley (Assistant Director), William Bates, Stephen Brown, Emily Chalmers, Eric Charles, DuEwa Kamara, Jamila Kennedy, John McGrail, John Mingus, Colleen Moffatt, Marc Molino, Bob Pollard, and Mark Ramage made key contributions to this report.

End Notes

[1] See GAO, *Characteristics and Performance of Nonprime Mortgages*, GAO-09-848R (Washington, D.C.: July 28, 2009).

[2] Our analysis was based on a 2 percent random sample of nonprime mortgages from 2005.

[3] LP is a unit of First American CoreLogic, Incorporated.

[4] Nonagency mortgage-backed securities (MBS), also known as private-label MBS, are backed by nonconforming conventional mortgages securitized primarily by investment banks. Nonconforming mortgages are those that do not meet the purchase requirements of Fannie Mae or Freddie Mac because they are too large or do not

meet their underwriting criteria. About 75 percent of subprime and Alt-A mortgages originated from 2001 through 2007 were securitized.

[5] The LP database has a loan-level indicator for loan class (i.e., subprime or Alt-A), but it is not well populated. Therefore, we used the pool-level classification. According to mortgage researchers, some of the loans in subprime pools may not be subprime loans, and some of the loans in Alt-A pools may not be Alt-A loans.

[6] Unless otherwise noted, we treat delinquent loans, loans in default, and loans in the foreclosure process as mutually exclusive categories. We considered a loan to have completed the foreclosure process if it was in real estate-owned status as of June 30, 2009, or was paid off after being either 90 or more days delinquent, in the foreclosure process, or in real estate-owned status.

[7] A loan cohort is a group of loans that originated in the same year. For a description of our methodology for estimating performance by congressional district, see GAO-09-848R.

[8] The FHFA index, comprising separate indexes for 384 metropolitan areas, is based on sales and appraisal data for properties with mortgages purchased or securitized by Fannie Mae or Freddie Mac (conforming mortgages). To be eligible for purchase by these entities, loans (and borrowers receiving the loans) must meet specified requirements.

[9] The S&P/Case-Shiller index, comprising separate indexes for 17 metropolitan areas, is based on sales data for homes purchased with both conforming and nonconforming mortgages.

[10] More specifically, short-term hybrid ARMs represented about 70 percent of the subprime mortgages originated from 2000 through 2007.

[11] Payment-option ARMs accounted for about 17 percent of the Alt-A mortgages originated from 2000 through 2007.

[12] There is no uniform definition of default across the lending industry. For purposes of this report, we use the definition provided.

[13] As previously noted, the data we used for our analysis do not cover the entire nonprime market but do cover the large majority of nonagency securitized mortgages within that market.

[14] Because many of these loans were prepaid as a consequence of refinancing, the number of loans reported exceeds the number of borrowers.

[15] Although defaults and foreclosures also increased in other market segments, the serious delinquency rate for the mortgage market as a whole was substantially lower. According to the Mortgage Bankers Association, the serious delinquency rate for the broader mortgage market was approximately 8 percent as of the end of the second quarter of 2009.

[16] Ellen Schloemer, Wei Li, Keith Ernst, and Kathleen Keest, *Losing Ground: Foreclosures in the Subprime Market,* Center for Responsible Lending (December 2006) and Center for Responsible Lending, *Updated Projections of Subprime Foreclosures in the United States and their Impact on Home Values and Communities* (August 2008); Rod Dubitsky, Larry Yang, Stevan Stevanovic, and Thomas Suehr, *Foreclosure Update: Over 8 Million Foreclosures Expected*, Credit Suisse (December 4, 2008); Jan Hatzius and Michael Marschoun, *Global Economics Paper No. 177,* Goldman Sachs (January 13, 2009); and Shane Sherlund, *The Past, Present, and Future of Subprime Mortgages*, Finance and Economics Discussion Series 2008-63, Federal Reserve Board (November 2008).

[17] Schloemer and others, *Losing Ground: Foreclosures in the Subprime Market,* provides a cumulative estimate of subprime foreclosures for the nation, state, and metropolitan statistical areas. Dubitsky and others, *Foreclosure Update: Over 8 Million Foreclosures Expected,* provides baseline yearly estimates of foreclosure starts for the subprime market and the whole mortgage market, as well as estimates of the effects of unemployment and loan modifications on the whole mortgage market. Hatzius and Marschoun, *Global Economics Paper No. 177,* provides quarterly estimates of defaults for three house price scenarios for the whole market. Sherlund, *The Past, Present and Future of Subprime Mortgages*, provides yearly estimates of subprime foreclosure starts, as well as cumulative performance by loan vintage.

[18] Dubitsky and others, *Foreclosure Update*, 2.

[19] For example, GAO, *Home Mortgages: Provisions in a 2007 Mortgage Reform Bill (H.R. 3915) Would Strengthen Borrower Protections, but Views on Their Long-term Impact Differ,* GAO-09-741 (Washington, D.C.: July 31, 2009).

[20] For example, Christopher Foote, Kristopher Gerardi, and Paul S. Willen, *Negative Equity and Foreclosure: Theory and Evidence,* Public Policy Discussion Paper 08-3, Federal Reserve Board (June 5, 2008).

[21] The remaining study assumed an overall decrease in house prices but did not indicate specifically when prices would stop falling.

[22] For example, as of September 2009, IHS Global Insight was projecting a decline in the national FHFA house price index through the third quarter of 2010. Additionally, as of October 2009, Freddie Mac was projecting a decline in the national S&P/Case-Shiller index through the end of 2010.

[23] With a forbearance plan, a lender agrees not to exercise the legal right of foreclosure if the borrower agrees to a payment plan that will resolve the borrower's deficiency for a set period of time.

[24] GAO, *Treasury Actions Needed to Make the Home Affordable Modification Program More Transparent and Accountable,* GAO-09-837 (Washington, D.C.: July 2009).

[25] As previously noted, our estimates using the FHFA index likely understate the extent of negative equity. Across the 15 metropolitan areas for which the FHFA and S&P/Case-Shiller indexes use the same geographic boundaries, the estimated percentage of borrowers with negative equity was nearly two times higher using the S&P/Case-Shiller index compared with estimates using the FHFA index.

[26] Due to data limitations, our analysis did not account for any second liens that the borrowers had on their properties. To the extent that borrowers had second liens, our analysis may understate the extent of negative home equity.

[27] As of November 2009 the S&P/Case-Shiller index did not include 2009 data for the Cleveland, Ohio metropolitan area. As a result, we did not estimate negative equity for that area.

[28] We excluded nonprime loans on properties not in these metropolitan areas from our analysis. As a result, our estimates cover 4.5 million of the 4.9 million nonprime loans that were active as of June 30, 2009.

[29] To illustrate, across the 15 metropolitan areas for which the FHFA and S&P/Case-Shiller indexes use the same geographic boundaries, the estimated percentage of borrowers with negative equity was about 34 percent using the FHFA index and 66 percent using the S&P/Case-Shiller index.

[30] The five metropolitan areas were Merced, California (87.4 percent); Stockton, California (85.6 percent); Modesto, California (83.5 percent); Vallejo-Fairfield, California (83.4 percent); and Las Vegas-Paradise, Nevada (83.4 percent).

[31] As discussed in our July 2009 report, average LTV ratios at loan origination peaked in 2006 at about 86 percent for subprime mortgages and 82 percent for Alt-A mortgages. See GAO-09-848R.

[32] Unlike the FHFA indexes, the S&P/Case-Shiller indexes do not always use the same geographic boundaries as the Office of Management and Budget's definitions of metropolitan areas. For example, S&P/Case-Shiller's geographic boundaries are more expansive for the New York City metropolitan area and more restrictive for the Chicago metropolitan area.

[33] For a detailed discussion of this issue, see Office of Federal Housing Enterprise Oversight (OFHEO), *Revisiting the Differences between the OFHEO and S&P/Case-Shiller House Price Indexes: New Explanations, (January 2008).*

[34] FHFA also publishes house price indexes that use sales data only. These "purchase-only" indexes are available for the nation as a whole, for each Census division and state, and for 25 metropolitan areas.

[35] Both indexes also have identical coverage for the Cleveland, Ohio metropolitan area, but as of November 2009 the S&P/Case-Shiller index did not include 2009 data for that area. As a result, we did not estimate negative home equity for the Cleveland metropolitan area.

[36] For this reason, we excluded 379,230 records (7.7 percent) from our analysis of 384 metropolitan areas using the FHFA index.

[37] A minimum of 1,000 observations per quarter are required for an MSA to be included in FHFA's index, so the number of MSAs the index includes can fluctuate from quarter to quarter.

[38] Our estimates of negative equity nationwide only reflect mortgaged properties in the 384 MSAs captured by the FHFA index. These MSAs account for about 84 percent of the U.S. population.

[39] In this report, we use the race and ethnicity categories defined in the HMDA data. As previously noted, the LP data we used for our analysis do not cover the entire nonprime market but do cover the large majority of nonagency securitized mortgages within that market.

[40] In our data tables we combined these racial groups into an "other" category.

[41] Individuals who classify themselves as Hispanic or Latino include people of different racial backgrounds.

[42] The debt-service-to-income ratio is the borrower's total monthly debt service payments divided by monthly gross income.

[43] We also included some loans with origination dates in December 2004 or January 2006 if there was evidence to suggest those loans might have originated in January 2005 or December 2005, respectively, and therefore match to loans in the 2005 HMDA file. We discuss this origination month issue later.

[44] For privacy reasons, the origination date is omitted from each HMDA record when it is publicly released. We requested and obtained the date fields from the Federal Financial Institutions Examination Council, which compiles and publishes the HMDA data.

[45] This pattern reflects LP's practice of imputing the origination month for some loans based on the month in which the first payment is due. In these cases, LP records the origination date as the first day of the imputed origination month.

ISBN: 978-1-61122-918-9
© 2011 Nova Science Publishers, Inc.

Chapter 3

STATE-LEVEL INFORMATION ON NEGATIVE HOME EQUITY AND LOAN PERFORMANCE IN THE NONPRIME MORTGAGE MARKET

United States Government Accountability Office

May 14, 2010

The Honorable Carolyn B. Maloney
Chair
Joint Economic Committee
House of Representatives

The Honorable Charles E. Schumer
Vice Chairman
Joint Economic Committee
United States Senate

Subject: State-Level Information on Negative Home Equity and Loan Performance in the Nonprime Mortgage Market

The decline of home prices in many parts of the country has left millions of homeowners with negative home equity, meaning that their outstanding mortgage balances exceed the current value of their homes. As we reported to you previously, a substantial proportion of borrowers with active nonprime mortgages (including subprime and Alt-A loans) had negative equity in their homes as of June 30, 2009.[1] For example, among the 16 metropolitan areas examined, we estimated that the percentage of nonprime borrowers with negative equity ranged from about 9 percent (Denver, Colorado) to more than 90 percent (Las Vegas, Nevada). Research indicates that negative home equity substantially increases the risk of mortgage delinquency, making it an important dimension of ongoing problems in the nonprime market.

To provide insight into how negative equity and loan performance among nonprime borrowers have varied by location and over time, this report examines, at the state level, the estimated proportion of nonprime borrowers with active loans that were in a negative equity position and the proportion that were seriously delinquent on their loan payments from 2006 through the end of 2009.[2] This report is part of our broader examination of the evolution and condition of the nonprime market segment.[3] As agreed with your offices, in a subsequent report we will provide more detailed information on the performance of nonprime mortgages through the end of 2009, the influence of nonprime loan and borrower characteristics and economic conditions on the likelihood of mortgage default, and the features and limitations of primary sources of data on nonprime mortgage performance and borrower characteristics.

To conduct our work, we used data from CoreLogic's (formerly LoanPerformance) Asset-Backed Securities Database for nonprime loans originated from 2000 through 2007 and CoreLogic's state-level Single Family Combined House Price Index (CoreLogic index). The CoreLogic database contains loan-level data on a large majority of nonagency securitized mortgages in subprime and Alt-A pools.[4] For example, for the period January 2001 through July 2007 the CoreLogic database contains information covering, in dollar terms, an estimated 87 percent of securitized subprime loans and 98 percent of securitized Alt-A loans. Researchers have found that nonprime mortgages that were not securitized (i.e., mortgages that lenders held in their portfolios) may have less risky characteristics and better performance histories than those that were securitized. For purposes of our analysis, we defined a subprime loan as a loan in a subprime pool and an Alt-A loan as a loan in an Alt-A pool.[5] We focused our analysis on first-lien purchase and refinance mortgages for one-to-four-family residential units. We included only loans that were active in a given quarter; loans that were inactive because they had been paid off or had completed the foreclosure process were excluded.

The CoreLogic index, like other house price indexes, measures house price changes in a geographic area based on sales of the same properties at different points in time. The use of repeat transactions on the same homes helps to control for differences in the quality of the houses in the data. The CoreLogic index is based on all usable transactions from CoreLogic's public record, servicing, and securities databases of single family attached and detached homes with all types of financing, including prime and nonprime loans.[6]

To estimate the proportion of nonprime borrowers with active loans that had negative equity, we used the CoreLogic index to adjust the appraised value of each home at loan origination to an estimated value at the end of each quarter from March 2006 through December 2009, the most recent quarterly data that we could analyze within the time frames of our review. We then subtracted the unpaid mortgage balance from the estimated house value as of each quarter to estimate the borrower's home equity. We divided the number of nonprime borrowers with negative home equity by the total number of active nonprime loans in each quarter to determine the proportion with negative equity (negative equity rate).[7] Due to data limitations, our analysis did not account for nonprime borrowers with second liens or multiple mortgaged properties.[8] Additionally, the CoreLogic index that we used represents price trends at the state level. Depending on the degree to which homes financed with nonprime loans were concentrated in areas with house price trends that differed from statewide trends, our estimates could overstate or understate the number of nonprime borrowers with negative equity.

To determine the proportion of nonprime borrowers that were seriously delinquent on their mortgage payments, we divided the number of nonprime loans that were more than 90 days past due or were in the foreclosure process by the total number of active nonprime loans in each quarter (serious delinquency rate). In addition, we analyzed the extent to which changes in estimated negative equity rates were associated with changes in serious delinquency rates from the first quarter of 2006 through the end of 2009. Specifically, we measured the statistical correlation between percentage point changes in the estimated proportion of nonprime borrowers with negative equity in each state and the proportion of nonprime borrowers that were seriously delinquent in each state.[9]

We assessed the reliability of the data used in this report by reviewing documentation on the process CoreLogic uses to collect and ensure the reliability and integrity of the data and by conducting reasonableness checks on data elements to identify any missing, erroneous, or outlying data. We also interviewed CoreLogic representatives to discuss the interpretation of various data fields. We concluded that the data we used were sufficiently reliable for our purposes. We conducted this engagement in Washington, D.C., and Chicago, Illinois, from March 2010 through May 2010 in accordance with generally accepted government auditing standards. Those standards require that we plan and perform the audit to obtain sufficient, appropriate evidence to provide a reasonable basis for our findings and conclusions based on our audit objective. We believe that the evidence obtained provides a reasonable basis for our findings and conclusions based on our audit objective.

SUMMARY

For most states and the District of Columbia, the estimated percentage of nonprime borrowers with active loans that were in a negative equity position increased from 2006 through mid-2008 and then remained fairly stable through the end of 2009. Growth in negative equity rates during that period varied widely among the states. Negative equity rates rose by at least 30 percentage points in 7 states, by 10 to 29.9 percentage points in 17 states, and by 5 to 9.9 percentage points in 9 states. Eighteen states' negative equity rates grew by less than 5 percentage points, including 3 states where the percentage of nonprime borrowers with negative equity increased negligibly.

For all states and the District of Columbia, the percentage of nonprime borrowers that were seriously delinquent—90 days or more late in payments or in the foreclosure process—increased from the first quarter of 2006 through the end of 2009, with growth ranging from 5.3 percentage points in Louisiana to 43.3 percentage points in Florida. Additionally, across all states and the District of Columbia, our measures for increases in estimated negative equity and serious delinquency rates exhibited a positive statistical correlation. Consistent with this observation, 6 of the 10 states that experienced the largest percentage point increases in negative equity rates also were among the 10 states with the largest percentage point increases in serious delinquency rates. However, the remaining 4 states ranked from 12th to 26th in their increases in serious delinquency rates.

BACKGROUND

The nonprime mortgage market has two segments:

- **Subprime**. Generally serves borrowers with blemished or limited credit histories, and the loans feature higher interest rates and fees than prime loans.
- **Alt-A**. Generally serves borrowers whose credit histories are close to prime, but the loans have one or more high-risk features, such as limited documentation of income or assets or the option of making monthly payments that are lower than would be required for a fully amortizing loan.

Active mortgages can fall into any one of several payment categories:

- **Current**. The borrower is meeting scheduled payments.
- **Delinquent**. The borrower has missed one or more scheduled payments.
- **Default**. The borrower is 90 days or more delinquent.[10] At this point, foreclosure proceedings against the borrower become a strong possibility.
- **In the foreclosure process**. The borrower has been delinquent for more than 90 days, and the lender has elected to foreclose in what is an often lengthy process with several possible outcomes. For instance, the borrower may sell the property or the lender may repossess the home.

In this report, we describe borrowers whose mortgages are in default or in the foreclosure process as "seriously delinquent."

Typically, home equity—that is, the difference between the value of a property and the amount still owed on the mortgage—increases over time as the mortgage balance is paid down and home values appreciate. However, if the home value falls below the mortgage balance, the borrower will be in a position of negative equity. Borrowers with nonprime loans may be particularly vulnerable to negative equity because they typically make small down payments and thus have less equity at the outset than a typical prime borrower. Also, some nonprime borrowers have loans with payment options that allow them to defer payment of accrued interest, thereby increasing the outstanding loan balance and decreasing equity.

In general, lower levels of home equity (as a percentage of home value) are associated with relatively poorer loan performance. Homeowners with negative equity may find it difficult to sell or refinance the property to avoid foreclosure. They may also have incentives to stop making mortgage payments to minimize their financial losses.

ACROSS STATES, NEGATIVE HOME EQUITY GENERALLY INCREASED FROM 2006 THROUGH MID-2008 BEFORE LEVELING OFF, WHILE SERIOUS DELINQUENCY RATES CONTINUED TO GROW THROUGH THE END OF 2009

Estimated Rates of Negative Equity Generally Increased through Mid-2008 and then Remained Relatively Stable

The estimated percentage of nonprime borrowers in a negative equity position generally increased from 2006 through mid-2008, with negative equity rates holding more steady through the end of 2009.[11] Across all states and the District of Columbia, the estimated percentage of nonprime borrowers with negative equity increased from 13 percent in the first quarter of 2006 to 35 percent in the first quarter of 2008, and then remained between 36 and 37 percent through the end of 2009 (see Figure 1).[12] The number of nonprime borrowers in a negative equity position increased from about 940,000 in the first quarter of 2006 to about 2.52 million at the end of 2007, and then declined to about 1.86 million by the end of 2009.[13] The percentage of nonprime borrowers with negative equity remained relatively stable while the number with negative equity decreased because the total number of active nonprime loans also decreased from mid-2007 through the end of 2009, as mortgages were prepaid or completed foreclosure.

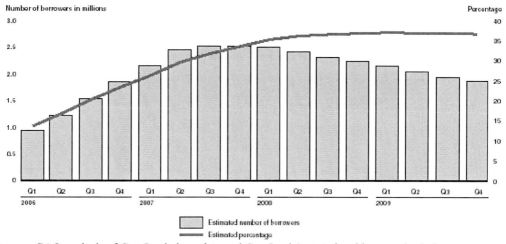

Source: GAO analysis of CoreLogic loan data and CoreLogic's state-level house price index.

Note: The analysis includes nonprime loans originated from 2000 through 2007, so the number of active nonprime loans increased from about 7 million in the first quarter of 2006 to nearly 8.4 million in the second quarter of 2007. As loans became inactive as a result of prepayment and completed foreclosures, the number of active nonprime loans decreased to about 5.1 million by the end of 2009. The decrease in the number of active loans accounts for the stable percentage of nonprime borrowers with negative equity even as the number decreased.

Figure 1. Estimated Number and Percentage of Nonprime Borrowers with Negative Home Equity from March 31, 2006, through December 31, 2009.

The extent to which estimated negative equity rates increased varied widely among the states. Seven states had an increase of at least 30 percentage points from the first quarter of 2006 through the end of 2009 (see Figure 2). The largest increases occurred in Arizona and Florida, each of which saw negative equity rates rise by 44 percentage points (from 24 percent to 68 percent in Arizona and from 28 percent to 72 percent in Florida). Eighteen states had an increase of less than 5 percentage points during the period—including North Dakota, South Dakota, and Oklahoma, which had negligible increases of less than 1 percentage point. Across all states, the median increase was about 9 percentage points, represented by South Carolina (rising from 1.6 percent to 10.4 percent).[14] In general, the states' negative equity rates grew through the second quarter of 2008 and then held relatively steady through the end of 2009.[15] For example, California's negative equity rate increased by 4.2 percentage points per quarter from the first quarter of 2006 through the second quarter of 2008 (rising from 23.5 to 60.9 percent), and then grew just slightly (0.06 percentage points per quarter) to end 2009 at 61.3 percent. See Enclosure I for quarterly information on the estimated number and percentage of nonprime borrowers with negative equity in each state from 2006 through 2009.

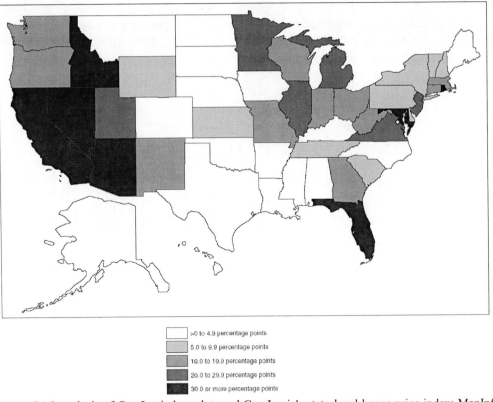

>0 to 4.9 percentage points

5.0 to 9.9 percentage points

10.0 to 19.9 percentage points

20.0 to 29.9 percentage points

30.0 or more percentage points

Source: GAO analysis of CoreLogic loan data and CoreLogic's state-level house price index; MapInfo (map).

Note: Our quarterly estimates of negative equity include only nonprime borrowers whose loans were active at the end of each quarter.

Figure 2. Percentage Point Change in the Estimated Percentage of Nonprime Borrowers with Negative Home Equity by State, March 31, 2006, through December 31, 2009.

Serious Delinquency Rates Rose from 2006 through 2009, and Some States with the Most Growth in Negative Equity Rates Were among Those with the Most Growth in Serious Delinquency Rates

From 2006 through 2009, serious delinquency rates among nonprime borrowers increased in all states and the District of Columbia. Across the states, the serious delinquency rate—the percentage of nonprime borrowers with active loans that were at least 90 days delinquent or in foreclosure—increased throughout the period, from 4 percent (280,000 loans) in the first quarter of 2006 to 28 percent (1.4 million loans) at the end of 2009. Among the states, the growth in serious delinquency rates ranged from 5 percentage points (Louisiana) to 43 percentage points (Florida). Michigan's increase of 17.1 percentage points represented the median change. Enclosure I includes quarterly information on serious delinquencies in each state from 2006 through 2009.

Across all states and the District of Columbia, our measures for increases in estimated negative equity and serious delinquency rates exhibited a positive statistical correlation.[16] Consistent with this observation, 6 of the 10 states with the largest percentage point increases in negative equity rates from 2006 through 2009 also were among the 10 states with the largest percentage point increases in serious delinquency rates over that same period.[17] For example, Arizona experienced the largest increase in negative equity rate (rising by 44.3 percentage points over the 4-year period) and the fifth largest increase in serious delinquency rate (rising 28.7 percentage points) (see Figure 3). However, the remaining 4 states ranked from 12th to 26th in their increases in serious delinquency rates.[18]

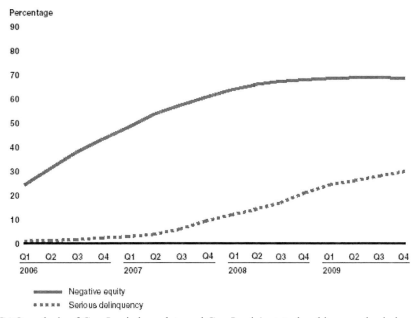

Source: GAO analysis of CoreLogic loan data and CoreLogic's state-level house price index.

Figure 3. Estimated Percentage of Nonprime Borrowers with Negative Home Equity and Seriously Delinquent in Arizona, March 31, 2006, through December 31, 2009.

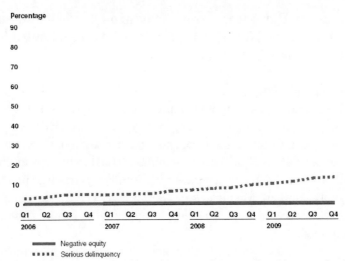

Source: GAO analysis of CoreLogic loan data and CoreLogic's state-level house price index.

Figure 4. Estimated Percentage of Nonprime Borrowers with Negative Home Equity and Seriously Delinquent in North Dakota, March 31, 2006, through December 31, 2009.

In addition, 5 of the 10 states with the smallest growth in negative equity rates also were among the 10 with the smallest growth in serious delinquency rates.[19] North Dakota, for instance, had virtually no increase in its negative equity rate from 2006 through 2009 (0.2 percentage points) and the fourth smallest increase in serious delinquency rate (10.5 percentage points) (see Figure 4). However, the remaining 5 states (including the District of Columbia) ranked from 11th to 41st in their increases in serious delinquency rates.[20]

Research has shown that negative equity is one of several factors that affect loan performance. As previously noted, in a forthcoming report, we will examine the influence of a broader range of factors—including loan and borrower characteristics and economic conditions—on the likelihood of mortgage default.

As agreed with your offices, unless you publicly announce its contents earlier, we plan no further distribution of this report until 30 days from the report date. At that time, we will send copies of this report to interested congressional parties and other interested parties. In addition, the report will be available at no charge on GAO's Web site at http://www.gao.gov.

If you or your staff have any questions about this report, please contact me at (202) 512-8678 or shearw@gao.gov. Contact points for our Offices of Congressional Relations and Public Affairs may be found on the last page of this report. In addition to the individual named above, Steve Westley (Assistant Director), William Bates, Jan Bauer, Julianne Dieterich, DuEwa Kamara, John McGrail, Marc Molino, Bob Pollard, and Jennifer Schwartz made key contributions to this report.

William B. Shear
Director, Financial Markets and Community Investment
Enclosure

ENCLOSURE I. ESTIMATED NEGATIVE EQUITY AND SERIOUS DELINQUENCY RATES BY STATE AND QUARTER FROM 2006 THROUGH 2009

Figure 5 contains the results of our analysis of the extent to which borrowers with active nonprime mortgages were estimated to be in a negative equity position or were seriously delinquent on their payments—that is, they were 90 days or more late on payments or were in the foreclosure process. The analysis uses CoreLogic's loan-level data and the CoreLogic state-level house price index and covers nonprime mortgages originated from 2000 through 2007. Due to data limitations, we could not identify borrowers with multiple mortgaged properties. For purposes of this analysis, we treat the number of borrowers and the number of loans as equal. To the extent that some nonprime borrowers had more than one mortgaged property, our results may overstate the number of individual nonprime borrowers with negative equity. For additional information on the methodology for this analysis, see pages 2 and 3.

		Number of borrowers			Percentage of borrowers	
		With active loans	With negative equity (estimated)	Seriously delinquent	With negative equity (estimated)	Seriously delinquent
Alabama						
2006	Q1	66,043	253	4,409	0.4%	6.7%
	Q2	69,426	591	4,496	0.9	6.5
	Q3	72,756	1,026	4,917	1.4	6.8
	Q4	75,749	1,433	5,468	1.9	7.2
2007	Q1	78,174	1,868	5,122	2.4	6.6
	Q2	78,222	2,361	5,581	3.0	7.1
	Q3	74,314	2,433	6,367	3.3	8.6
	Q4	70,271	2,444	7,120	3.5	10.1
2008	Q1	66,014	2,443	7,046	3.7	10.7
	Q2	62,150	2,423	7,050	3.9	11.3
	Q3	58,877	2,416	7,313	4.1	12.4
	Q4	56,183	2,393	8,074	4.3	14.4
2009	Q1	53,510	2,325	8,161	4.3	15.3
	Q2	51,228	2,259	8,609	4.4	16.8
	Q3	49,156	2,156	9,052	4.4	18.4
	Q4	47,390	2,047	9,441	4.3	19.9
Alaska						
2006	Q1	7,388	26	189	0.4%	2.6%
	Q2	7,970	58	211	0.7	2.6
	Q3	8,485	105	261	1.2	3.1
	Q4	8,965	146	274	1.6	3.1
2007	Q1	9,295	230	311	2.5	3.3
	Q2	9,433	306	377	3.2	4.0
	Q3	8,927	332	452	3.7	5.1
	Q4	8,340	343	462	4.1	5.5
2008	Q1	7,716	342	533	4.4	6.9
	Q2	7,133	315	599	4.4	8.4
	Q3	6,698	297	573	4.4	8.6
	Q4	6,383	292	573	4.6	9.0
2009	Q1	6,015	282	686	4.7	11.4
	Q2	5,710	267	771	4.7	13.5
	Q3	5,426	257	820	4.7	15.1
	Q4	5,184	245	814	4.7	15.7

Figure 5. (Continued)

		Number of borrowers			Percentage of borrowers	
Arizona		With active loans	With negative equity (estimated)	Seriously delinquent	With negative equity (estimated)	Seriously delinquent
2006	Q1	250,669	60,434	2,329	24.1%	0.9%
	Q2	263,808	81,307	2,661	30.8	1.0
	Q3	278,330	104,068	4,039	37.4	1.5
	Q4	290,056	124,323	6,358	42.9	2.2
2007	Q1	304,221	145,515	8,272	47.8	2.7
	Q2	313,893	167,351	11,429	53.3	3.6
	Q3	301,036	171,296	17,281	56.9	5.7
	Q4	285,604	172,180	25,876	60.3	9.1
2008	Q1	268,869	170,713	31,438	63.5	11.7
	Q2	251,238	165,159	35,217	65.7	14.0
	Q3	234,256	157,036	38,675	67.0	16.5
	Q4	219,628	148,678	45,771	67.7	20.8
2009	Q1	205,511	140,407	49,669	68.3	24.2
	Q2	191,908	131,626	49,616	68.6	25.9
	Q3	179,696	123,239	49,883	68.6	27.8
	Q4	169,016	115,576	50,139	68.4	29.7
Arkansas						
2006	Q1	26,943	207	1,494	0.8%	5.5%
	Q2	28,141	418	1,560	1.5	5.5
	Q3	29,159	657	1,778	2.3	6.1
	Q4	30,221	899	1,996	3.0	6.6
2007	Q1	31,244	1,141	2,005	3.7	6.4
	Q2	32,000	1,365	2,224	4.3	7.0
	Q3	30,501	1,405	2,612	4.6	8.6
	Q4	28,950	1,415	2,980	4.9	10.3
2008	Q1	27,295	1,411	2,911	5.2	10.7
	Q2	25,798	1,384	2,915	5.4	11.3
	Q3	24,532	1,360	3,097	5.5	12.6
	Q4	23,476	1,327	3,237	5.7	13.8
2009	Q1	22,498	1,273	3,274	5.7	14.6
	Q2	21,581	1,219	3,321	5.6	15.4
	Q3	20,792	1,164	3,546	5.6	17.1
	Q4	20,095	1,126	3,738	5.6	18.6

		Number of borrowers			Percentage of borrowers	
California		With active loans	With negative equity (estimated)	Seriously delinquent	With negative equity (estimated)	Seriously delinquent
2006	Q1	1,393,739	327,653	17,551	23.5%	1.3%
	Q2	1,436,446	418,205	23,109	29.1	1.6
	Q3	1,497,959	525,337	34,584	35.1	2.3
	Q4	1,557,729	629,943	51,901	40.4	3.3
2007	Q1	1,618,116	730,228	66,909	45.1	4.1
	Q2	1,660,868	835,340	90,456	50.3	5.4
	Q3	1,602,499	860,913	129,363	53.7	8.1
	Q4	1,527,338	866,385	179,176	56.7	11.7
2008	Q1	1,439,545	859,456	214,118	59.7	14.9
	Q2	1,345,041	819,290	227,611	60.9	16.9
	Q3	1,258,514	769,797	231,392	61.2	18.4
	Q4	1,197,317	734,364	263,312	61.3	22
2009	Q1	1,139,357	702,661	295,535	61.7	25.9
	Q2	1,076,878	664,010	301,484	61.7	28.0
	Q3	1,024,339	630,152	308,240	61.5	30.1
	Q4	976,522	598,342	309,926	61.3	31.7
Colorado						
2006	Q1	190,855	2,151	8,051	1.1%	4.2%
	Q2	196,712	2,959	8,277	1.5	4.2
	Q3	201,457	4,307	9,511	2.1	4.7
	Q4	206,397	5,659	11,556	2.7	5.6
2007	Q1	209,060	6,868	12,239	3.3	5.9
	Q2	207,172	8,499	12,640	4.1	6.1
	Q3	196,009	8,914	13,683	4.5	7.0
	Q4	183,880	9,058	15,250	4.9	8.3
2008	Q1	172,297	8,850	15,669	5.1	9.1
	Q2	162,451	8,458	16,157	5.2	9.9
	Q3	153,535	8,074	15,353	5.3	10.0
	Q4	146,052	7,772	15,970	5.3	10.9
2009	Q1	139,274	7,366	17,119	5.3	12.3
	Q2	132,319	6,744	18,134	5.1	13.7
	Q3	126,302	6,418	18,955	5.1	15.0
	Q4	120,889	6,156	19,308	5.1	16.0

Figure 5. (Continued)

Connecticut

		Number of borrowers			Percentage of borrowers	
		With active loans	With negative equity (estimated)	Seriously delinquent	With negative equity (estimated)	Seriously delinquent
2006	Q1	78,883	5,428	2,859	6.9%	3.6%
	Q2	80,912	7,466	3,125	9.2	3.9
	Q3	83,505	9,909	3,843	11.9	4.6
	Q4	85,530	12,055	4,769	14.1	5.6
2007	Q1	87,695	13,956	5,147	15.9	5.9
	Q2	89,238	16,287	5,950	18.3	6.7
	Q3	85,334	16,877	7,319	19.8	8.6
	Q4	80,821	17,060	8,645	21.1	10.7
2008	Q1	76,450	16,973	9,516	22.2	12.4
	Q2	72,430	16,705	9,842	23.1	13.6
	Q3	69,087	16,574	10,546	24.0	15.3
	Q4	66,520	16,421	11,963	24.7	18.0
2009	Q1	64,240	16,120	13,073	25.1	20.4
	Q2	61,873	15,511	13,947	25.1	22.5
	Q3	59,704	15,087	15,204	25.3	25.5
	Q4	57,749	14,728	16,363	25.5	28.3

Delaware

		With active loans	With negative equity (estimated)	Seriously delinquent	With negative equity (estimated)	Seriously delinquent
2006	Q1	18,349	195	700	1.1%	3.8%
	Q2	19,117	336	754	1.8	3.9
	Q3	20,232	553	902	2.8	4.5
	Q4	21,056	785	1,090	3.7	5.2
2007	Q1	21,927	1,041	1,184	4.7	5.4
	Q2	22,499	1,390	1,397	6.2	6.2
	Q3	21,437	1,454	1,719	6.8	8.0
	Q4	20,256	1,488	2,073	7.3	10.2
2008	Q1	19,086	1,481	2,251	7.8	11.8
	Q2	18,057	1,464	2,434	8.1	13.5
	Q3	17,251	1,452	2,622	8.4	15.2
	Q4	16,569	1,433	2,965	8.6	17.9
2009	Q1	15,964	1,402	3,143	8.8	19.7
	Q2	15,378	1,356	3,360	8.8	21.8
	Q3	14,870	1,302	3,628	8.8	24.4
	Q4	14,450	1,267	3,829	8.8	26.5

District of Columbia

		Number of borrowers			Percentage of borrowers	
		With active loans	With negative equity (estimated)	Seriously delinquent	With negative equity (estimated)	Seriously delinquent
2006	Q1	13,556	82	199	0.6%	1.5%
	Q2	14,279	130	231	0.9	1.6
	Q3	15,186	208	327	1.4	2.2
	Q4	15,975	254	503	1.6	3.1
2007	Q1	16,521	321	595	1.9	3.6
	Q2	16,847	414	724	2.5	4.3
	Q3	16,044	441	943	2.7	5.9
	Q4	15,184	450	1,180	3.0	7.8
2008	Q1	14,379	446	1,347	3.1	9.4
	Q2	13,616	432	1,459	3.2	10.7
	Q3	12,995	417	1,612	3.2	12.4
	Q4	12,505	407	1,837	3.3	14.7
2009	Q1	12,018	387	1,987	3.2	16.5
	Q2	11,525	360	2,052	3.1	17.8
	Q3	11,040	346	2,109	3.1	19.1
	Q4	10,698	339	2,211	3.2	20.7

Florida

		With active loans	With negative equity (estimated)	Seriously delinquent	With negative equity (estimated)	Seriously delinquent
2006	Q1	674,480	189,875	16,067	28.2%	2.4%
	Q2	718,506	253,744	17,116	35.3	2.4
	Q3	771,416	325,472	21,839	42.2	2.8
	Q4	816,521	391,736	31,410	48.0	3.8
2007	Q1	858,558	455,416	41,534	53.0	4.8
	Q2	889,755	519,200	59,833	58.4	6.7
	Q3	881,511	531,149	88,123	61.7	10.3
	Q4	828,517	533,978	128,129	64.5	15.5
2008	Q1	793,343	530,627	158,712	66.9	20.0
	Q2	758,163	520,674	183,040	68.7	24.1
	Q3	726,083	507,176	206,769	69.9	28.3
	Q4	697,365	492,655	233,105	70.6	33.4
2009	Q1	668,623	476,629	250,640	71.3	37.5
	Q2	641,838	460,255	258,295	71.7	40.2
	Q3	615,464	442,367	265,387	71.9	43.1
	Q4	590,632	424,319	269,721	71.8	45.7

Figure 5. (Continued)

Georgia		Number of borrowers			Percentage of borrowers	
		With active loans	With negative equity (estimated)	Seriously delinquent	With negative equity (estimated)	Seriously delinquent
2006	Q1	248,154	16,058	12,020	6.5%	4.8%
	Q2	260,866	20,209	12,853	7.7	4.9
	Q3	274,104	26,534	15,359	9.7	5.6
	Q4	285,691	32,266	18,371	11.3	6.4
2007	Q1	293,092	38,606	18,941	13.2	6.5
	Q2	294,337	45,092	21,618	15.3	7.3
	Q3	279,569	46,461	25,219	16.6	9.0
	Q4	262,943	46,870	28,492	17.8	10.8
2008	Q1	246,510	46,407	29,047	18.8	11.8
	Q2	232,692	45,464	29,377	19.5	12.6
	Q3	221,129	44,532	30,350	20.1	13.7
	Q4	211,277	43,675	33,879	20.7	16.0
2009	Q1	202,014	42,172	35,477	20.9	17.6
	Q2	193,825	40,149	37,377	20.7	19.3
	Q3	186,390	38,736	40,021	20.8	21.5
	Q4	179,534	37,523	42,383	20.9	23.6
Hawaii						
2006	Q1	33,186	49	351	0.1%	1.1%
	Q2	34,436	138	410	0.4	1.2
	Q3	36,285	303	553	0.8	1.5
	Q4	37,645	473	806	1.3	2.1
2007	Q1	38,849	575	1,048	1.5	2.7
	Q2	40,289	802	1,264	2.0	3.1
	Q3	38,884	849	1,670	2.2	4.3
	Q4	37,201	887	2,213	2.4	5.9
2008	Q1	35,365	883	2,629	2.5	7.4
	Q2	33,725	865	2,935	2.6	8.7
	Q3	32,501	843	3,570	2.6	11.0
	Q4	31,506	823	4,519	2.6	14.3
2009	Q1	30,342	799	5,402	2.6	17.8
	Q2	29,187	733	6,064	2.5	20.8
	Q3	28,123	649	6,542	2.3	23.3
	Q4	27,142	596	6,925	2.2	25.5

Idaho		Number of borrowers			Percentage of borrowers	
		With active loans	With negative equity (estimated)	Seriously delinquent	With negative equity (estimated)	Seriously delinquent
2006	Q1	38,986	1,287	761	3.3%	2.0%
	Q2	41,043	3,008	761	7.3	1.9
	Q3	42,956	5,007	854	11.7	2.0
	Q4	45,126	7,068	1,072	15.7	2.4
2007	Q1	46,712	9,194	1,216	19.7	2.6
	Q2	47,158	11,566	1,430	24.5	3.0
	Q3	44,684	12,057	1,893	27.0	4.2
	Q4	42,053	12,220	2,488	29.1	5.9
2008	Q1	39,346	12,194	2,928	31.0	7.4
	Q2	36,842	12,081	3,134	32.8	8.5
	Q3	34,890	11,894	3,577	34.1	10.3
	Q4	33,293	11,726	4,389	35.2	13.2
2009	Q1	31,508	11,426	4,961	36.3	15.7
	Q2	29,778	10,854	5,397	36.5	18.1
	Q3	28,224	10,285	5,638	36.4	20.0
	Q4	26,767	9,743	5,619	36.4	21.0
Illinois						
2006	Q1	265,717	20,386	14,768	7.7%	5.6%
	Q2	275,236	28,174	16,108	10.2	5.9
	Q3	285,198	38,808	19,120	13.6	6.7
	Q4	291,620	49,727	23,029	17.1	7.9
2007	Q1	296,968	61,007	24,196	20.5	8.1
	Q2	297,740	72,645	27,194	24.4	9.1
	Q3	280,788	74,864	32,957	26.7	11.7
	Q4	261,732	75,334	38,222	28.8	14.6
2008	Q1	244,188	74,856	40,305	30.7	16.5
	Q2	228,493	73,495	41,408	32.2	18.1
	Q3	216,023	72,273	43,292	33.5	20.0
	Q4	206,161	71,237	47,414	34.6	23.0
2009	Q1	197,355	69,725	50,173	35.3	25.4
	Q2	188,519	66,854	52,246	35.5	27.7
	Q3	181,216	65,108	55,919	35.9	30.9
	Q4	174,749	63,587	58,667	36.4	33.6

Figure 5. (Continued)

	Number of borrowers			Percentage of borrowers	
Indiana	With active loans	With negative equity (estimated)	Seriously delinquent	With negative equity (estimated)	Seriously delinquent
2006 Q1	124,601	10,737	11,555	8.6%	9.3%
Q2	128,730	13,366	12,047	10.4	9.4
Q3	132,245	16,522	12,915	12.5	9.8
Q4	134,667	19,325	14,262	14.4	10.6
2007 Q1	137,193	22,326	14,328	16.3	10.4
Q2	136,111	25,200	15,237	18.5	11.2
Q3	129,015	25,701	16,972	19.9	13.2
Q4	121,978	25,854	18,900	21.2	15.5
2008 Q1	114,902	25,732	18,547	22.4	16.1
Q2	107,865	24,819	17,993	23.0	16.7
Q3	101,874	23,912	18,015	23.5	17.7
Q4	96,751	23,024	18,407	23.8	19.0
2009 Q1	92,424	21,926	18,277	23.7	19.8
Q2	88,286	20,656	18,715	23.4	21.2
Q3	84,593	19,879	19,091	23.5	22.6
Q4	81,466	19,222	19,290	23.6	23.7
Iowa					
2006 Q1	34,071	171	2,397	0.5%	7.0%
Q2	34,642	241	2,508	0.7	7.2
Q3	35,255	362	2,815	1.0	8.0
Q4	35,755	485	3,098	1.4	8.7
2007 Q1	36,281	561	2,975	1.5	8.2
Q2	35,976	608	3,199	1.7	8.9
Q3	33,612	628	3,662	1.9	10.9
Q4	31,307	629	3,956	2.0	12.6
2008 Q1	29,358	625	3,940	2.1	13.4
Q2	27,554	561	3,826	2.0	13.9
Q3	26,033	561	3,842	2.2	14.8
Q4	24,794	554	3,906	2.2	15.8
2009 Q1	23,622	514	3,781	2.2	16.0
Q2	22,635	471	3,811	2.1	16.8
Q3	21,713	453	3,964	2.1	18.3
Q4	20,891	447	4,142	2.1	19.8

	Number of borrowers			Percentage of borrowers	
Kansas	With active loans	With negative equity (estimated)	Seriously delinquent	With negative equity (estimated)	Seriously delinquent
2006 Q1	38,605	856	2,044	2.2%	5.3%
Q2	39,556	1,208	2,147	3.1	5.4
Q3	40,282	1,665	2,243	4.1	5.6
Q4	40,931	2,082	2,582	5.1	6.3
2007 Q1	41,075	2,525	2,486	6.1	6.1
Q2	40,568	3,008	2,647	7.4	6.5
Q3	38,244	3,123	2,913	8.2	7.6
Q4	35,959	3,140	3,237	8.7	9.0
2008 Q1	33,776	3,137	3,151	9.3	9.3
Q2	31,699	3,065	3,128	9.7	9.9
Q3	30,057	2,995	3,101	10.0	10.3
Q4	28,713	2,928	3,369	10.2	11.7
2009 Q1	27,504	2,801	3,353	10.2	12.2
Q2	26,253	2,710	3,458	10.3	13.2
Q3	25,170	2,597	3,718	10.3	14.8
Q4	24,196	2,487	3,799	10.3	15.7
Kentucky					
2006 Q1	53,606	610	3,890	1.1%	7.3%
Q2	55,849	954	4,109	1.7	7.4
Q3	57,950	1,428	4,596	2.5	7.9
Q4	59,592	1,836	5,173	3.1	8.7
2007 Q1	61,170	2,215	5,194	3.6	8.5
Q2	60,536	2,514	5,740	4.2	9.5
Q3	57,255	2,562	6,434	4.5	11.2
Q4	53,947	2,571	6,970	4.8	12.9
2008 Q1	50,654	2,525	6,878	5.0	13.6
Q2	47,463	2,390	6,776	5.0	14.3
Q3	44,765	2,303	6,693	5.1	15.0
Q4	42,427	2,192	6,803	5.2	16.0
2009 Q1	40,524	2,056	6,574	5.1	16.2
Q2	38,723	1,900	6,733	4.9	17.4
Q3	37,133	1,796	7,142	4.8	19.2
Q4	35,684	1,738	7,286	4.9	20.4

Figure 5. (Continued)

Louisiana	Number of borrowers			Percentage of borrowers	
	With active loans	With negative equity (estimated)	Seriously delinquent	With negative equity (estimated)	Seriously delinquent
2006 Q1	57,946	174	10,691	0.3%	18.4%
Q2	59,327	359	8,661	0.6	14.6
Q3	61,079	650	7,922	1.1	13.0
Q4	62,442	1,032	7,702	1.7	12.3
2007 Q1	63,736	1,349	6,981	2.1	11.0
Q2	64,273	1,640	6,793	2.6	10.6
Q3	61,310	1,592	7,027	2.8	11.5
Q4	58,506	1,706	7,597	2.9	13.0
2008 Q1	55,432	1,696	7,398	3.1	13.3
Q2	52,642	1,621	7,492	3.1	14.2
Q3	50,445	1,601	7,952	3.2	15.8
Q4	48,685	1,598	8,563	3.3	17.6
2009 Q1	47,005	1,508	8,354	3.2	17.8
Q2	45,491	1,431	8,647	3.1	19.0
Q3	44,060	1,422	9,400	3.2	21.3
Q4	42,832	1,392	10,165	3.3	23.7

Maine	Number of borrowers			Percentage of borrowers	
	With active loans	With negative equity (estimated)	Seriously delinquent	With negative equity (estimated)	Seriously delinquent
2006 Q1	19,950	93	953	0.5%	4.8%
Q2	20,652	144	1,122	0.7	5.4
Q3	21,264	229	1,387	1.1	6.5
Q4	21,821	350	1,653	1.6	7.6
2007 Q1	22,549	420	1,834	1.9	8.1
Q2	23,163	573	2,167	2.5	9.4
Q3	21,994	611	2,484	2.8	11.3
Q4	20,854	620	2,858	3.0	13.7
2008 Q1	19,679	617	3,166	3.1	16.1
Q2	18,600	588	3,221	3.2	17.3
Q3	17,780	569	3,314	3.2	18.6
Q4	17,091	546	3,522	3.2	20.6
2009 Q1	16,436	519	3,603	3.2	21.9
Q2	15,772	486	3,660	3.1	23.2
Q3	15,213	472	3,797	3.1	25.0
Q4	14,664	462	3,947	3.2	26.9

Maryland	Number of borrowers			Percentage of borrowers	
	With active loans	With negative equity (estimated)	Seriously delinquent	With negative equity (estimated)	Seriously delinquent
2006 Q1	166,555	7,912	2,858	4.8%	1.7%
Q2	174,591	15,377	3,379	8.8	1.9
Q3	185,017	25,114	4,622	13.6	2.5
Q4	192,580	35,041	6,289	18.2	3.3
2007 Q1	201,872	45,486	7,285	22.5	3.6
Q2	206,749	56,024	9,711	27.1	4.7
Q3	195,745	57,965	13,381	29.6	6.8
Q4	183,743	58,596	17,569	31.9	9.6
2008 Q1	171,413	58,343	19,943	34.0	11.6
Q2	161,994	57,925	22,573	35.8	13.9
Q3	155,307	57,391	26,379	37.0	17.0
Q4	149,385	56,811	30,400	38.0	20.4
2009 Q1	142,977	56,052	32,376	39.2	22.6
Q2	136,653	53,955	33,242	39.5	24.3
Q3	131,508	52,168	35,142	39.7	26.7
Q4	126,717	50,372	36,273	39.8	28.6

Massachusetts	Number of borrowers			Percentage of borrowers	
	With active loans	With negative equity (estimated)	Seriously delinquent	With negative equity (estimated)	Seriously delinquent
2006 Q1	122,395	12,072	4,941	9.9%	4.0%
Q2	125,077	14,463	5,658	11.6	4.5
Q3	128,304	17,116	7,162	13.3	5.6
Q4	131,021	19,452	9,053	14.8	6.9
2007 Q1	134,003	21,367	9,888	15.9	7.4
Q2	135,646	23,455	11,237	17.3	8.3
Q3	129,094	23,679	13,849	18.3	10.7
Q4	121,824	23,572	16,680	19.3	13.7
2008 Q1	114,471	23,064	18,220	20.1	15.9
Q2	108,067	22,295	19,156	20.6	17.7
Q3	103,170	21,710	19,972	21.0	19.4
Q4	99,268	21,202	21,575	21.4	21.7
2009 Q1	95,736	20,560	22,880	21.5	23.9
Q2	92,244	19,265	23,996	20.9	26.0
Q3	89,035	18,721	25,568	21.0	28.7
Q4	85,826	18,182	26,542	21.2	30.9

Figure 5. (Continued)

Michigan

		Number of borrowers			Percentage of borrowers	
		With active loans	With negative equity (estimated)	Seriously delinquent	With negative equity (estimated)	Seriously delinquent
2006	Q1	232,899	109,511	17,627	47.0%	7.6%
	Q2	239,929	122,205	19,195	50.9	8.0
	Q3	247,109	135,628	21,975	54.9	8.9
	Q4	251,685	147,213	24,983	58.5	9.9
2007	Q1	253,611	157,779	24,211	62.2	9.5
	Q2	251,169	164,983	26,345	65.7	10.5
	Q3	236,715	162,939	29,829	68.8	12.6
	Q4	221,865	159,259	32,567	71.8	14.7
2008	Q1	206,931	153,321	31,174	74.1	15.1
	Q2	193,870	145,035	29,473	74.8	15.2
	Q3	182,737	137,548	29,025	75.3	15.9
	Q4	173,418	131,191	30,309	75.7	17.5
2009	Q1	165,720	125,721	31,421	75.9	19.0
	Q2	157,965	119,942	32,541	75.9	20.6
	Q3	151,101	114,887	34,940	76.0	23.1
	Q4	144,262	109,720	36,607	76.1	24.7

Minnesota

		With active loans	With negative equity (estimated)	Seriously delinquent	With negative equity (estimated)	Seriously delinquent
2006	Q1	114,018	15,624	5,733	13.7%	5.0%
	Q2	117,636	19,604	6,344	16.7	5.4
	Q3	122,531	24,381	7,661	19.9	6.3
	Q4	126,102	28,626	9,212	22.7	7.3
2007	Q1	128,951	32,297	9,892	25.0	7.7
	Q2	128,899	35,593	11,248	27.6	8.7
	Q3	121,364	35,951	13,334	29.6	11.0
	Q4	112,977	35,845	14,411	31.7	12.8
2008	Q1	105,123	35,358	14,544	33.6	13.8
	Q2	97,870	34,189	13,993	34.9	14.3
	Q3	91,831	33,227	13,755	36.2	15.0
	Q4	86,619	32,308	14,146	37.3	16.3
2009	Q1	82,169	31,272	14,723	38.1	17.9
	Q2	78,097	29,287	15,577	37.5	19.9
	Q3	74,284	27,629	15,811	37.2	21.3
	Q4	70,801	26,377	15,821	37.3	22.3

Mississippi

		Number of borrowers			Percentage of borrowers	
		With active loans	With negative equity (estimated)	Seriously delinquent	With negative equity (estimated)	Seriously delinquent
2006	Q1	34,556	221	5,589	0.6%	16.2%
	Q2	35,898	480	5,081	1.3	14.2
	Q3	37,022	799	5,059	2.2	13.7
	Q4	37,932	1,165	5,079	3.1	13.4
2007	Q1	38,686	1,563	4,518	4.0	11.7
	Q2	39,049	1,867	4,531	4.8	11.6
	Q3	37,184	1,910	4,950	5.1	13.3
	Q4	35,324	1,927	5,514	5.5	15.6
2008	Q1	33,496	1,915	5,378	5.7	16.1
	Q2	31,759	1,851	5,103	5.8	16.1
	Q3	30,267	1,796	5,239	5.9	17.3
	Q4	29,070	1,678	5,613	5.8	19.3
2009	Q1	27,998	1,545	5,609	5.5	20.0
	Q2	27,051	1,408	5,821	5.2	21.5
	Q3	26,157	1,297	6,183	5.0	23.6
	Q4	25,399	1,243	6,547	4.9	25.8

Missouri

		With active loans	With negative equity (estimated)	Seriously delinquent	With negative equity (estimated)	Seriously delinquent
2006	Q1	115,077	6,073	5,990	5.3%	5.2%
	Q2	118,999	8,295	6,286	7.0	5.3
	Q3	122,501	10,898	7,490	8.9	6.1
	Q4	125,452	13,569	8,751	10.8	7.0
2007	Q1	127,364	16,200	8,290	12.7	6.5
	Q2	126,689	18,769	9,462	14.8	7.5
	Q3	118,813	19,190	10,944	16.2	9.2
	Q4	110,428	19,142	11,869	17.3	10.7
2008	Q1	102,554	18,754	11,303	18.3	11.0
	Q2	95,806	17,970	10,836	18.8	11.3
	Q3	90,216	17,343	11,460	19.2	12.7
	Q4	85,442	16,762	12,378	19.6	14.5
2009	Q1	81,349	15,930	12,310	19.6	15.1
	Q2	77,659	14,941	12,570	19.2	16.2
	Q3	74,372	14,293	13,465	19.2	18.1
	Q4	71,430	13,775	14,089	19.3	19.7

Figure 5. (Continued)

Montana		Number of borrowers			Percentage of borrowers	
		With active loans	With negative equity (estimated)	Seriously delinquent	With negative equity (estimated)	Seriously delinquent
2006	Q1	11,890	9	311	0.1%	2.6%
	Q2	12,457	27	320	0.2	2.6
	Q3	13,057	69	342	0.5	2.6
	Q4	13,775	114	396	0.8	2.9
2007	Q1	14,258	170	397	1.2	2.8
	Q2	14,182	256	467	1.8	3.3
	Q3	13,393	287	511	2.1	3.8
	Q4	12,549	296	604	2.4	4.8
2008	Q1	11,632	296	690	2.5	5.9
	Q2	10,771	289	741	2.7	6.9
	Q3	10,119	283	813	2.8	8.0
	Q4	9,642	274	976	2.8	10.1
2009	Q1	9,082	257	1,137	2.8	12.5
	Q2	8,536	245	1,267	2.9	14.8
	Q3	8,073	228	1,329	2.8	16.5
	Q4	7,713	224	1,374	2.9	17.8
Nebraska						
2006	Q1	22,872	239	1,243	1.0%	5.4%
	Q2	23,647	334	1,315	1.4	5.6
	Q3	24,213	470	1,467	1.9	6.1
	Q4	24,599	597	1,716	2.4	7.0
2007	Q1	24,938	723	1,642	2.9	6.6
	Q2	24,651	805	1,725	3.3	7.0
	Q3	23,207	823	1,938	3.5	8.4
	Q4	21,805	825	2,162	3.8	9.9
2008	Q1	20,565	794	2,149	3.9	10.4
	Q2	19,338	732	2,018	3.8	10.4
	Q3	18,344	705	2,066	3.8	11.3
	Q4	17,534	673	2,168	3.8	12.4
2009	Q1	16,854	641	2,155	3.8	12.8
	Q2	16,153	600	2,281	3.7	14.1
	Q3	15,479	574	2,392	3.7	15.5
	Q4	14,861	551	2,428	3.7	16.3

Nevada		Number of borrowers			Percentage of borrowers	
		With active loans	With negative equity (estimated)	Seriously delinquent	With negative equity (estimated)	Seriously delinquent
2006	Q1	157,510	63,160	2,424	40.1%	1.5%
	Q2	168,728	77,034	3,066	45.7	1.8
	Q3	180,208	91,447	4,374	50.7	2.4
	Q4	186,621	103,996	6,729	54.8	3.5
2007	Q1	198,269	116,268	8,716	58.6	4.4
	Q2	202,603	128,247	11,543	63.3	5.7
	Q3	195,372	130,380	15,894	66.7	8.1
	Q4	186,439	130,498	22,090	70.0	11.8
2008	Q1	176,541	129,173	25,873	73.2	14.7
	Q2	165,632	123,624	27,842	74.6	16.8
	Q3	154,792	117,104	29,484	75.7	19.0
	Q4	145,350	111,158	34,330	76.5	23.6
2009	Q1	136,066	105,424	38,765	77.5	28.5
	Q2	126,796	99,550	40,390	78.5	31.9
	Q3	117,823	93,492	40,795	79.4	34.6
	Q4	111,225	88,965	42,239	80.0	38.0
New Hampshire						
2006	Q1	27,619	1,033	878	3.7%	3.2%
	Q2	28,288	1,314	1,069	4.6	3.8
	Q3	29,341	1,681	1,365	5.7	4.7
	Q4	30,138	2,024	1,547	6.7	5.1
2007	Q1	31,093	2,289	1,714	7.4	5.5
	Q2	31,505	2,603	2,058	8.3	6.5
	Q3	29,857	2,638	2,411	8.8	8.1
	Q4	28,071	2,615	2,780	9.3	9.9
2008	Q1	26,402	2,549	2,900	9.7	11.0
	Q2	24,967	2,445	2,826	9.8	11.3
	Q3	23,767	2,358	2,948	9.9	12.4
	Q4	22,767	2,270	3,358	10.0	14.7
2009	Q1	21,877	2,171	3,492	9.9	16.0
	Q2	20,982	2,020	3,681	9.6	17.5
	Q3	20,835	1,947	4,086	9.6	20.2
	Q4	19,508	1,897	4,343	9.7	22.3

Figure 5. (Continued)

New Jersey

		Number of borrowers			Percentage of borrowers	
		With active loans	With negative equity (estimated)	Seriously delinquent	With negative equity (estimated)	Seriously delinquent
2006	Q1	166,581	8,331	5,832	5.0%	3.5%
	Q2	171,893	12,842	6,645	7.5	3.9
	Q3	179,419	19,026	8,271	10.6	4.6
	Q4	185,242	24,516	10,289	13.2	5.6
2007	Q1	192,289	29,517	12,001	15.4	6.2
	Q2	198,238	34,973	14,467	17.6	7.3
	Q3	189,113	36,047	18,466	19.1	9.8
	Q4	178,894	36,328	23,057	20.3	12.9
2008	Q1	168,194	36,012	26,325	21.4	15.7
	Q2	159,115	35,564	28,853	22.4	18.1
	Q3	152,217	35,136	31,157	23.1	20.5
	Q4	147,112	34,759	34,946	23.6	23.8
2009	Q1	141,968	34,278	38,927	24.1	27.4
	Q2	136,511	33,418	41,330	24.5	30.3
	Q3	131,742	32,573	43,834	24.7	33.3
	Q4	127,617	31,858	45,699	25.0	36.8

New Mexico

		With active loans	With negative equity (estimated)	Seriously delinquent	With negative equity (estimated)	Seriously delinquent
2006	Q1	30,688	94	920	0.3%	3.0%
	Q2	31,805	315	961	1.0	3.0
	Q3	32,944	737	986	2.2	3.0
	Q4	34,111	1,234	1,098	3.6	3.2
2007	Q1	35,367	1,930	1,126	5.5	3.2
	Q2	35,910	2,878	1,276	8.0	3.6
	Q3	33,917	3,124	1,493	9.2	4.4
	Q4	31,889	3,163	1,933	9.9	6.1
2008	Q1	29,824	3,155	2,193	10.6	7.4
	Q2	28,010	3,088	2,369	11.0	8.5
	Q3	26,643	3,025	2,606	11.4	9.8
	Q4	25,490	2,941	3,042	11.5	11.9
2009	Q1	24,414	2,851	3,346	11.7	13.7
	Q2	23,367	2,743	3,594	11.7	15.4
	Q3	22,399	2,633	3,793	11.8	16.9
	Q4	21,556	2,534	3,961	11.8	18.4

New York

		Number of borrowers			Percentage of borrowers	
		With active loans	With negative equity (estimated)	Seriously delinquent	With negative equity (estimated)	Seriously delinquent
2006	Q1	256,904	4,278	10,892	1.7%	4.2%
	Q2	264,774	7,440	12,212	2.8	4.6
	Q3	277,069	11,332	14,957	4.1	5.4
	Q4	287,638	15,299	18,266	5.3	6.4
2007	Q1	299,792	19,558	20,647	6.5	6.9
	Q2	310,238	24,470	24,340	7.9	7.8
	Q3	300,685	25,650	29,921	8.5	10.0
	Q4	288,844	25,991	36,123	9.0	12.5
2008	Q1	276,456	25,866	40,068	9.4	14.5
	Q2	265,129	25,734	43,160	9.7	16.3
	Q3	255,980	25,526	46,766	10.0	18.3
	Q4	249,082	25,308	52,936	10.2	21.3
2009	Q1	242,280	25,030	58,519	10.3	24.2
	Q2	234,900	24,450	62,725	10.4	26.7
	Q3	228,274	23,858	66,911	10.5	29.3
	Q4	222,570	23,333	71,234	10.5	32.0

North Carolina

		With active loans	With negative equity (estimated)	Seriously delinquent	With negative equity (estimated)	Seriously delinquent
2006	Q1	146,359	350	7,145	0.2%	4.9%
	Q2	152,973	653	7,614	0.4	5.0
	Q3	159,767	1,392	8,458	0.9	5.3
	Q4	165,586	2,128	9,650	1.3	5.8
2007	Q1	170,128	3,044	9,175	1.8	5.4
	Q2	171,411	4,363	10,055	2.5	5.9
	Q3	162,733	4,664	11,551	2.9	7.1
	Q4	153,294	4,782	13,199	3.1	8.6
2008	Q1	143,104	4,771	13,226	3.3	9.2
	Q2	133,882	4,713	12,874	3.5	9.6
	Q3	127,369	4,699	13,578	3.7	10.7
	Q4	122,244	4,675	15,286	3.8	12.5
2009	Q1	117,739	4,605	16,530	3.9	14.0
	Q2	113,022	4,421	17,678	3.9	15.6
	Q3	108,823	4,309	19,139	4.0	17.6
	Q4	105,043	4,170	20,346	4.0	19.4

Figure 5. (Continued)

North Dakota		Number of borrowers			Percentage of borrowers	
		With active loans	With negative equity (estimated)	Seriously delinquent	With negative equity (estimated)	Seriously delinquent
2006	Q1	3,743	0	102	0.0%	2.7%
	Q2	3,935	1	133	0.0	3.4
	Q3	4,162	2	192	0.0	4.6
	Q4	4,393	6	209	0.1	4.8
2007	Q1	4,590	8	210	0.2	4.6
	Q2	4,604	8	227	0.2	4.9
	Q3	4,332	8	218	0.2	5.0
	Q4	4,077	7	256	0.2	6.3
2008	Q1	3,852	6	265	0.2	6.9
	Q2	3,566	6	270	0.2	7.6
	Q3	3,328	6	262	0.2	7.9
	Q4	3,168	6	297	0.2	9.4
2009	Q1	3,013	6	305	0.2	10.1
	Q2	2,852	6	315	0.2	11.0
	Q3	2,693	6	343	0.2	12.7
	Q4	2,564	6	338	0.2	13.2

Ohio		Number of borrowers			Percentage of borrowers	
		With active loans	With negative equity (estimated)	Seriously delinquent	With negative equity (estimated)	Seriously delinquent
2006	Q1	219,060	31,149	23,434	14.2%	10.7%
	Q2	225,814	35,745	24,746	15.8	11.0
	Q3	231,493	41,518	27,480	17.9	11.9
	Q4	236,397	46,439	30,315	19.6	12.8
2007	Q1	240,557	50,757	30,390	21.1	12.6
	Q2	238,436	53,780	32,371	22.6	13.6
	Q3	226,976	53,619	35,382	23.6	15.6
	Q4	215,063	52,990	37,976	24.6	17.7
2008	Q1	203,161	51,521	37,139	25.4	18.3
	Q2	192,071	48,957	35,793	25.5	18.6
	Q3	182,235	47,538	34,556	26.1	19.0
	Q4	173,962	45,985	34,664	26.4	19.9
2009	Q1	167,197	43,733	34,589	26.2	20.7
	Q2	160,533	40,762	34,688	25.4	21.6
	Q3	154,560	39,131	35,986	25.3	23.3
	Q4	148,838	37,767	36,286	25.4	24.4

Oklahoma		Number of borrowers			Percentage of borrowers	
		With active loans	With negative equity (estimated)	Seriously delinquent	With negative equity (estimated)	Seriously delinquent
2006	Q1	51,526	69	3,268	0.1%	6.3%
	Q2	53,797	100	3,372	0.2	6.3
	Q3	55,782	132	3,614	0.2	6.5
	Q4	57,348	168	3,990	0.3	7.0
2007	Q1	58,965	194	4,092	0.3	7.0
	Q2	59,406	223	4,330	0.4	7.3
	Q3	56,649	226	4,812	0.4	8.5
	Q4	53,951	227	5,405	0.4	10.0
2008	Q1	51,247	225	5,440	0.4	10.6
	Q2	48,439	225	5,258	0.5	10.9
	Q3	45,889	223	5,175	0.5	11.3
	Q4	43,781	223	5,323	0.5	12.2
2009	Q1	41,999	219	5,553	0.5	13.2
	Q2	40,201	209	5,761	0.5	14.3
	Q3	38,469	205	6,125	0.5	15.9
	Q4	37,029	202	6,369	0.5	17.2

Oregon		Number of borrowers			Percentage of borrowers	
		With active loans	With negative equity (estimated)	Seriously delinquent	With negative equity (estimated)	Seriously delinquent
2006	Q1	100,485	654	1,936	0.7%	1.9%
	Q2	103,473	1,718	1,911	1.7	1.8
	Q3	106,757	3,533	2,106	3.3	2.0
	Q4	111,349	5,614	2,492	5.0	2.2
2007	Q1	115,616	7,813	2,797	6.8	2.4
	Q2	117,029	10,843	3,475	9.3	3.0
	Q3	111,095	11,631	4,384	10.5	3.9
	Q4	104,577	11,930	5,568	11.4	5.3
2008	Q1	97,952	11,912	6,625	12.2	6.8
	Q2	91,759	11,822	7,288	12.9	7.9
	Q3	86,785	11,714	8,158	13.5	9.4
	Q4	82,590	11,555	9,753	14.0	11.8
2009	Q1	78,719	11,353	11,799	14.4	15.0
	Q2	74,571	10,868	12,685	14.6	17.0
	Q3	70,930	10,365	13,136	14.6	18.5
	Q4	67,718	9,973	13,412	14.7	19.8

Figure 5. (Continued)

Pennsylvania		Number of borrowers			Percentage of borrowers	
		With active loans	With negative equity (estimated)	Seriously delinquent	With negative equity (estimated)	Seriously delinquent
2006	Q1	182,236	1,812	10,890	1.0%	6.0%
	Q2	189,003	2,799	11,489	1.5	6.1
	Q3	197,878	4,455	12,922	2.3	6.5
	Q4	205,029	6,405	14,598	3.1	7.1
2007	Q1	212,495	8,221	14,760	3.9	6.9
	Q2	216,417	10,023	16,241	4.6	7.5
	Q3	207,437	10,399	18,557	5.0	8.9
	Q4	197,475	10,514	21,263	5.3	10.8
2008	Q1	187,588	10,458	22,095	5.6	11.8
	Q2	178,608	10,255	22,890	5.7	12.8
	Q3	170,969	10,088	23,901	5.9	14.0
	Q4	164,677	9,941	25,864	6.0	15.7
2009	Q1	159,116	9,743	26,812	6.1	16.9
	Q2	153,823	9,444	28,471	6.1	18.5
	Q3	149,022	9,191	30,527	6.2	20.5
	Q4	144,506	8,995	32,362	6.2	22.4

Rhode Island		Number of borrowers			Percentage of borrowers	
2006	Q1	27,133	5,193	928	19.1%	3.4%
	Q2	27,701	6,561	1,128	23.7	4.1
	Q3	28,321	8,090	1,402	28.6	5.0
	Q4	28,461	9,364	1,820	32.9	6.4
2007	Q1	28,799	10,609	2,020	36.8	7.0
	Q2	28,919	11,753	2,454	40.6	8.5
	Q3	27,144	11,899	2,952	43.8	10.9
	Q4	25,261	11,847	3,465	46.9	13.7
2008	Q1	23,390	11,625	3,553	49.7	15.2
	Q2	21,860	11,320	3,573	51.8	16.3
	Q3	20,669	11,038	3,707	53.4	17.9
	Q4	19,600	10,538	3,940	53.8	20.1
2009	Q1	18,674	10,042	3,995	53.8	21.4
	Q2	17,853	9,605	4,077	53.8	22.8
	Q3	17,180	9,244	4,364	53.8	25.4
	Q4	16,590	8,925	4,596	53.8	27.7

South Carolina		Number of borrowers			Percentage of borrowers	
		With active loans	With negative equity (estimated)	Seriously delinquent	With negative equity (estimated)	Seriously delinquent
2006	Q1	74,095	1,184	4,633	1.6%	6.3%
	Q2	77,637	1,956	4,678	2.5	6.0
	Q3	80,981	3,071	5,156	3.8	6.4
	Q4	83,608	3,944	5,847	4.7	7.0
2007	Q1	86,335	5,158	5,810	6.0	6.7
	Q2	87,757	6,608	6,358	7.5	7.2
	Q3	83,852	6,900	7,370	8.2	8.8
	Q4	79,414	6,979	8,401	8.8	10.6
2008	Q1	74,573	6,921	8,456	9.3	11.3
	Q2	70,201	6,763	8,502	9.6	12.1
	Q3	66,779	6,665	8,689	10.0	13.0
	Q4	64,096	6,541	9,500	10.2	14.8
2009	Q1	61,487	6,366	9,859	10.4	16.0
	Q2	59,391	6,132	10,608	10.3	18.2
	Q3	57,321	5,930	11,695	10.3	20.4
	Q4	55,452	5,775	12,294	10.4	22.2

South Dakota		Number of borrowers			Percentage of borrowers	
2006	Q1	5,977	7	267	0.1%	4.5%
	Q2	6,257	14	298	0.2	4.8
	Q3	6,533	19	371	0.3	5.7
	Q4	6,767	24	427	0.4	6.3
2007	Q1	6,947	31	410	0.4	5.9
	Q2	6,865	33	434	0.5	6.3
	Q3	6,410	34	524	0.5	8.2
	Q4	5,968	34	548	0.6	9.2
2008	Q1	5,563	33	529	0.6	9.5
	Q2	5,157	17	538	0.3	10.4
	Q3	4,832	17	521	0.4	10.8
	Q4	4,529	17	526	0.4	11.6
2009	Q1	4,281	17	544	0.4	12.7
	Q2	4,042	17	589	0.4	14.6
	Q3	3,827	17	602	0.4	15.7
	Q4	3,644	17	605	0.5	16.6

Figure 5. (Continued)

Tennessee		With active loans	With negative equity (estimated)	Seriously delinquent	With negative equity (estimated)	Seriously delinquent
		Number of borrowers			**Percentage of borrowers**	
2006	Q1	124,054	720	7,766	0.6%	6.3%
	Q2	130,056	1,476	8,227	1.1	6.3
	Q3	135,739	2,514	9,649	1.9	7.1
	Q4	141,100	3,621	11,122	2.6	7.9
2007	Q1	145,102	5,037	10,757	3.5	7.4
	Q2	145,855	6,327	12,219	4.3	8.4
	Q3	138,431	6,559	13,726	4.7	9.9
	Q4	130,718	6,636	15,341	5.1	11.7
2008	Q1	122,819	6,626	15,069	5.4	12.3
	Q2	115,450	6,531	15,100	5.7	13.1
	Q3	109,391	6,461	15,963	5.9	14.6
	Q4	104,082	6,382	17,114	6.1	16.4
2009	Q1	99,021	6,134	17,185	6.2	17.4
	Q2	94,680	5,798	17,721	6.1	18.7
	Q3	90,781	5,597	18,539	6.2	20.4
	Q4	87,268	5,404	19,011	6.2	21.8
Texas						
2006	Q1	476,668	3,511	25,183	0.7%	5.3%
	Q2	504,222	7,042	26,621	1.4	5.3
	Q3	525,598	11,389	28,877	2.2	5.5
	Q4	548,152	15,439	31,926	2.8	5.8
2007	Q1	569,197	19,706	31,515	3.5	6.5
	Q2	577,337	25,317	34,221	4.4	6.9
	Q3	556,051	26,364	39,490	4.7	7.1
	Q4	533,337	26,580	45,081	5.0	8.5
2008	Q1	507,667	26,623	44,077	5.2	8.7
	Q2	483,433	25,846	42,459	5.3	8.8
	Q3	464,006	24,975	44,830	5.4	9.7
	Q4	448,503	24,145	51,594	5.4	11.5
2009	Q1	432,332	23,058	50,081	5.3	11.6
	Q2	417,210	22,068	52,452	5.3	12.6
	Q3	403,092	21,387	57,460	5.3	14.3
	Q4	389,891	20,590	61,809	5.3	15.9

Utah		With active loans	With negative equity (estimated)	Seriously delinquent	With negative equity (estimated)	Seriously delinquent
		Number of borrowers			**Percentage of borrowers**	
2006	Q1	75,194	200	2,336	0.3%	3.1%
	Q2	78,183	730	2,083	0.9	2.7
	Q3	81,113	1,832	2,093	2.3	2.6
	Q4	84,501	3,487	2,280	4.1	2.7
2007	Q1	87,599	6,383	2,264	7.3	2.6
	Q2	88,619	10,948	2,525	12.4	2.8
	Q3	82,612	12,050	3,097	14.6	3.7
	Q4	76,011	12,372	4,027	16.3	5.3
2008	Q1	69,437	12,350	4,613	17.8	6.6
	Q2	63,439	12,220	5,022	19.3	7.9
	Q3	58,640	12,029	5,566	20.5	9.5
	Q4	54,611	11,779	6,507	21.6	11.9
2009	Q1	50,940	11,463	7,475	22.5	14.7
	Q2	47,642	10,841	8,271	22.8	17.4
	Q3	44,886	10,333	8,774	23.0	19.5
	Q4	42,389	9,837	9,045	23.2	21.3
Vermont						
2006	Q1	6,404	67	229	1.0%	3.6%
	Q2	6,502	96	270	1.5	4.2
	Q3	6,659	146	319	2.2	4.8
	Q4	6,817	229	391	3.4	5.7
2007	Q1	7,063	290	441	4.1	6.2
	Q2	7,245	388	485	5.4	6.7
	Q3	6,847	417	573	6.1	8.4
	Q4	6,515	428	666	6.6	10.2
2008	Q1	6,170	425	756	6.9	12.3
	Q2	5,850	417	764	7.1	13.1
	Q3	5,577	401	762	7.2	13.7
	Q4	5,356	389	845	7.3	15.8
2009	Q1	5,169	382	893	7.4	17.3
	Q2	4,929	356	927	7.2	18.8
	Q3	4,731	345	987	7.3	20.9
	Q4	4,580	342	1,068	7.5	23.3

Figure 5. (Continued)

Virginia		Number of borrowers			Percentage of borrowers	
		With active loans	With negative equity (estimated)	Seriously delinquent	With negative equity (estimated)	Seriously delinquent
2006	Q1	182,012	26,285	3,127	14.4%	1.7%
	Q2	192,710	36,103	3,608	18.7	1.9
	Q3	204,395	46,654	4,844	22.8	2.4
	Q4	213,736	55,880	6,651	26.1	3.1
2007	Q1	222,857	63,574	7,902	28.5	3.5
	Q2	226,632	70,337	10,549	31.0	4.7
	Q3	215,130	71,258	14,503	33.1	6.7
	Q4	202,000	71,122	18,888	35.2	9.4
2008	Q1	187,931	70,069	20,604	37.3	11.0
	Q2	174,658	68,064	20,857	39.0	11.9
	Q3	164,209	66,111	21,239	40.3	12.9
	Q4	156,343	63,355	23,778	40.5	15.2
2009	Q1	148,449	59,621	25,289	40.2	17.0
	Q2	140,879	55,888	25,725	39.7	18.3
	Q3	134,210	52,766	26,243	39.3	19.6
	Q4	128,789	50,596	26,715	39.3	20.7

Washington						
2006	Q1	181,739	739	4,100	0.4%	2.3%
	Q2	187,261	2,472	4,174	1.3	2.2
	Q3	193,217	5,644	4,802	2.9	2.5
	Q4	201,197	9,358	5,562	4.7	2.8
2007	Q1	206,084	13,723	5,987	6.6	2.9
	Q2	210,721	19,826	6,713	9.4	3.2
	Q3	199,751	21,645	8,548	10.8	4.3
	Q4	187,108	22,351	10,663	11.9	5.7
2008	Q1	174,642	22,351	12,053	12.8	6.9
	Q2	163,169	22,222	13,174	13.6	8.1
	Q3	154,490	22,045	14,696	14.3	9.5
	Q4	147,331	21,843	17,897	14.8	12.1
2009	Q1	140,487	21,512	21,440	15.3	15.3
	Q2	133,385	20,721	23,696	15.5	17.8
	Q3	127,317	20,020	25,251	15.7	19.8
	Q4	122,290	19,452	26,660	15.9	21.8

West Virginia		Number of borrowers			Percentage of borrowers	
		With active loans	With negative equity (estimated)	Seriously delinquent	With negative equity (estimated)	Seriously delinquent
2006	Q1	10,516	1,142	647	10.9%	6.2%
	Q2	10,994	1,320	682	12.0	6.2
	Q3	11,612	1,640	747	14.1	6.4
	Q4	12,336	1,948	827	15.8	6.7
2007	Q1	12,716	2,220	737	17.5	5.8
	Q2	12,961	2,465	825	19.0	6.4
	Q3	12,411	2,499	1,040	20.1	8.4
	Q4	11,751	2,449	1,290	20.8	11.0
2008	Q1	11,108	2,404	1,254	21.6	11.3
	Q2	10,556	2,331	1,305	22.1	12.4
	Q3	10,124	2,281	1,464	22.5	14.5
	Q4	9,722	2,252	1,557	23.2	16.0
2009	Q1	9,355	2,214	1,571	23.7	16.8
	Q2	8,943	2,122	1,589	23.7	17.8
	Q3	8,581	2,039	1,618	23.8	18.9
	Q4	8,273	1,972	1,689	23.8	20.4

Wisconsin						
2006	Q1	71,766	2,400	4,477	3.3%	6.2%
	Q2	74,395	3,451	4,886	4.6	6.6
	Q3	77,953	5,002	5,822	6.4	7.5
	Q4	80,259	6,368	6,789	7.9	8.5
2007	Q1	82,682	7,802	7,131	9.4	8.6
	Q2	83,282	9,094	8,188	10.9	9.8
	Q3	78,243	9,305	9,706	11.9	12.4
	Q4	72,957	9,362	10,948	12.8	15.0
2008	Q1	67,914	9,158	11,181	13.5	16.5
	Q2	63,384	8,803	11,056	13.9	17.4
	Q3	59,768	8,626	11,338	14.4	19.0
	Q4	56,623	8,447	11,592	14.9	20.5
2009	Q1	53,803	8,180	11,608	15.2	21.6
	Q2	51,303	7,657	11,912	14.9	23.2
	Q3	48,998	7,362	12,531	15.0	25.6
	Q4	46,992	7,114	12,770	15.1	27.2

Figure 5. (Continued)

	Number of borrowers			Percentage of borrowers	
	With active loans	With negative equity (estimated)	Seriously delinquent	With negative equity (estimated)	Seriously delinquent
Wyoming					
2006 Q1	7,989	30	173	0.4%	2.2%
Q2	8,294	64	213	0.8	2.6
Q3	8,563	118	243	1.4	2.8
Q4	8,918	173	259	1.9	2.9
2007 Q1	9,311	274	261	2.9	2.8
Q2	9,291	414	275	4.5	3.0
Q3	8,654	448	336	5.2	3.9
Q4	8,012	464	387	5.8	4.8
2008 Q1	7,425	464	401	6.2	5.4
Q2	6,832	460	396	6.7	5.8
Q3	6,375	459	406	7.2	6.4
Q4	5,970	448	449	7.5	7.5
2009 Q1	5,655	441	486	7.8	8.6
Q2	5,330	421	575	7.9	10.8
Q3	5,039	396	657	7.9	13.0
Q4	4,792	370	659	7.7	13.8
Total (all states and the District of Columbia)					
2006 Q1	7,042,247	940,794	279,177	13.4%	4.0%
Q2	7,332,583	1,215,056	299,930	16.6	4.1
Q3	7,660,361	1,539,004	354,594	20.1	4.6
Q4	7,949,339	1,845,318	431,636	23.2	5.4
2007 Q1	8,221,852	2,145,353	469,503	26.1	5.7
Q2	8,358,373	2,453,835	558,255	29.4	6.7
Q3	7,992,184	2,514,270	703,786	31.5	8.8
Q4	7,577,782	2,523,852	876,555	33.3	11.6
2008 Q1	7,143,347	2,497,956	969,626	35.0	13.6
Q2	6,726,294	2,412,956	1,021,676	35.9	15.2
Q3	6,374,170	2,314,600	1,077,138	36.3	16.9
Q4	6,090,063	2,229,881	1,204,241	36.6	19.8
2009 Q1	5,821,670	2,143,119	1,294,916	36.8	22.2
Q2	5,555,210	2,039,041	1,342,852	36.7	24.2
Q3	5,319,566	1,946,828	1,400,282	36.6	26.3
Q4	5,106,683	1,861,880	1,439,903	36.5	28.2

Source: GAO analysis of CoreLogic loan data and CoreLogic's state-level house price index.

Figure 5. Nonprime Borrowers with Negative Equity and Seriously Delinquent Loans by State and Quarter, 2006 through 2009.

End Notes

[1] GAO, *Loan Performance and Negative Home Equity in the Nonprime Mortgage Market,* GAO-10-146R (Washington, D.C.: Dec. 16, 2009).

[2] We considered loans to be seriously delinquent if borrowers were 90 days or more late on their mortgage payments or in the foreclosure process.

[3] See GAO-10-146R and GAO, *Characteristics and Performance of Nonprime Mortgages,* GAO-09-848R (Washington, D.C.: July 28, 2009).

[4] Nonagency mortgage-backed securities (MBS), also known as private-label MBS, are backed by nonconforming conventional mortgages securitized primarily by investment banks. Nonconforming mortgages are those that do not meet the purchase requirements of Fannie Mae or Freddie Mac because they are too large or do not meet their underwriting criteria. About 75 percent of subprime and Alt-A mortgages originated from 2001 through 2007 were securitized.

[5] The CoreLogic database has a loan-level indicator for loan class (i.e., subprime or Alt-A), but it is not well populated. Therefore, we used the pool-level classification. According to mortgage researchers, some of the loans in subprime pools may not be subprime loans, and some of the loans in Alt-A pools may not be Alt-A loans.

[6] Single family attached and detached homes include condominiums, townhouses, and cooperatives. Newly constructed homes are necessarily excluded from the index because they have not been sold repeatedly. The CoreLogic index uses a value-weighted regression model that gives greater weight to price trends for more expensive homes than other homes. To limit the influence of atypical changes in the value of individual homes, the CoreLogic index also excludes certain transactions, such as nonarms length sales, those with outlier prices, closely spaced sales that may represent investor churning or "flipping," and sales with unusually high appreciation rates that likely indicate significant property improvements.

[7] Our analysis focused on whether or not a nonprime borrower was in a negative equity position. We did not estimate the extent to which a nonprime borrower's outstanding loan balance exceeded the estimated value of the home, a factor that could affect the probability of serious delinquency for a given loan.

[8] To the extent that nonprime borrowers had second liens, our analysis may understate the extent of negative home equity. To the extent that some nonprime borrowers had more than one mortgaged property, our results may overstate the actual number of individual nonprime borrowers with negative home equity.

[9] Correlation is the degree to which two variables' movements are associated. Our analysis used a statistical measure of association—the Pearson's correlation coefficient—which ranges in value from negative 1 to positive 1, with negative 1 indicating a perfect negative correlation, 0 an absence of correlation, and positive 1 a perfect positive correlation.

[10] There is no uniform definition of default across the lending industry. For purposes of this report, we use the definition provided.

[11] Our quarterly estimates of negative equity include only borrowers whose loans were active at the end of each quarter.

[12] Using a different house price index, we previously estimated that 25 percent of borrowers who obtained nonprime mortgages from 2000 through 2007 and whose loans were active as of June 30, 2009, had negative equity as of that date (see GAO-10-146R). That estimate used the Federal Housing Finance Agency's (FHFA) All-Transactions Index for 384 metropolitan areas covering approximately 84 percent of the U.S. population. The FHFA index does not include data for homes with certain types of financing, including subprime mortgages. We noted that our estimates using the FHFA index likely understated the extent of negative equity among nonprime borrowers. The CoreLogic state-level house price index, by contrast, includes all types of financing and transactions outside of metropolitan areas.

[13] At the end of 2009, 66 percent of the borrowers with negative equity had mortgages on homes in Arizona, California, Florida, and Nevada, the four states with the largest percentage point increases in negative equity rates.

[14] That is, South Carolina ranked in the middle (26th) among the 50 states and the District of Columbia in the increase in negative equity rates.

[15] Some states experienced a modest decrease in their negative equity rates from the second quarter of 2008 through the end of 2009. For example, Hawaii's rate decreased by 0.4 percentage points, Kentucky's decreased by 0.2 percentage points, and Mississippi's decreased by 0.9 percentage points.

[16] Specifically, the correlation coefficient between our measures for increases in negative equity rates and serious delinquency rates was 0.72. (The correlation coefficient is a statistical measure of association, with a value of 1 indicating a perfect positive correlation.)

[17] The six states were Arizona, California, Florida, Illinois, Maryland, and Nevada.

[18] The four states were Idaho, Michigan, Rhode Island, and Virginia.

[19] The five states were Louisiana, Nebraska, North Dakota, Oklahoma, and South Dakota.

[20] The five were the District of Columbia, Hawaii, Iowa, Maine, and Montana.

In: Mortgage Markets and the Role of Nonprime Loans   ISBN: 978-1-61122-918-9
Editor: Eric J. Carlson   © 2011 Nova Science Publishers, Inc.

Chapter 4

NONPRIME MORTGAGES: ANALYSIS OF LOAN PERFORMANCE, FACTORS ASSOCIATED WITH DEFAULTS, AND DATA SOURCES

United States Government Accountability Office

WHY GAO DID THIS STUDY

The surge in mortgage foreclosures that began in late 2006 and continues today was initially driven by deterioration in the performance of nonprime (subprime and Alt-A) loans. Nonprime mortgage originations increased dramatically from 2000 through 2006, rising from about 12 percent ($125 billion) of all mortgage originations to about 34 percent ($1 trillion). The nonprime market contracted sharply in mid-2007, partly in response to increasing defaults and foreclosures for these loans.

This report (1) provides information on the performance of nonprime loans through December 31, 2009; (2) examines how loan and borrower characteristics and economic conditions influenced the likelihood of default (including foreclosure) of nonprime loans; and (3) describes the features and limitations of primary sources of data on nonprime loan performance and borrower characteristics, and discusses federal government efforts to improve the availability or use of such data. To do this work, GAO analyzed a proprietary database of securitized nonprime loans and Home Mortgage Disclosure Act data, and reviewed information on mortgage data sources maintained by private firms and the federal government.

WHAT GAO RECOMMENDS

GAO makes no recommendations in this report.

WHAT GAO FOUND

The number of active nonprime loans originated from 2000 through 2007 that were seriously delinquent (90 or more days late or in the foreclosure process) increased from 1.1 million at the end of 2008 to 1.4 million at the end of 2009. Serious delinquency rates were higher for certain adjustable-rate products common in the subprime and Alt-A market segments than they were for fixed-rate products. The number of nonprime loans that were 90 or more days late grew throughout 2009, accounting for most of the overall growth in the number of serious delinquencies. By comparison, the number of active loans in the foreclosure process grew in the first half of the year, and then began to decline somewhat. Additionally, 475,000 nonprime mortgages completed the foreclosure process during 2009. The persistently weak performance of nonprime loans suggests that problems in the nonprime market will not be resolved quickly, and underscores the importance of federal efforts to assist distressed borrowers and prevent a recurrence of the aggressive lending practices that helped precipitate the foreclosure crisis.

In addition to performance differences between mortgage products, GAO found across product types that house price changes, loan amount, the ratio of the amount of the loan to the value of the home, and borrower credit score were among the variables that influenced the likelihood of default on nonprime loans originated from 2004 through 2006. In addition, loans that lacked full documentation of borrower income and assets were associated with increased default probabilities, and the influence of borrowers' reported income varied with the level of documentation. GAO found that borrower race and ethnicity were associated with the probability of default, particularly for loans used to purchase rather than to refinance a home. However, these associations should be interpreted with caution because GAO lacks data on factors that may influence default rates and that may also be associated with race and ethnicity, such as borrower wealth and first-time homebuyer status.

Existing sources of data on nonprime mortgages contain a range of information to support different uses. While these data sources offer some similar elements, they vary in their coverage of loan, property, and borrower attributes. The data sources generally lack information on certain attributes that could help inform policy decisions or regulatory efforts to mitigate risk. For example, first-time homebuyers are not identified in any of the data sources, limiting the ability of analysts to compare the marginal effect of prior homeownership experience on default probabilities. In addition, most of the data sources do not cover the entire nonprime mortgage market. Ongoing federal efforts have the potential to provide data that may not have some of the constraints of the existing sources. For example, officials from the Board of Governors of the Federal Reserve System and Freddie Mac are collaborating on a pilot project to develop a publicly available National Mortgage Database, which would compile data on a representative sample of outstanding mortgages and provide more comprehensive data than are currently available.

ABBREVIATIONS

ABS	asset-backed securities
ARM	adjustable-rate mortgage

BLS	Bureau of Labor Statistics
CLTV	combined loan-to-value
CoreLogic LP	CoreLogic LoanPerformance
DTI	debt-service-to-income
FFIEC	Federal Financial Institutions Examination Council
FHA	Federal Housing Administration
FHFA	Federal Housing Finance Agency
HMDA	Home Mortgage Disclosure Act
HPA	house price appreciation
HPI	house price index
HUD	Department of Housing and Urban Development
LLS	Loan Level Servicing
LPS	Lender Processing Services
LTV	loan-to-value
MBS	mortgage-backed securities
NMDB	National Mortgage Database
SFDW	Single Family Data Warehouse

August 24, 2010

The Honorable Carolyn B. Maloney
Chair
The Honorable Charles E. Schumer
Vice Chairman
Joint Economic Committee
United States Congress

The surge in mortgage foreclosures that began in late 2006 and continues today was initially driven by deterioration in the performance of nonprime (subprime and Alt-A) loans.[1] Nonprime mortgage originations increased dramatically from 2000 through 2006, rising from about 12 percent ($125 billion) of all mortgage originations to about 34 percent ($1 trillion).[2] The nonprime market contracted sharply in mid-2007, partly in response to increasing default and foreclosure rates for these mortgages. As economic conditions deteriorated in 2008 and 2009, growing numbers of borrowers—including those with both nonprime and prime loans—entered foreclosure, exacerbating stresses in the mortgage and housing markets.

Researchers and policymakers have sought to understand the causes of the foreclosure crisis and develop policy responses to reduce foreclosures and prevent similar crises in the future. However, data limitations have complicated efforts to analyze the nonprime mortgage market, in part because no one database provides complete information on the features and performance of nonprime loans and the characteristics of borrowers. Furthermore, questions have been raised about whether timely access to more comprehensive information on the nonprime mortgage market could have helped federal banking regulators anticipate the foreclosure crisis or respond to it more quickly and effectively.

To inform congressional oversight and decision making about efforts to address problems in the mortgage market, you requested that we examine the evolution and condition of the nonprime market segment. In prior reports, we discussed certain characteristics of nonprime loans and borrowers; the performance of nonprime mortgages as of March 31, 2009, and June 30, 2009; the extent of negative equity among nonprime borrowers in selected metropolitan areas and nationwide as of June 30, 2009; and the proportion of nonprime borrowers with negative equity and seriously delinquent loans, by state, from 2006 through 2009.[3] This report (1) provides information on the performance of nonprime loans through December 31, 2009; (2) examines how loan and borrower characteristics and economic conditions influenced the likelihood of default and foreclosure of nonprime loans; and (3) describes the features and limitations of primary sources of data on nonprime loan performance and borrower characteristics, and discusses federal government efforts to improve the availability or use of such data. An electronic supplement to this report provides additional information on the performance of nonprime mortgages by annual loan cohort, product type, Census division, state, and congressional district as of December 31, 2009.[4]

To examine the recent performance of nonprime mortgages, we used data from CoreLogic LoanPerformance's (CoreLogic LP) Asset-Backed Securities Database for nonprime loans originated from 2000 through 2007 (the last year in which substantial numbers of nonprime mortgages were made). The CoreLogic LP database contains loan-level data on a large majority of nonagency securitized mortgages in subprime and Alt-A pools.[5] For the purposes of our analysis, we defined a subprime loan as a loan in a subprime pool and an Alt-A loan as a loan in an Alt-A pool.[6] We focused our analysis on first-lien purchase and refinance mortgages for one- to four-family residential units. For the nonprime market as a whole, and for the subprime and Alt-A market segments, we calculated the number and percentage of nonprime mortgages that were in different performance categories—for example, current (up to date on payments); delinquent (30 to 89 days behind); in default (90 or more days behind); in the foreclosure process; or having completed the foreclosure process—at the end of each quarter from December 31, 2008, through December 31, 2009, the most recent quarterly data that we could analyze within the time frame of our review.[7] We classified mortgages in default or in the foreclosure process as "seriously delinquent." We also examined mortgage performance as of December 31, 2009, by loan cohort; product type; and geographic areas, including Census divisions, states, and congressional districts.[8] These latter analyses are reported in detail in the electronic supplement to this report.[9]

To analyze the influence of loan and borrower characteristics and economic conditions on the performance of nonprime loans, we developed a statistical model to estimate the relationship between relevant variables and the probability of loan default or foreclosure within 24 months after the borrower's first payment. We define a loan as being in default or foreclosure if it was delinquent by at least 90 days, in the foreclosure process (including loans identified as in real-estate-owned status), paid off after being 90-days delinquent or in foreclosure, or already terminated with evidence of a loss. We analyzed nonprime loans originated from 2004 to 2006, using records from the CoreLogic LP database that we matched to records in the Home Mortgage Disclosure Act (HMDA) database compiled by the Federal Financial Institutions Examination Council (FFIEC) from information reported by lenders.[10] Combining the information in these two data sources yielded a data set with loan-level information on loan characteristics (mortgage type and key mortgage terms); loan performance (payment status at particular times); and certain borrower characteristics (such as borrower race, ethnicity, reported income, and credit score).[11] In addition, we used the Federal Housing Finance Agency's (FHFA) house price indexes (HPI) for metropolitan areas to incorporate data on house price appreciation.[12] We also used employment data from the

Bureau of Labor Statistics (BLS) and Census tract-level data from the 2000 Census to control for various economic conditions and neighborhood characteristics. Appendix I contains additional information on the methodology for this statistical model.

To identify sources of data on nonprime loans and borrowers, we reviewed research literature on mortgage markets and interviewed knowledgeable private sector and federal agency officials. For data sources that are national in scope, provide loan-level information on nonprime loans, and are widely available for free or a fee, we reviewed database documentation and related research and interviewed agency and company officials to determine the scope and features of each data source. We also collected and reviewed similar documentation for data on loans insured by the Department of Housing and Urban Development's (HUD) Federal Housing Administration (FHA) because borrowers served by FHA earlier in the decade had some similar characteristics to subprime borrowers. We also used our review of documentation and research and interviews to identify limitations in data availability and federal government efforts to address them or to improve the use of such data.

We tested the reliability of the data used in this report by reviewing documentation on the process that the data providers use to collect and ensure the reliability and integrity of their data, and by conducting reasonableness checks on data elements to identify any missing, erroneous, or outlying data. We also interviewed CoreLogic LP representatives to discuss the interpretation of various data fields. We concluded that the data we used were sufficiently reliable for our purposes.

We conducted this engagement in Washington, D.C., and Chicago, Illinois, from December 2009 through August 2010 in accordance with generally accepted government auditing standards. Those standards require that we plan and perform the audit to obtain sufficient, appropriate evidence to provide a reasonable basis for our findings and conclusions based on our audit objectives. We believe that the evidence obtained provides a reasonable basis for our findings and conclusions based on our audit objectives.

BACKGROUND

The nonprime mortgage market has two segments:

- *Subprime*: Generally serves borrowers with blemished or limited credit histories, and the loans feature higher interest rates and fees than prime loans.
- *Alt-A*: Generally serves borrowers whose credit histories are close to prime, but the loans have one or more high-risk features, such as limited documentation of income or assets or the option of making monthly payments that are lower than would be required for a fully amortizing loan.

Of the 14.5 million nonprime loans originated from 2000 through 2007, 9.4 million (65 percent) were subprime loans and 5.1 million (35 percent) were Alt-A loans.

In both of these market segments, two types of loans are common: fixed-rate mortgages, which have unchanging interest rates, and adjustable-rate mortgages (ARM), which have interest rates that can adjust periodically on the basis of changes in a specified index. Specific types of ARMs are prevalent in each market segment. "Short-term hybrid ARMs" accounted for 70 percent of subprime mortgage originations from 2000 through 2007 (see Figure 1). These loans have a fixed interest rate for an initial period (2 or 3 years) but then "reset" to an adjustable rate for the remaining term of the loan. In the Alt-A segment, "payment-option ARMs" are a common adjustable-rate product, accounting for 17 percent of Alt-A mortgage originations from 2000 through 2007. For an initial period of typically 5 years, or until the loan balance reaches a specified cap, this product provides the borrower with multiple payment options each month, including minimum payments that are lower than what would be needed to cover any of the principal or all of the accrued interest. After the initial period, payments are "recast" to include an amount that will fully amortize the outstanding balance over the remaining loan term.

Several payment categories describe the performance of mortgages, including nonprime mortgages:

- *Current*: The borrower is meeting scheduled payments.
- *Delinquent*: The borrower is 30 to 89 days behind in scheduled payments.
- *Default*: The borrower is 90 days or more delinquent.[13] At this point, foreclosure proceedings against the borrower become a strong possibility.
- *In the foreclosure process*: The borrower has been delinquent for more than 90 days, and the lender has elected to foreclose in what is often a lengthy process. The loan is considered active during the foreclosure process.
- *Completed the foreclosure process*: The borrower's loan terminates and foreclosure proceedings end with one of several possible outcomes. For example, the borrower may sell the property or the lender may repossess the home.
- *Prepaid*: The borrower has paid off the entire loan balance before it is due. Prepayment often occurs as a result of the borrower selling the home or refinancing into a new mortgage.

In this report, we describe mortgages in default or in the foreclosure process as "seriously delinquent."

As we have stated in previous reports, a combination of falling house prices, aggressive lending practices, and weak economic conditions have contributed to the increase in troubled mortgages. For example, in 2009, we noted that falling house prices had left a substantial proportion of nonprime borrowers in a negative equity position—that is, their mortgage balances exceeded the current value of their homes—limiting their ability to sell or refinance their homes in the event they could not stay current on their mortgage payments.[14] Additionally, we reported that an easing of underwriting standards and wider use of certain loan features associated with poorer loan performance contributed to increases in mortgage delinquencies and foreclosures.[15] These features included mortgages with higher loan-to-value (LTV) ratios (the amount of the loan divided by the value of the home at loan origination), adjustable interest rates, limited or no documentation of borrower income or assets, and deferred payment of principal or interest. Also, in some cases, mortgage originators engaged in questionable sales practices that resulted in loans with onerous terms and conditions that made repayment more difficult for some borrowers. Furthermore, rising unemployment has contributed to mortgage defaults and foreclosures because job loss directly affects a borrower's ability to make mortgage payments.

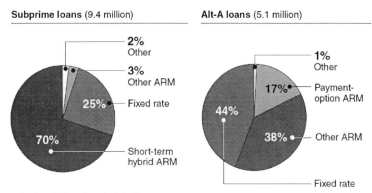

Source: GAO analysis of CoreLogic LP data.

Figure 1. Percentage of Subprime and Alt-A Loans Originated from 2000 through 2007, by Product Type.

The foreclosure crisis has imposed significant costs on borrowers, neighborhoods, and taxpayers. For example, vacant and foreclosed properties have contributed to neighborhood blight and reduced property values in many communities. Additionally, foreclosures affecting minority populations and the high incidence of subprime lending to members of these groups have heightened concerns that these groups have received disparate treatment in mortgage lending. In light of these costs and concerns, Congress and federal agencies have taken a number of steps to address and prevent a recurrence of ongoing problems in the mortgage market. These efforts include programs to modify or refinance the loans of distressed borrowers and legislation to strengthen mortgage-lending standards and prevent mortgage originators from steering borrowers into high-risk or high-cost mortgages.

NONPRIME LOAN PERFORMANCE DETERIORATED THROUGH THE END OF 2009 AND VARIED BY MARKET SEGMENT, PRODUCT TYPE, COHORT YEAR, AND LOCATION

The Worsening Performance of Nonprime Loans Was Reflected in Increases in Serious Delinquencies

As of December 31, 2009, 63 percent of the 14.50 million nonprime loans originated from 2000 through 2007 (the last year in which substantial numbers of nonprime mortgages were made) was no longer active. Fifty percent of the nonprime loans originated during this period had prepaid, and 13 percent had completed foreclosure (see Figure 2).[16]

Among the 4.59 million nonprime loans that remained active as of the end of 2009, about 16 percent was in default (90 or more days late) and about 14 percent was in the foreclosure process, for a total serious delinquency rate of 30 percent (see Figure 3).[17] About 12 percent was in a less serious stage of delinquency (30 to 89 days late), and the remaining 58.5 percent was current.

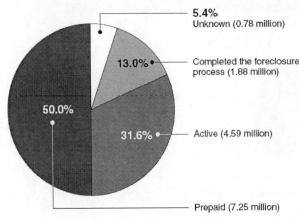

Source: GAO analysis of CoreLogic LP data.
Note: The percentages in this figure were calculated from unrounded numbers.

Figure 2. Status of Nonprime Loans Originated from 2000 through 2007 as of December 31, 2009.

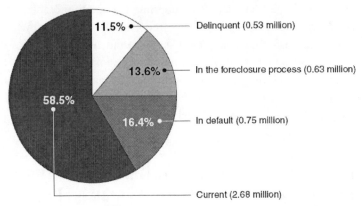

Source: GAO analysis of CoreLogic LP data.
Note: The percentages in this figure were calculated from unrounded numbers.

Figure 3. Active Nonprime Loans by Performance Category as of December 31, 2009.

The performance of nonprime mortgages originated from 2000 through 2007 deteriorated from the end of 2008 through the end of 2009. At the end of 2009, 1.38 million active nonprime loans were seriously delinquent, compared with 1.10 million at the end of 2008.[18] Over the 12-month period, the serious delinquency rate rose from 21 percent to 30 percent. About three-quarters of the year-over-year change in the number of serious delinquencies was due to an increase in defaults, while the remainder was due to an increase in loans in the foreclosure process. As shown in figure 4, the number of active nonprime loans in default grew each quarter, with the largest increases occurring in the third and fourth quarters of 2009. By comparison, the number of active nonprime loans in the foreclosure process grew in the first two quarters of the year, held almost steady in the third quarter, and declined in the last quarter of 2009. The decline in the number of loans in the foreclosure process may be attributable to decisions by lenders not to begin foreclosure proceedings on defaulted loans.

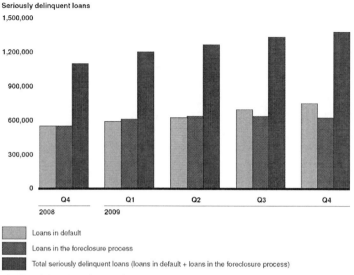

Source: GAO analysis of CoreLogic LP data.

Figure 4. Number of Seriously Delinquent Nonprime Loans, December 31, 2008, through December 31, 2009.

In addition, among all nonprime loans originated from 2000 through 2007, the cumulative percentage that had completed the foreclosure process increased from 10 percent at the end of 2008 to 13 percent at the end of 2009. About 475,000 nonprime loans completed foreclosure in 2009, or roughly 119,000 per quarter. Most (63 percent) of the 759,000 decline in the number of active loans in 2009 was attributable to loans completing foreclosure, rather than to prepayments.

Loan Performance Varied by Market Segment, Product Type, Cohort Year, and Location

In 2009, the performance of nonprime loans differed between the subprime and Alt-A market segments and, within each segment, among product types (fixed-rate mortgages versus ARMs). Nonprime loan performance also varied by the year of loan origination (cohort year) and by location.

Loan Performance by Market Segment and Product Type

In general, the subprime market segment performed worse than the Alt-A segment in 2009.

- Of the 2.76 million subprime loans that were active at the end of 2008, 10 percent (267,000) completed foreclosure in 2009. By comparison, 8 percent (208,000) of the 2.59 million Alt-A loans that were active at the end of 2008 completed foreclosure in 2009.

- Cumulatively, 15 percent (1.41 million) of subprime loans originated from 2000 through 2007 had completed foreclosure as of December 31, 2009, compared with 9 percent (474,000) of Alt-A loans.
- Among active loans at the end of 2009, 36 percent (858,000) of subprime loans were seriously delinquent, compared with 23 percent (517,000) of Alt-A loans.

However, Alt-A loans accounted for 55 percent (152,000) of the 277,000 year-over-year increase in the number of seriously delinquent loans.

Within the subprime and Alt-A market segments, loan performance varied by product type. As we stated in a previous report, serious delinquency rates were higher for certain adjustable-rate products common in the subprime and Alt-A market segments than they were for fixed-rate products or the market as a whole.[19] Although many nonprime borrowers with adjustable-rate loans fell behind on their mortgages before their payments increased, the higher serious delinquency rates for these products may partly reflect the difficulties some borrowers had in making their payments when their interest rates reset to higher levels or when their monthly payments recast to fully amortizing amounts. In the subprime market segment, the serious delinquency rate for short-term hybrid ARMs was 48 percent at the end of 2009, compared with 21 percent for fixed-rate mortgages and 36 percent for all active subprime loans (see Figure 5). The serious delinquency rate increased by 11 percentage points for short-term hybrid ARMs in 2009, compared with 8 percentage points for fixed-rate mortgages and 10 percentage points for all active subprime loans. However, the year-over-year increase in the number of fixed-rate mortgages that were seriously delinquent (over 62,000) was greater than the corresponding increase among short-term hybrid ARMs (over 47,000), even though short-term hybrid ARMs were more prevalent than fixed-rate mortgages among subprime loans.

In the Alt-A segment, the serious delinquency rate at the end of 2009 was higher for payment-option ARMs (38 percent) than for fixed-rate mortgages (15 percent) and active Alt-A mortgages as a whole (23 percent) (see Figure 6). The serious delinquency rate increased by 14 percentage points for payment-option ARMs in 2009, compared with 7 percentage points for fixed-rate mortgages and 9 percentage points for all active Alt-A mortgages. Although the serious delinquency rate grew faster for payment-option ARMs than for fixed-rate mortgages, the year-over-year increase in the number of seriously delinquent loans was greater for fixed-rate mortgages (about 63,000) than for payment-option ARMs (over 36,000), reflecting the preponderance of fixed-rate mortgages in the Alt-A market segment.
Source: GAO analysis of CoreLogic LP data.

	Serious delinquency rate as of December 31, 2009	Change in serious delinquency from year-end 2008 to year-end 2009	
		By percentage point	By number of loans
Total subprime market	36%	+10	+126,308
Short-term hybrid ARMs	48	+11	+47,413
Fixed-rate loans	21	+8	+62,328

Source: GAO analysis of CoreLogic LP data.

Figure 5. Serious Delinquency Rates for Subprime Loans as of December 31, 2009, and Year-over-Year Changes in Serious Delinquency (Dec. 31, 2008-Dec. 31, 2009).

	Serious delinquency rate as of December 31, 2009	Change in serious delinquency from year-end 2008 to year-end 2009	
		By percentage point	By number of loans
Total Alt-A market	23%	+9	+152,168
Payment-option ARMs	38	+14	+36,216
Fixed-rate loans	15	+7	+62,948

Source: GAO analysis of CoreLogic LP data.

Figure 6. Serious Delinquency Rates for Alt-A Loans as of December 31, 2009, and Year-over-Year Changes in Serious Delinquency (Dec. 31, 2008-Dec. 31, 2009).

Loan Performance by Cohort Year

Nonprime mortgages originated from 2004 through 2007 accounted for most of the distressed loans at the end of 2009. Of the active subprime loans originated from 2000 through 2007, 94 percent of those that were seriously delinquent as of December 31, 2009, were from those four cohorts. In addition, loans from these cohorts made up 77 percent of the subprime loans that had completed the foreclosure process. This pattern was more pronounced in the Alt-A market, where 98 percent of the loans that were seriously delinquent as of December 31, 2009, were from the 2004 through 2007 cohorts. Similarly, 95 percent of the Alt-A loans that had completed the foreclosure process were from those cohorts.

Also, within each market segment, the percentage of mortgages completing the foreclosure process generally increased for each successive loan cohort (see Figure 7). Within 3 years of loan origination, 5 percent of subprime loans originated in 2004 had completed the foreclosure process, compared with 8 percent of the 2005 cohort and 16 percent each of the 2006 and 2007 cohorts. Among Alt-A loans, 1 percent of the 2004 cohort had completed the foreclosure process within 3 years of origination, compared with 2 percent of the 2005 cohort, 8 percent of the 2006 cohort, and 13 percent of the 2007 cohort.

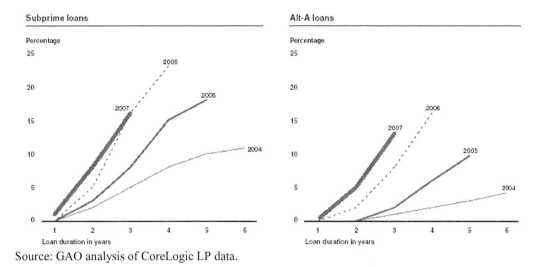

Source: GAO analysis of CoreLogic LP data.

Figure 7. Cumulative Percentage of Subprime and Alt-A Loans That Completed the Foreclosure Process by Cohort Year, 2004 through 2007.

This trend is partly attributable to a decline in the appreciation of or an absolute decline in house prices in much of the country beginning in 2005 and worsening in subsequent years. This situation made it more difficult for some borrowers to sell or refinance their homes to avoid default or foreclosure. In addition, borrowers who purchased homes but came to owe more than the properties were worth, had incentives to stop making mortgage payments to minimize their financial losses. The deterioration in loan performance for the successive cohorts may also reflect an increase in riskier loan and borrower characteristics over time, such as limited documentation of borrower income and higher ratios of debt to household income.

Loan Performance by Location

The proportion of active nonprime loans that were seriously delinquent as of December 31, 2009, varied across the states. Four states—Florida, Illinois, Nevada, and New Jersey—had serious delinquency rates above 35 percent at the end of 2009. Seven states had serious delinquency rates between 30 and 35 percent; 9 states had serious delinquency rates between 25 and 30 percent; and 19 states had serious delinquency rates between 20 and 25 percent. The remaining 12 states had serious delinquency rates of less than 20 percent, including Wyoming's rate of 15 percent, which was the lowest in the country. Detailed data on the performance of nonprime loans by cohort year and location, as well as by market segment and product type, are available in the electronic supplement to this report.[20]

HOUSE PRICE CHANGES AND CERTAIN LOAN AND BORROWER CHARACTERISTICS WERE ASSOCIATED WITH DEFAULT RATES

House price changes and loan and borrower characteristics, such as loan amount, combined LTV (CLTV) ratio, and borrower credit score, were among the variables that we found influenced the likelihood of default on nonprime loans originated from 2004 through 2006, the peak years of nonprime mortgage lending.[21] In addition, nonprime loans that lacked full documentation of borrower income and assets were associated with increased default probabilities, and the influence of borrowers' reported income varied by product type, loan purpose, and the level of documentation. For purchase loans in particular, borrower race and ethnicity were associated with the probability of default. However, these associations should be interpreted with caution because we lack data on factors—such as borrower wealth, first-time homebuyer status, and employment status—that may influence default rates and that may also be associated with race and ethnicity.

Description of our Statistical Model

Prior research has shown that various loan, borrower, and economic variables influence the performance of a mortgage.[22] We developed a statistical model to examine the relationship between such variables and the probability of a loan defaulting within 24 months after the borrower's first payment. We focused on the probability of a loan defaulting within 24 months as our measure of performance because a large proportion of nonprime borrowers had hybrid ARMs and prepaid their loans (e.g., by refinancing) within 2 years. For the purposes of this analysis, we defined a loan as being in default if it was delinquent by at least 90 days, in the foreclosure process (including loans identified as in real-estate-owned status), paid off after being 90 days delinquent or in foreclosure, or already terminated with evidence of a loss.[23]

We developed the statistical model using data on nonprime mortgages originated from 2004 through 2006. To include more information on borrower demographics (i.e., race, ethnicity, and reported income) than is available in the CoreLogic LP data, we matched CoreLogic LP records to HMDA records.[24] Although we matched about three-quarters of the CoreLogic LP loans, and the loans that we could match were similar in important respects to the loans that we could not match, our estimation results may not be fully representative of the securitized portion of the nonprime market or the nonprime market as a whole. (See app. II for additional information on our matching methodology.)

We produced separate estimates for the three most prevalent nonprime loan products: (1) short-term hybrid ARMs, representing 51 percent of nonprime loans originated during this period; (2) longer-term ARMs—those with interest rates that were fixed for 5, 7, or 10 years before adjusting (11 percent of originations); and (3) fixed-rate mortgages (27 percent of originations). For each product type, we produced separate estimates for purchase and refinance loans and for loans to owner-occupants and investors.[25] Twenty-four months after the first loan payment, default rates were highest for short-term hybrid ARMs and, across product types, were generally higher for purchase loans than refinance loans. Appendix I provides additional information about our model and estimation results.

Across Product Types, Changes in House Prices Influenced Default Probabilities

Consistent with prior research, we found that lower rates of house price appreciation or declines in house prices were strongly associated with a higher likelihood of default for each product type and loan purpose.[26] To illustrate the role of this variable, we estimated the default probability assuming house price changes that resembled the actual patterns in certain metropolitan areas, all else being equal.[27] For example, for short-term hybrid ARMs used for home purchases, house price appreciation of 25 percent in the 1st year of the loan and then 20 percent in the 2nd year was associated with about a 5 percent estimated default probability, all else being equal (see Figure 8).[28] Assuming instead that house prices stayed about level in the 1st year of the loan and then dropped by about 10 percent in the 2nd year, the estimated default probability for short-term hybrid ARM purchase loans increased by about 26 percentage points, to 31 percent. These two scenarios approximate the actual house price changes in Los Angeles beginning in early 2004 and mid-2005, respectively, and are emblematic of a number of markets in which a period of substantial house price growth was followed by a period of decline. Assuming that house prices rose by a modest 2 percent per year—approximating the pattern in a number of midwestern markets—the estimated default probability was about 22 percent. As shown in figure 8, the influence of house prices changes on estimated default probabilities was greater for short-term hybrid ARMs than for other mortgage products.

	Estimated probability of default for house price appreciation assumptions (year 1 / year 2)		
	25% / 20% appreciation	2% / 2% appreciation	0% / (10%) appreciation
Short-term hybrid ARMs	5.0%	22.2%	30.9%
	4.1	15.1	20.4
Longer-term ARMs	1.1	4.8	7.7
	0.8	3.9	5.9
Fixed-rate mortgages	1.2	5.4	8.3
	1.4	5.1	7.2

Purchase loan
Refinance loan

Source: GAO analysis of CoreLogic LP, HMDA, FHFA, Census, and BLS data.

Note: This figure compares the estimated probability of default assuming the house price change values shown in the 1st and 2nd year of the loan, all else being equal. The results presented are for owner-occupants. The estimated default probabilities that we present do not necessarily reflect the ultimate performance of any product type.

Figure 8. Estimated Probability of Nonprime Mortgages Defaulting within 24 Months under Different House Price Appreciation Assumptions in the First 2 Years of the Loan, 2004 through 2006 Loans.

House price changes may also reflect broader economic trends, thereby affecting the precision of estimated impacts of other broad economic variables, such as employment growth, on mortgage defaults. In our model, we included a variable for state-level employment growth and noted that the variable was positively correlated with the variable for house price changes.[29] With that in mind, we found that for purchase and refinance loans of all product types, lower rates of employment growth were associated with somewhat higher estimated default probabilities. For example, for short-term hybrid ARM purchase loans, moving from a 4 percent employment growth rate over 24 months to a zero percent employment growth rate was associated with about a 1 percentage point increase in estimated default probabilities. For each of the other product types and loan purposes, the corresponding change was between 1 and 2 percentage points.

Loan Amount, CLTV Ratio, and Credit Score Also Were Associated with the Likelihood of Default for All Product Types

In general, we found that higher loan amounts, higher CLTV ratios, and lower credit scores also were strongly associated with higher likelihoods of default.[30] For example:

- *Loan amount*: For each product type and loan purpose, we estimated the default probability assuming a loan amount near the 25th percentile for that product and purpose and compared this with the estimated default probability assuming a loan amount near the 75th percentile for that product and purpose. For short-term hybrid ARMs used for home purchases, moving from a loan amount of $125,000 to $300,000 was associated with a 6 percentage point increase in estimated default probability, all else being equal (see Figure 9). A similar pattern held across product types, with a larger effect for purchase loans than refinance loans.
- *CLTV ratio*: For each product type and loan purpose, we estimated the default probability assuming a CLTV ratio close to the 25th percentile for that product and

purpose and compared this with the estimated default probability assuming a CLTV ratio close to the 75th percentile for that product and purpose. For short-term hybrid ARMs used for home purchases, moving from a CLTV ratio between 80 and 90 percent to a CLTV ratio of 100 percent or more was associated with a 10 percentage point increase in estimated default probability, all else being equal (see Figure 9). For short-term hybrid ARMs used for refinancing, moving from a CLTV ratio of less than 80 percent to a CLTV ratio of 90 percent was associated with a 7 percentage point increase in estimated default probability. For the other product types, the effects of increasing the CLTV ratio were smaller for both purchase and refinance loans.

- *Borrower credit score*: For each product type and loan purpose, we estimated the default probability assuming a borrower credit score near the 75th percentile for that product and purpose and compared this with the estimated default probability assuming a loan amount near the 25th percentile for that product and purpose. For short-term hybrid ARMs used for home purchases, moving from the higher credit score to the lower one was associated with a 10 percentage point increase in estimated default probability, all else being equal (see Figure 9). For the other product types (whether for home purchase or refinancing), the effects were smaller.

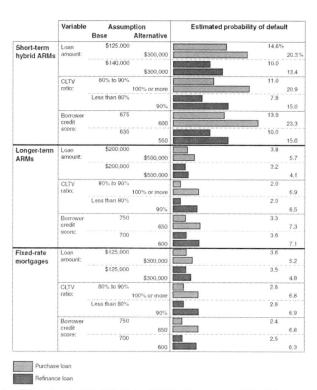

Source: GAO analysis of CoreLogic LP, HMDA, FHFA, Census, and BLS data.
Note: For each variable presented, the figure compares the estimated probability of default assuming values near the 25th and 75th percentile for the respective product type and loan purpose, all else being equal. The results presented in this figure are for loans to owner-occupants.

Figure 9. Estimated Probability of Nonprime Mortgages Defaulting within 24 Months under Different Loan Amount, CLTV Ratio, and Credit Score Assumptions, 2004 through 2006 Loans.

We also found that the difference between the loan's initial interest rate and the relevant interest rate index (interest rate spread) had a significant influence on estimated default probabilities, which is generally consistent with other economic research showing a positive relationship between higher interest rates and default probabilities for nonprime mortgages.[31] Across product types and loan purposes, the interest rate spread had a statistically significant influence on estimated default probabilities. For example, for short-term hybrid ARMs, moving from a spread of 3.0 percent (near the 25th percentile for that product) to a spread of 4.5 percent (near the 75th percentile) was associated with about a 4 percentage point increase in default probability for purchase and refinance loans, all other things being equal.

We also estimated the effect of the debt-service-to-income (DTI) ratio at origination and found that for all product types, this variable did not have a strong influence on the probability of default within 24 months.[32] This relatively weak association, based on the DTI ratio at origination, could differ from the impact of changes to the DTI ratio after origination due, in part, to changes in borrower income or indebtedness. For example, a mortgage that is affordable to the borrower at origination may become less so if the borrower experiences a decline in income or takes on additional nonmortgage debt.[33]

Level of Income Documentation Influenced Default Probabilities, and Associations between Income and Defaults Varied by Product Type, Loan Purpose, and Documentation Level

Loans originated with limited documentation of borrowers' income or assets became prevalent in the nonprime mortgage market, particularly in the Alt-A market segment. We found that documentation of borrower income and assets influenced the probability of default of nonprime loans originated from 2004 through 2006. For purchase and refinance loans of all product types, limited documentation of income and assets was associated with a 1 to 3 percentage point increase in the estimated probability of default, all other things being equal. Our results are generally consistent with prior research showing an association between a lack of documentation and higher default probabilities.[34]

Because our data indicated that borrowers with full documentation loans had different reported risk characteristics (e.g., credit score, CLTV ratio, and reported income) than borrowers with limited documentation loans, we more closely explored the relationship between documentation level and default for short-term hybrid ARMs (the most common nonprime product) taking these differences into account. On average, short-term hybrid ARM purchase loans with limited documentation went to borrowers with higher credit scores, higher reported incomes, and somewhat lower CLTV ratios, compared with borrowers who had full documentation loans.[35] To account for these differences, we estimated default probabilities separately for borrowers with full and limited documentation loans, usi0ng the mean credit score, reported income, and CLTV ratio values specific to each group.[36] Using this method, the expected default probability for the limited documentation group was 3 percentage points *lower* than for the full documentation group, reflecting their better reported risk characteristics. However, *in reality*, borrowers with limited documentation loans had a 5 percentage point *higher* default rate than borrowers with full documentation loans. The differences between the estimated and actual default probabilities for these borrowers suggest that the reported risk characteristics—particularly income—may be misstated, or that other unobserved factors may be associated with the use of the limited documentation feature. For example, mortgage originators or borrowers may have used the limited documentation feature in some cases to overstate the financial resources of borrowers and qualify them for larger, potentially unaffordable loans. In addition, borrowers who used the feature could have experienced decreases in their income after loan origination, thereby making it more difficult for them to stay current on their payments.

We also found that the influence of borrowers' reported income varied by product type and loan purpose and, in some cases, depended on whether the loan had full documentation. For example, for short-term hybrid ARMs used for home purchases and refinancing, moving from $60,000 to $100,000 in reported income was associated with an 1 percentage point decrease in the estimated default probability for loans with full documentation, all else being equal (see Figure 10). However, for loans with limited documentation, the same change in reported income was associated with a slight increase (0.2 percentage points) in estimated default probability for purchase loans and a small decrease (0.5 percentage points) for refinance loans. For fixed-rate mortgages used for purchase and refinancing, moving from $60,000 to $100,000 in reported income was associated with small decreases in estimated default probabilities for both full and limited documentation loans, although the decreases were slightly smaller for loans with limited documentation. For longer-term ARMs, moving from the lower to the higher income level generally did not affect the estimated default probabilities for purchase or refinance loans, regardless of the level of documentation.

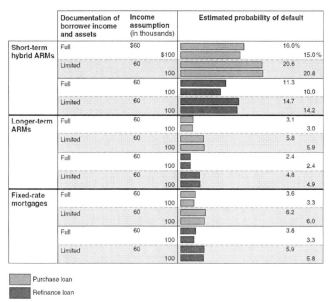

Source: GAO analysis of CoreLogic LP, HMDA, FHFA, Census, and BLS data.

Note: This figure compares the estimated probability of default assuming different levels of reported income, with all other variables for each product type and loan purpose being equal. The results presented in this figure are for owner-occupants.

Figure 10. Estimated Probability of Nonprime Mortgages Defaulting within 24 Months under Different Reported Income Assumptions for Borrowers with and without Full Documentation, 2004 through 2006 Loans.

Associations between Race and Ethnicity and the Likelihood of Default Varied by Product Type and Loan Purpose, but Other Unobserved Variables May Help to Explain these Associations

Some researchers and market observers have noted that the foreclosure crisis has hit minority borrowers particularly hard. We found that, for certain product types and loan purposes, reported race and ethnicity were associated with the probability of default for nonprime mortgages. Not controlling for other variables, black or African-American borrowers had higher 24-month default rates across product types than white borrowers, especially for purchase loans.[37] For example, for short-term hybrid ARMs, black or African-American borrowers had about a 12 percentage point higher default rate than white borrowers for purchase loans and about a 2 percentage point higher default rate for refinance loans (see Figure 11). Additionally, Hispanic or Latino borrowers (of all races) generally had higher default rates than (non-Hispanic) white borrowers. For example, Hispanic or Latino borrowers had about an 8 percentage point higher default rate than white borrowers for short-term hybrid ARM purchase loans and about a 2 percentage point higher default rate for refinance loans. For fixed-rate refinance loans, however, Hispanic borrowers had essentially the same default rate as white borrowers.

Various factors may help to explain some of the observed differences in the default rates between racial and ethnic groups. Across product types, black or African-American borrowers had lower average credit scores and reported incomes than white and Hispanic or Latino borrowers. Also, black or African-American borrowers generally were more likely than white borrowers to have CLTV ratios of 90 percent or more. For short-term hybrid ARMs and longer-term ARMs, black or African-American and Hispanic or Latino borrowers were less likely to have loans that originated in 2004, when house price appreciation was still strong in many parts of the country. In addition, Hispanic or Latino borrowers had a higher incidence of limited documentation loans and were concentrated in California, where house price declines in a number of areas were particularly severe.

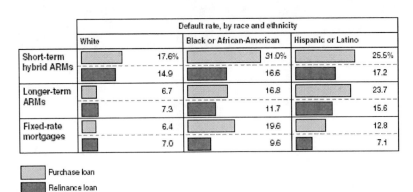

Source: GAO analysis of CoreLogic LP and HMDA data.

Note: The White category excludes people who identified their ethnicity as Hispanic or Latino. The Black or African-American category includes people of all ethnicities. The Hispanic or Latino category includes people of all races. The results presented in this figure are for owner-occupants.

Figure 11. Default Rates for Nonprime Mortgages 24 Months after First Payment, by Race and Ethnicity, Not Controlling for Other Variables, 2004 through 2006 Loans.

Controlling for these variations, we found that the differences in estimated default probabilities by racial and ethnic group were still significant but considerably smaller than the actual observed differences (i.e., the differences without the statistical controls in place). Taking short-term hybrid ARMs used for home purchases as an example, when we estimated default probabilities by racial and ethnic group holding the other variables in our model to the mean values for each group, we found that the estimated default probability for black or African-American borrowers was about 7 percentage points higher than for white borrowers, compared with the observed 12 percentage point difference that we have previously discussed (see Figure 12).[38] Using the same assumptions, the corresponding default probability for Hispanic or Latino borrowers was about 4 percentage points higher than for white borrowers. For short-term hybrid ARMs used for refinancing, black or African-American borrowers had only about a 1 percentage point higher estimated default probability than white borrowers, while Hispanic or Latino borrowers had about the same estimated default probability as white borrowers. d about the same estimated default probability as white borrowers.

Inferences drawn from these statistical results should be viewed with caution because we lack data for variables that may help to explain the remaining differences in estimated default probabilities between borrowers of different racial and ethnic groups. Unobserved factors that may influence the likelihood of default may also be associated with race and ethnicity. For example:

- *First-time homebuyer*: We could not determine which nonprime borrowers were first-time homebuyers, but other evidence suggests that members of minority groups are disproportionately first-time homebuyers.[39] To the extent that black or African-American and Hispanic or Latino borrowers with purchase loans were disproportionately first-time homebuyers, their higher estimated default probabilities may partly reflect limited experience with the risks and costs of homeownership. As shown in figure 12, we found that the differences in estimated default rates between racial and ethnic groups were much smaller for nonprime refinance loans—which, by definition, exclude first-time homebuyers—than they were for purchase loans.

- *Employment status*: We did not have data on the employment status of nonprime borrowers, but unemployment rates are generally higher for black or African-American and Hispanic or Latino workers than for white workers.[40] The higher estimated default probabilities that we found for black or African-American and Hispanic or Latino borrowers may reflect that nonprime borrowers from minority groups were disproportionately affected by unemployment in recent years.

- *Wealth*: Although we obtained data on reported income by matching CoreLogic LP and HMDA records, we did not have information on nonprime borrowers' savings or other assets, which may affect their ability to keep up with their mortgage payments if faced with job loss or other unexpected changes in income or expenses. However, according to the Survey of Consumer Finances, nonwhite and Hispanic families generally are less likely to save or hold financial assets than non-Hispanic white families.[41] Furthermore, the median value of assets for nonwhite and Hispanic families having financial assets is dramatically less than for non-Hispanic white families.[42]

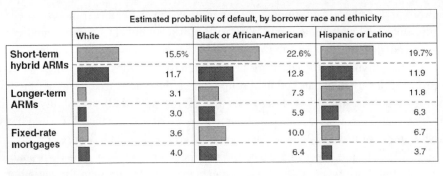

	Estimated probability of default, by borrower race and ethnicity		
	White	Black or African-American	Hispanic or Latino
Short-term hybrid ARMs	15.5%	22.6%	19.7%
	11.7	12.8	11.9
Longer-term ARMs	3.1	7.3	11.8
	3.0	5.9	6.3
Fixed-rate mortgages	3.6	10.0	6.7
	4.0	6.4	3.7

☐ Purchase loan

■ Refinance loan

Source: GAO analysis of CoreLogic LP, HMDA, FHFA, Census, and BLS data.

Note: The White category excludes people who identified their ethnicity as Hispanic or Latino. The Black or African-American category includes people of all ethnicities. The Hispanic or Latino category includes people of all races. The results presented in this figure are for owner-occupants. We estimated the default probability for each group of borrowers setting all variables to their mean values for the respective group.

Figure 12. Estimated Probability of Nonprime Mortgages Defaulting within 24 Figure 12: Estimated Probability of Nonprime Mortgages Defaulting within 24 Months, by Borrower Race and Ethnicity, 2004 through 2006 Loans.

- *Origination channel or lender steering to higher-cost or riskier loans*: We did not have data on whether the nonprime loans were originated by mortgage brokers (intermediaries between borrowers and lenders) or directly by a lender's retail branch, or how the loans were marketed to the borrowers. Some evidence suggests that broker-originated loans were associated with higher default rates and that, at least in some markets, minority families were more likely to access the mortgage market through brokers rather than through retail lenders.[43] In addition, some researchers and market observers have raised concerns that some nonprime loan originators used questionable marketing tactics in lower-income and minority neighborhoods.[44] Such practices may have led borrowers to take out higher-cost or riskier loans than necessary, which may have increased their probability of default.

AVAILABLE NONPRIME MORTGAGE DATA SOURCES PROVIDE USEFUL INFORMATION BUT HAVE CONSTRAINTS THAT MAY BE ADDRESSED, IN PART, BY ONGOING EFFORTS

Several Private and Public Sector Data Sources Cover Nonprime Loans

Mortgage market participants, financial regulators, investors, and public policy analysts use mortgage data for a variety of purposes. Some of the broad uses of such data include monitoring and modeling the performance of mortgages and mortgage-backed securities, assessing the soundness of financial institutions with mortgage-related holdings, and examining fair lending and consumer protection issues. For example, in a 2009 report, we used loan-level mortgage data to assess the implications of proposed mortgage reform legislation on consumer protections and on the availability of mortgage credit.[45] Existing sources of data on nonprime mortgages contain a range of information to support these different uses. Loan-level data with broad national coverage of the nonprime market segment are available from several sources: four mortgage databases (three maintained by private firms and one by the federal government) and two major credit reporting agencies.[46] For comparison, we also reviewed information on a HUD database of FHA-insured mortgages, because the borrower populations served by FHA and the nonprime market earlier in the decade had some similarities (e.g., relatively low credit scores) and the database is rich in detail.

- *CoreLogic LP Asset-Backed Securities (ABS) Database*: A private sector database of nonprime loans that contains information on nonagency securitized mortgages in subprime and Alt-A pools.[47] The data are supplied by a number of different parties, including loan servicers; broker-dealers; and security issuers, trustees, and administrators.
- *CoreLogic LP Loan Level Servicing (LLS) database*: A private sector database of prime, nonprime, and government-guaranteed mortgages that contains data supplied by participating loan servicers.[48] The mortgages include loans in agency and nonagency securitizations and loans held in lenders' portfolios.[49]
- *Lender Processing Services (LPS) Loan Level Data*: Similar to the LLS database, this private sector database contains data supplied by participating loan servicers on prime, nonprime, and government-guaranteed mortgages, including loans in agency and nonagency securitization and loans held in lenders' portfolios.
- *Consumer credit file data*: Two national credit reporting agencies—both private firms—provide anonymous data from consumer credit files that include information on prime, nonprime, and government-guaranteed mortgages.
- *FFIEC HMDA data*: A federal government database that contains information reported by lenders on about 80 percent of all mortgages funded each year, including nonprime loans.
- *HUD Single Family Data Warehouse (SFDW)*: A federal government database with information on mortgages insured by FHA.[50]

Among the data sources that include nonprime mortgages, the private databases and extracts of credit file data can be licensed or purchased for a fee. Recent HMDA data can be acquired at no charge. Some of these data may be subject to use restrictions determined by the provider. The private companies and credit reporting agencies update data on a daily or monthly basis and provide the updated data to users within 1 month or upon request. HMDA data are updated annually with a lag of 9 months.[51]

While these data sources currently offer some similar data elements, the sources vary in their coverage of loan, property, and borrower attributes.[52] In part, this variation reflects the different primary purposes of the data sets. For example, the HMDA database is intended to provide the public with loan data that can assist in identifying potential risks for discriminatory patterns to help enforce antidiscrimination laws and evaluate bank community reinvestment initiatives. Accordingly, the HMDA data provide relatively detailed information about mortgage borrowers but no information about the performance of the loans. By contrast, the CoreLogic LP and LPS databases offer performance data to support the benchmarking and analysis of loans or mortgage-backed securities. Figure 13 presents some of the available data elements, with a focus on data that may assist in evaluating the probability of mortgage default and differences in mortgage outcomes across demographic groups.[53] All of the nonprime data sources report on loan amount. The sources vary in their coverage of other loan attributes, such as mortgage type and performance status. All of the nonprime data sources report the property location at the ZIP code or Census-tract level, while coverage of other property attributes, such as property type and appraised value, varies. In the category of borrower attributes, all but one of the nonprime data sources provide borrower credit score at loan origination and owner-occupancy status. Among the nonprime data sources, only the HMDA data and credit reporting agency data provide additional demographic information on borrowers.

Several other sources of mortgage data provide useful information about the mortgage market, including nonprime loans, but do not provide loan-level detail or, in some cases, lack broad national data coverage. For example, the Mortgage Bankers Association's National Delinquency Survey provides quarterly summary statistics on the performance of the overall mortgage market and different market segments, including subprime loans. RealtyTrac offers data on the number of properties in some stage of the foreclosure process but not data on all active loans. Additionally, federal banking regulators and the government-sponsored enterprises produce free or comparatively low-cost data that are typically aggregated and only cover mortgages within their regulatory jurisdiction.

Limitations in Data Sources Constrain Analysis of Some Aspects of Nonprime Mortgages

Although the selected data sources that include nonprime mortgages contain important loan, property, and borrower characteristics, the sources have a number of constraints. First, the data sources generally lack information on certain attributes that could help inform policy decisions or regulatory efforts to mitigate risk, including the following:

- *Loan attributes*: Although three of the five nonprime data sources provide information on the initial interest rates of the mortgages (and, in some cases, how those interest rates can change over the life of the loan), they do not provide information on other mortgage costs, such as points and fees paid at loan closing.[54] For example, one study that found no evidence of adverse pricing of subprime loans by race, ethnicity, or gender noted that an important caveat to the analysis was the lack of data on points and fees.[55] Consequently, data users have limited ability to evaluate the influence of loan costs on default probabilities or to examine fair lending concerns regarding loan pricing. In addition, while the CoreLogic LP LLS and LPS Loan Level Data databases indicate whether a mortgage was originated by a broker or directly by a lender's retail branch, the other data sources do not. As we have previously noted, some research has suggested associations between origination channel and mortgage performance.

	CoreLogic LP		LPS	Equifax and Experian[a]	FFIEC	HUD
	ABS (Nonagency securitized mortgages in subprime and Alt-A pools)	**LLS** (Prime, nonprime, and government-guaranteed mortgages serviced by participating servicers)	**Loan Level Data** (Prime, nonprime, and government-guaranteed mortgages serviced by participating servicers)	**Credit file information** (Prime, nonprime, and government-guaranteed mortgages as reported to credit reporting agencies by lenders and loan servicers)	**HMDA** (Prime, nonprime, and government-guaranteed mortgages originated by lenders required to report)	**SFDW** (FHA-insured mortgages)
Loan attributes						
Loan amount	X	X	X	X	X	X
Loan start date[b]	X	X	X	X	X	X
Loan purpose (i.e., purchase or refinance)	X	X	X		X	X
Loan status (e.g., delinquent, in foreclosure)	X	X	X	X		X
Outstanding loan balance	X	X	X	X		X
Initial interest rate	X	X	X			X
Loan-to-value ratio at loan origination	X	X	X			X
Product type (e.g., fixed or adjustable rate)	X	X	X			X
Debt service-to-income ratio	X	X				X
Property attributes						
Lowest level geographic indicator	ZIP code	ZIP code	ZIP code	ZIP code	Census tract	ZIP code
Property type (e.g., single unit, multiunit)	X	X	X		X	X
Appraised value at origination or sale price	X	X	X			X
Borrower attributes						
Credit score at loan origination	X	X	X	X		X
Investor or owner-occupant	X	X	X		X	X
Age or date of birth				X		X
Race and ethnicity					X	X
Reported income				Estimates of income are available	X	X
Sex					X	X
First-time homebuyer				May be imputed from borrower's credit account history		X

Source: GAO analysis of information provided by CoreLogic LP, LPS, Experian, Equifax, FFIEC, and HUD.

[a] For all data elements, an "X" indicates that both credit reporting agencies provide the information, and a blank cell indicates that neither agency provides the information. Analysts may be able to calculate values for some data elements without an "X," such as LTV and DTI ratios, depending on the availability of supplemental or estimated information.

[b] Loan start date represents either the loan origination date or, for the credit reporting agencies, the date that the credit account was opened. The specificity of the loan start date varies by data source. The publicly available HMDA data provide the year only, and the credit reporting agencies and one other source provide at least the month and year. The remaining two nonprime data sources provide the day, month, and year; but for some loans, the origination date is imputed from the date of the first loan payment.

Figure 13. Examples of Available Data in Selected Mortgage Data Sources.

- *Borrower attributes*: A number of borrower characteristics that may be associated with default risk generally does not appear in the nonprime data sources we reviewed. For example, first-time homebuyers are not directly identified in any of the nonprime data sources, limiting the ability of analysts to compare the marginal effect of prior homeownership experience on default probabilities. (By comparison, SFDW identifies first-time homebuyers with FHA-insured mortgages and contains data on loan performance.) In addition, none of the nonprime data sources contain information on borrower wealth (savings and other assets), a factor that could affect a borrower's ability to continue making mortgage payments in times of economic stress. With the exception of the credit reporting agencies, the data sources also do not always directly provide information on the amount of borrowers' other mortgage debt (second liens), which may constrain accurate assessment of the relationship between home equity and default.[56] Similarly, data on nonmortgage credit obligations are unavailable, except from the credit reporting agencies, which may limit researchers' understanding of how borrowers' total debt burden affects the mortgages they obtain and their ability to meet mortgage obligations. Also, the data sources lack information on borrower life events that may influence the probability of mortgage default, such as job loss or divorce.

A second type of constraint is that analysts may not be able to generalize their results to the entire nonprime market because certain data sources do not cover all segments of the market and some mortgage originators, securitizers, or servicers do not contribute information. For example, the CoreLogic LP ABS database contains information on a large majority of nonprime mortgages that were securitized but not those that lenders hold in their portfolios. As we have previously noted, researchers have found that nonprime mortgages that were not securitized may have less risky characteristics than those that were securitized. Private sector databases that contain information on both securitized and nonsecuritized mortgages (CoreLogic LP LLS and LPS Loan Level Data) cover the majority of the market but do not provide complete market coverage because not all servicers contribute information to the databases. Similarly, because mortgage originators located outside of metropolitan areas are not required to report their loan information, the HMDA data do not capture many mortgages made in rural areas. By contrast, the credit reporting agencies have broader market coverage but lack data on key mortgage attributes, such as loan type and purpose.

The third constraint we identified is that the existing nonprime data sources cannot readily be combined to create a single database with a more comprehensive set of variables. Merging data sources enables researchers to more thoroughly analyze lending patterns and factors influencing loan performance. However, due to competition and privacy concerns, the selected data sources either elect not to provide or are restricted from providing certain key fields that could be used to merge databases, such as the property address. For example, to match loan records in the CoreLogic LP ABS database and HMDA data, we relied in part on loan origination date fields that are not publicly released due to privacy concerns.[57] Even with the origination date fields, we could not match all of the CoreLogic LP records to HMDA records.

Finally, a user of existing data sources may have the ability to track some specific loans over time but may not easily track a specific borrower or property. Tracking a specific borrower or property over time would provide insights into mortgage outcomes throughout a homeownership experience, even if a borrower refinances into a new mortgage.[58]

Ongoing Federal Efforts May Address Some Constraints in Mortgage Data Sources

Ongoing federal efforts could provide data on the entire mortgage market that potentially would not have some of the constraints that we identified in the existing sources of mortgage data. First, officials from the Board of Governors of the Federal Reserve System (Federal Reserve Board) and Freddie Mac are collaborating on a pilot project to develop a publicly available National Mortgage Database (NMDB). The officials are exploring the feasibility of developing a federally funded, loan-level, and representative database of first-lien mortgages designed to address mortgage-related policy, finance, and business concerns. NMDB would compile data on a representative sample of outstanding mortgages from a national credit reporting agency, supplement those data by matching records to existing mortgage databases (such as the HMDA data), and obtain data unavailable in any existing databases through a survey of borrowers. Since NMDB would include data from a variety of sources, it would provide more comprehensive data on the first-lien mortgage market than are currently available. If implemented, the combined database would contain loan-level information on (1) mortgage terms; (2) mortgage performance from origination to termination; (3) borrowers' other credit circumstances over the life of the loan; (4) borrower demographics; and (5) other borrower attributes, such as key life events and shopping behavior.

Second, the Dodd-Frank Wall Street Reform and Consumer Protection Act provides for additional compilation of HMDA data, such as borrower age and credit score, loan origination channel, and—as the Bureau of Consumer Financial Protection deems appropriate—a unique identifier for the loan originator and a universal loan identifier.[59] Additionally, the act includes the creation of a publicly available Default and Foreclosure database that would include Census tract-level information on the number and percentage of mortgages delinquent for more than 30 and 90 days, real-estate-owned properties, mortgages in the foreclosure process, mortgages with negative equity, and other information. If implemented, the universal loan identifier could facilitate matching among mortgage databases, and the HMDA data would become more comprehensive.

OBSERVATIONS

The growth of the nonprime market earlier in this decade was accompanied by a shift toward increasingly risky mortgage products. Nonprime loans provided homeownership and refinancing opportunities that may have benefited many households. However, many nonprime loans had features or were underwritten to standards that made them vulnerable to default and foreclosure, particularly in recent years when house prices began to stagnate and decline and economic conditions eroded more broadly. As a result, millions of nonprime borrowers have lost their homes or are in danger of doing so. These issues have particular salience for minority borrowers, who have experienced particularly high default rates.

The persistently weak performance of nonprime mortgages suggests that loan performance problems in the nonprime market will not be resolved quickly, and underscores the importance of federal efforts to assist distressed borrowers and prevent a recurrence of the aggressive lending practices that helped precipitate the foreclosure crisis. As lawmakers seek to reform mortgage lending practices, they will need to consider how their efforts may affect consumer protections, the availability of mortgage credit, and progress toward the goal of sustainable homeownership.

Data on the performance of nonprime loans and on the borrowing and lending practices associated with them can help analysts and policymakers assess the potential effects of proposed reforms and evaluate the results of their implementation. Although extensive data are available on nonprime loans, no one data source is comprehensive. Existing data sources can be combined with effort, but even then certain data that could inform understanding of the nonprime market—such as total mortgage costs and first-time homebuyer status—are not readily available. Having access to a more comprehensive set of data might have enhanced the ability of researchers, regulators, and investors to monitor lending practices, evaluate mortgage performance, and assess the mortgage outcomes for different groups of borrowers. Ongoing federal efforts, including the NMDB pilot project, may improve the quality and availability of mortgage market data going forward.

As agreed with your offices, unless you publicly announce its contents earlier, we plan no further distribution of this report until 30 days from the report date. At that time, we will send copies of this report to the appropriate congressional committees and other interested parties. In addition, the report will be made available at no charge on GAO's Web site at http://www.gao.gov.

If you or your staffs have any questions about this report, please contact me at (202) 512-8678 or shearw@gao.gov. Contact points for our Offices of Congressional Relations and Public Affairs may be found on the last page of this report. Key contributors to this report are listed in appendix III.

William B. Shear

William B. Shear
Director, Financial Markets
and Community Investment

APPENDIX I. DESCRIPTION OF THE ECONOMETRIC ANALYSIS OF NONPRIME MORTGAGE DEFAULT PROBABILITIES

This appendix describes the econometric model we developed to examine the relationship between variables representing loan attributes, borrower characteristics, and economic conditions and the probability of a nonprime loan entering default within 24 months after the first loan payment. Certain loan attributes and borrower characteristics have been associated with a higher risk of mortgage default. For example, lower down payments, lower borrower credit scores, and limited documentation of borrowers' income and assets have been cited as increasing the risk of default. Economic conditions, such as house price changes, have also been associated with default risk.

Since minority borrowers have accounted for a larger share of the nonprime mortgage market than the mortgage market as a whole, associations between race and ethnicity and nonprime mortgage performance also are of interest. However, data limitations have complicated efforts to analyze the demographic characteristics of nonprime borrowers, such as race, ethnicity, and income. Existing data sets either provide detailed information about nonprime loans but limited information about the borrowers (e.g., CoreLogic LoanPerformance (CoreLogic LP) data) or provide more extensive information about borrowers but not about loan performance over time (e.g., Home Mortgage Disclosure Act (HMDA) data). To include information on the demographic characteristics of nonprime borrowers in our model, we matched records in the CoreLogic LP data to HMDA records. For securitized first-lien nonprime loans originated from 2004 through 2006, we achieved a match rate of approximately 73 percent, representing about 6.9 million records. (App. II contains a more detailed discussion of our methodology.)

Of all the CoreLogic LP records that we matched to HMDA records, we used those for which the associated property was located in an area covered by the Federal Housing Finance Agency's (FHFA) house price indexes (HPI) for metropolitan areas, approximately 92 percent of loans.[60] Based on each associated property's state and Census tract, we also incorporated employment data from the Bureau of Labor Statistics (BLS) and data from the 2000 Census to control for various economic conditions and neighborhood characteristics. For each loan, we determined the performance status 24 months after the month of the first payment. We defined a loan as being in default if it was delinquent by at least 90 days, in the foreclosure process (including loans identified as in real-estate-owned status), paid off after being 90-days delinquent or in foreclosure, or already terminated with evidence of a loss.

We separately analyzed the three most prevalent types of nonprime loans: short-term hybrid adjustable-rate mortgages (ARM) (ARMs with initial 2- or 3-year fixed-rate periods followed by frequent interest rate adjustments); fixed-rate mortgages; and other longer-term ARMs (ARMs with initial 5-, 7-, or 10-year fixed-rate periods). For each product type, we estimated default probabilities for purchase money loans separately from loans for refinance, and for each product type and loan purpose, we examined separately loans made to owner-occupants and investors. Our primary reason for examining performance by product type, loan purpose, and occupancy status is that borrower incentives and motivations may vary for loans with different characteristics and purposes. For example, because of their early, frequent, and upward interest rate adjustments, short-term hybrid ARMs provide a stronger incentive for a borrower to exit earlier from a mortgage as compared with fixed-rate mortgages or longer-term ARMs. Also, an investor may not react the same way as an owner-occupant may react when facing similar economic circumstances.

We estimated separate default models for each mortgage product type, although the general underlying structure of the models was similar. We used a logistic regression model to explain the probability of loan default, based on the observed pattern of actual defaults and the values of variables representing loan attributes, borrower characteristics, and economic conditions (see table 1). Some variables describe conditions at the time of mortgage origination, such as the loan-to-value (LTV) ratio, the borrower's credit score, and the borrower's reported income. Other factors influencing loan performance vary over time in ways that can be observed, or at least approximated. For example, greater house price appreciation (HPA) contributes to greater housing equity, thus reducing the probability that a borrower, if facing financial distress, views defaulting on a loan as a better option than prepaying. More generally, greater house price appreciation creates equity that may induce a borrower to prepay, which eliminates any default risk that would remain if the loan were active. Some potentially significant determinants of mortgage default, such as job loss or illness, are not available for inclusion in our model. In addition, we lack data on certain factors—such as borrower wealth and first-time homebuyer status—that could be especially relevant to explaining actual loan performance.

Table 1. Variables Used in the Logistic Regression Models.

Variable	Variable description
Mortgage default (dependent variable)	One if the mortgage was in default by 24 months after the month of first payment, 0 otherwise. We defined a loan as in default if it was delinquent by at least 90 days, in the foreclosure process (including loans identified as in real-estate-owned status), paid off after being 90-days delinquent or in foreclosure, or with evidence of a loss.
Loan origination period indicator	A series of 0-1 categorical variables indicating whether the loan originated in the first or second half of 2004, 2005, or 2006. The omitted category was early 2005.
Loan amount	Defined as a continuous variable representing the original loan amount.
House price appreciation	Defined using FHFA's metropolitan house price indexes and split into time periods measuring (1) appreciation during the 1st year of the loan and (2) the difference in appreciation between the 1st and 2nd years of the loan. We assigned each loan to a metropolitan area using the property ZIP code information in the CoreLogic LP database and data that relate ZIP codes to Core-based Statistical Areas.
Combined loan-to-value (CLTV) ratio	This represents the amount of the mortgage and any known associated second lien, divided by the house value. Because the CoreLogic LP data do not capture all second liens, the reported CLTV ratios are likely understated for some loans. This complicates interpretation of CLTV in continuous form, since many loans with a value of exactly 80 may have "true" CLTV values of 90 or 100. Therefore, we defined a series of 0-1 categorical variables indicating the specific CLTV value or range, as follows: less than 80, equal to 80, more than 80 and less than 90, equal to 90, more than 90 and less than 100, and greater than or equal to 100. The omitted category was "equal to 80."
Debt-service-to-income (DTI) ratio	This represents the borrower's total monthly debt service pay-ments, divided by monthly gross income. Since this information is not available for many loans, we constructed a set of 0-1 cate-gorical variables indicating the DTI range, as follows: less than 35 percent, 35 to 41 percent, greater than 41 percent, and missing. The omitted category was "35 to 41 percent."
FICO score	FICO score (at loan origination) represents a measure of the borrower's credit history. Defined as a single continuous variable for fixed-rate mortgages and as a set of continuous variables split into low, middle, and high ranges for the two types of adjustable-rate mortgages. Specifically, for short-term hybrid ARMs, the low FICO range was either 600 or the FICO score itself if the FICO score was below 600; the middle range varied between 0 and 60, with a minimum of 0 if the FICO score was 600 or less, a maximum of 60 if the FICO score was above 660, and between 0 and 60 if the FICO score was between 600 and 660; and the high range was 0 for FICO scores of 660 or less and the difference between the FICO score and 660 for FICO scores above 660. Because Alt-A borrowers generally

Table 1. (Continued)

Variable	Variable description
FICO score	had higher credit scores, the range boundaries for longer-term ARMs were 680 and 740, rather than 600 and 660.
High cost spread	This variable incorporates information about the loan's high cost status as reported in the HMDA data. For fixed-rate and longer-term adjustable rate mortgages, we defined this to be a 0-1 variable in which the value of 1 indicates whether the loan's annual percentage rate as calculated by the loan's originator exceeded a benchmark rate by at least 3 percentage points, and 0 other-wise. For short-term hybrid ARMs, we defined a series of 0-1 categorical variables based on the magnitude of this reported spread. The categories are as follows: miss-ing (an indication that the spread is presumed to be less than 3 percent); the spread is greater than or equal to 3 percent but is less than 4 percent; greater than or equal to 4 and less than 5 percent; greater than or equal to 5 and less than 6 percent; and greater than or equal to 6 percent. The omitted category was "is greater than or equal to 3 percent but is less than 4 percent."
Initial interest rate	Defined as a pair of continuous variables that split a loan's original interest rate into two parts: a relevant Treasury rate at the time of origination, and the difference between the loan's initial interest and that Treasury rate. For short-term hybrid ARMs, we used the 2-year Treasury constant maturity rate; for fixed rate mortgages, we used the 10-year Treasury constant maturity rate; and for longer-term ARMs, we used the 5-year Treasury constant maturity rate.
ARM initial fixed-rate period	For longer-term ARMs, we defined a set of categorical variables describing the number of years for which the initial interest rate is fixed. The categories are 5 years, 7 years, and 10 years. The omitted category was 5 years.
Documentation of borrower income and assets	One if full documentation, 0 otherwise.
Income if full documentation, and income if limited documentation	Defined as a pair of continuous variables permitting the possibility that the effects of reported income (from HMDA) differ depending on whether the . loan had full documentation of income or had limited documentation of income.
Race	Defined as a series of 0-1 categorical variables based on the borrower's reported race. The categories are as follows: Black (1 if black or African-American, 0 otherwise); Asian (1 if Asian, 0 otherwise); White (1 if white, 0 otherwise); and Other (1 if other reported category, 0 otherwise). We excluded observations for which borrower race was not available. The omitted category is White.
Ethnicity	One if Hispanic or Latino, 0 otherwise. We excluded observations for which borrower ethnicity was not available.
Change in employment growth	We cannot observe borrowers' employment status. As an indicator of economic conditions in the borrower's community, we used a state measure of employment growth over the 24- month performance window. These data are from BLS.

Table 1. (Continued)

Variable	Variable description
Census neighborhood characteristics[a]	We defined a series of 0-1 indicators representing high and low levels of education, unearned income (e.g., interest or dividends), new versus old housing, and housing vacancy rates that may provide information about housing and borrower characteristics in the Census tract where the property is located. Specifically, the indicators were as follows: • 1 if property is in a tract with a high incidence of less than high school education, 0 otherwise • 1 if property is in a tract with a high incidence of greater than college education, 0 otherwise • 1 if property is in a tract with a low incidence of unearned income, 0 otherwise • 1 if property is in a tract with a high incidence of unearned income, 0 otherwise • 1 if property is in a tract with a high incidence of very old housing, 0 otherwise • 1 if property is in a tract with a high incidence of vacant housing, 0 therwise
State	Defined as a series of 0-1 categorical variables based on the property's state. The omitted category is Texas.
Regulator	We defined a series of 0-1 indicators representing the regulatory agencies with oversight over the practices of the lending institutions reporting HMDA data. Specifically, the indicators were the Office of the Comptroller of the Currency, Federal Reserve System, Federal Deposit Insurance Corporation, Office of Thrift Supervision, and Department of Housing and Urban Development. We excluded loans made by institutions overseen by the National Credit Union Administration. The omitted category was the Federal Reserve System.

Source: GAO.

[a] For each of the Census neighborhood characteristics variables, we used information on the distribution of values across all Census tracts for the relevant Census data element. We defined cutoffs for a high or low incidence based on, approximately, the top or bottom 10 percent of the distribution for each data element.

Tables 2 through 4 provide information on the number of loans and mean values for each of the product types for which we estimated default probabilities. Short-term hybrid ARMs were the most prevalent type of mortgage, and purchase loans were more prevalent than refinance loans, except among fixed-rate mortgages. Default rates were highest for short-term hybrid ARMs and generally higher for purchase loans than for refinance loans, except for fixed-rate and longer-term ARM loans to investors.

Table 2. Mean Values for Short-term Hybrid ARMs.

	Purchase loans		Refinance loans	
	Owner-occupants	Investors	Owner-occupants	Investors
Number of observations	1,189,791	115,587	1,187,804	80,565
Mortgage in default by 24 months	0.227	0.233	0.157	0.203
Loan amount (thousands)	228.851	170.519	236.064	177.615
HPA: First year of the loan	1.084	1.087	1.089	1.076
HPA: Difference between 1st and 2nd year of the loan	0.081	0.075	0.085	0.071
Change in employment growth	1.026	1.026	1.025	1.023
DTI ratio missing	0.256	0.200	0.248	0.207
DTI ratio less than 35 percent	0.143	0.296	0.196	0.305
DTI ratio 35 percent to 41 percent	0.155	0.168	0.150	0.146
DTI ratio greater than 41 percent	0.446	0.335	0.406	0.343
FICO score	639.527	673.047	597.178	632.890
FICO score, low range	593.282	597.380	576.197	589.052
FICO score, middle range	32.969	45.423	16.970	31.269
FICO score, high range	13.276	30.245	4.011	12.570
CLTV ratio less than 80	0.034	0.056	0.346	0.368
CLTV ratio equal to 80	0.138	0.112	0.133	0.189
CLTV ratio between 80 and 90	0.035	0.111	0.193	0.194
CLTV ratio equal to 90	0.079	0.414	0.141	0.212
CLTV ratio between 90 and 100	0.151	0.234	0.101	0.035
CLTV ratio greater than or equal to 100	0.563	0.073	0.087	0.002
Full documentation	0.549	0.461	0.652	0.491
Reported income (thousands)	85.556	113.446	79.432	108.972
Reported income among borrowers with full documentation loans (thousands)	74.882	99.807	73.537	93.247
Reported income among borrowers with limited documentation loans (thousands)	98.558	125.119	90.479	124.118
High cost spread, less than 3 percent	0.196	0.225	0.190	0.189
High cost spread, between 3 and 4 percent	0.155	0.155	0.172	0.148
High cost spread, between 4 and 5 percent	0.216	0.186	0.205	0.178
High cost spread, between 5 and 6 percent	0.244	0.207	0.233	0.220
High cost spread, 6 percent or more	0.189	0.226	0.200	0.265
2-year Treasury constant maturity rate	3.784	3.664	3.658	3.682
Spread over 2-year Treasury constant maturity rate	3.765	4.479	4.019	4.502
High incidence of less than high school education	0.093	0.146	0.095	0.176
High incidence of more than college education	0.040	0.034	0.046	0.033
Low incidence of wealth	0.090	0.225	0.089	0.243
High incidence of wealth	0.051	0.037	0.063	0.029

Table 2. (Continued)

	Purchase loans		Refinance loans	
	Owner-occupants	Investors	Owner-occupants	Investors
High incidence of old housing	0.062	0.176	0.071	0.191
High incidence of vacant units	0.044	0.096	0.042	0.085
Asian	0.048	0.047	0.030	0.032
Black or African-American	0.206	0.301	0.196	0.343
Other race	0.022	0.015	0.021	0.018
Hispanic or Latino	0.279	0.157	0.191	0.152

Source: GAO analysis of CoreLogic LP, HMDA, FHFA, Census, and BLS data.

Table 3. Mean Values for Longer-term ARMs.

	Purchase loans		Refinance loans	
	Owner-occupants	Investors	Owner-occupants	Investors
Number of observations	227,066	52,070	127,675	26,171
Mortgage in default by 24 months	0.115	0.099	0.093	0.101
Loan amount (thousands)	341.356	223.645	386.097	260.090
HPA: First year of the loan	1.073	1.092	1.063	1.065
HPA: Difference between 1st and 2nd year of the loan	0.098	0.099	0.098	0.094
Change in employment growth	1.025	1.029	1.020	1.023
DTI ratio missing	0.334	0.322	0.297	0.335
DTI ratio less than 35 percent	0.190	0.294	0.245	0.304
DTI ratio 35 percent to 41 percent	0.201	0.170	0.194	0.160
DTI ratio greater than 41 percent	0.275	0.214	0.264	0.202
FICO score	711.103	726.171	689.428	710.290
FICO score, low range	672.704	677.005	663.126	673.242
FICO score, middle range	30.268	37.721	21.195	29.878
FICO score, high range	8.130	11.445	5.107	7.170
CLTV ratio less than 80	0.081	0.156	0.458	0.612
CLTV ratio equal to 80	0.190	0.241	0.162	0.210
CLTV ratio between 80 and 90	0.028	0.068	0.114	0.065
CLTV ratio equal to 90	0.064	0.192	0.074	0.077
CLTV ratio between 90 and 100	0.161	0.174	0.110	0.029
CLTV ratio greater than or equal to 100	0.476	0.169	0.081	0.007
Full documentation	0.383	0.390	0.426	0.312
Reported income (thousands)	129.498	184.110	132.477	187.598
Reported income among borrowers with full documentation loans (thousands)	109.492	158.083	111.412	157.090
Reported income among borrowers with limited documentation loans (thousands)	141.927	200.770	148.103	201.410
High cost spread indicator	0.143	0.222	0.206	0.197
5-year Treasury constant maturity rate	4.225	4.217	4.240	4.219

Table 3. (Continued)

	Purchase loans		Refinance loans	
	Owner-occupants	Investors	Owner-occupants	Investors
Spread over 5-year Treasury constant maturity rate	2.079	2.698	2.107	2.460
High incidence of less than high school education	0.057	0.075	0.059	0.106
High incidence of more than college education	0.127	0.079	0.140	0.096
Low incidence of wealth	0.043	0.090	0.040	0.116
High incidence of wealth	0.129	0.080	0.161	0.084
High incidence of old housing	0.050	0.070	0.049	0.096
High incidence of vacant units	0.051	0.093	0.046	0.075
Asian	0.076	0.063	0.059	0.056
Black or African-American	0.089	0.107	0.092	0.132
Other race	0.023	0.014	0.022	0.015
Hispanic or Latino	0.206	0.117	0.166	0.122

Source: GAO analysis of CoreLogic LP, HMDA, FHFA, Census, and BLS data.

Table 4. Mean Values for Fixed-rate Mortgages.

	Purchase loans		Refinance loans	
	Owner-occupants	Investors	Owner-occupants	Investors
Number of observations	350,486	104,889	621,968	96,326
Mortgage in default by 24 months	0.092	0.077	0.074	0.070
Loan amount (thousands)	230.568	151.556	233.057	161.606
HPA: First year of the loan	1.071	1.088	1.081	1.085
HPA: Difference between 1st and 2nd year of the loan	0.063	0.063	0.079	0.066
Change in employment growth	1.024	1.027	1.022	1.025
DTI ratio missing	0.538	0.576	0.410	0.535
DTI ratio less than 35 percent	0.129	0.181	0.188	0.211
DTI ratio 35 percent to 41 percent	0.115	0.098	0.125	0.091
DTI ratio greater than 41 percent	0.218	0.146	0.278	0.162
FICO score	691.031	721.308	643.810	694.148
CLTV ratio less than 80	0.111	0.165	0.500	0.639
CLTV ratio equal to 80	0.180	0.244	0.128	0.188
CLTV ratio between 80 and 90	0.035	0.065	0.151	0.083
CLTV ratio equal to 90	0.068	0.266	0.082	0.073
CLTV ratio between 90 and 100	0.170	0.136	0.084	0.014
CLTV ratio greater than or equal to 100	0.435	0.124	0.055	0.002
Full documentation	0.506	0.507	0.649	0.466
Reported income (thousands)	99.991	144.007	87.518	137.163

Table 4. (Continued)

	Purchase loans		Refinance loans	
	Owner-occupants	Investors	Owner-occupants	Investors
Reported income among borrowers with full documentation loans (thousands)	85.711	125.619	77.873	114.861
Reported income among borrowers with limited documentation loans (thousands)	114.641	162.941	105.313	156.605
High cost spread indicator	0.257	0.381	0.361	0.319
10-year Treasury constant maturity rate	4.498	4.451	4.477	4.440
Spread over 10-year Treasury constant maturity rate	2.546	2.775	2.725	2.640
High incidence of less than high school education	0.057	0.095	0.087	0.133
High incidence of more than college education	0.081	0.058	0.063	0.060
Low incidence of wealth	0.059	0.127	0.084	0.175
High incidence of wealth	0.097	0.055	0.083	0.049
High incidence of old housing	0.064	0.143	0.065	0.151
High incidence of vacant units	0.044	0.085	0.045	0.071
Asian	0.052	0.059	0.030	0.042
Black or African-American	0.126	0.143	0.167	0.192
Other race	0.016	0.012	0.020	0.016
Hispanic or Latino	0.176	0.103	0.166	0.113

Source: GAO analysis of CoreLogic LP, HMDA, FHFA, Census, and BLS data.

The results of our analysis are presented in tables 5 through 8. We ran 12 regressions: separate owner-occupant and investor regressions for purchase and refinance loans of three product types (short-term hybrid ARMs, fixed-rate mortgages, and longer-term ARMs). For short-term hybrid ARMs, the most prevalent product type, we present the results for purchase and refinance loans to owner-occupants (table 5) and investors (table 6). For the other product types, we present the results for purchase and refinance loans to owner-occupants only (tables 7 and 8); the results for investors were substantively similar. We present coefficient estimates as well as a transformation of the coefficients into a form that can be interpreted as the marginal effect of each variable on the estimated probability of default. This marginal effect is the calculation of the change in the estimated probability of default that would result if a variable's standard deviation were added to that variable's mean value, while all other variables are held at their mean values. This permits a comparison of the impact of different variables within and across product types. In general, HPA, loan amount, CLTV ratio, and FICO score had substantial marginal effects across different product types and loan purposes. Specifically, lower HPA, higher loan amount, higher CLTV ratio, and lower FICO scores were associated with higher likelihoods of default. The observed effects for DTI ratio were smaller. Documentation of borrower income and assets and a loan's interest rate spread over the applicable Treasury rate had substantial marginal effects. Limited documentation and higher interest rate spreads were associated with higher default probabilities.

Table 5. Estimation Results for Short-term Hybrid ARMs for Owner-Occupants.

	Purchase loans			Refinance loans		
	Coefficient	Significance	Marginal effect	Coefficient	Significance	Marginal effect
Number of observations: Purchase loans – 1,189,791 Refinance loans – 1,187,804						
Intercept	10.904	***		10.207	***	
Loan amount	0.002	***	5.11	0.002	***	3.24
HPA: First year of the loan	(7.974)	***	(8.51)	(6.752)	***	(5.31)
HPA: Difference between 1st and 2nd year of the loan	2.850	***	3.45	2.328	***	1.92
Change in employment growth	(2.246)	***	(0.81)	(3.994)	***	(1.03)
DTI ratio missing	0.023	***	0.15	0.024	**	0.11
DTI ratio less than 35 percent	(0.028)	***	(0.14)	(0.025)	**	(0.10)
DTI ratio greater than 41 percent	0.079	***	0.59	0.066	***	0.35
FICO score, low range	(0.006)	***	(1.39)	(0.005)	***	(1.55)
FICO score, middle range	(0.009)	***	3 (.08)	(0.006)	***	(1.32)
FICO score, high range	(0.006)	***	(2.18)	(0.007)	***	(1.04)
CLTV ratio less than 80	(0.962)	***	(2.42)	(0.498)	***	(2.28)
CLTV ratio between 80 and 90	(0.519)	***	(1.36)	0.028	***	0.12
CLTV ratio equal to 90	(0.361)	***	(1.38)	0.242	***	0.91
CLTV ratio between 90 and 100	(0.071)	***	(0.37)	0.386	***	1.28
CLTV ratio greater than or equal to 100	0.249	***	1.88	0.804	***	2.59
Full documentation	(0.174)	***	(1.24)	(0.159)	***	(0.77)
Reported income if full documentation	(0.002)	***	(1.32)	(0.003)	***	(1.61)
Reported income if limited documentation	0.0003	***	0.25	(0.001)	***	(0.56)
High cost spread, less than 3 percent	(0.167)	***	(0.95)	(0.116)	***	(0.47)
High cost spread, between 4 and 5 percent	0.106	***	0.65	0.066	***	0.28
High cost spread, between 5 and 6 percent	0.194	***	1.26	0.092	***	0.42
High cost spread, 6 percent or more	0.121	***	0.71	0.053	***	0.22
2-year Treasury constant maturity rate	0.195	***	2.87	0.259	***	2.95
Spread over 2-year Treasury constant maturity rate	0.160	***	3.02	0.251	***	3.93
High incidence of less than high school education	(0.015)		(0.06)	(0.023)	**	(0.07)
High incidence of more than college education	(0.141)	***	(0.40)	(0.115)	***	(0.25)
Low incidence of wealth	0.255	***	1.09	0.042	***	0.13
High incidence of wealth	(0.247)	***	(0.78)	(0.142)	***	(0.36)
High incidence of old housing	0.163	***	0.58	0.129	***	0.35
High incidence of vacant units	0.201	***	0.61	0.115	***	0.24
Asian	0.023	*	0.07	(0.047)	***	(0.08)
Black or African-American	0.483	***	3.05	0.042	***	0.17
Other race	0.081	***	0.18	(0.017)		(0.03)
Hispanic or Latino	0.188	***	1.27	0.093	***	0.39

Source: GAO analysis of CoreLogic LP, HMDA, FHFA, Census, and BLS data.

Note: In the "Significance" columns, the symbols *, **, and *** indicate statistical significance at the 10 percent, 5 percent, and 1 percent levels, respectively. A blank cell in these columns indicates that the coefficient for the variable was not statistically significant at these levels.

Table 6. Estimation Results for Short-term Hybrid ARMs for Investors.

	Purchase loans			Refinance loans		
	Coefficient	Significance	Marginal effect	Coefficient	Significance	Marginal effect
Number of observations: Purchase loans - 115,587 Refinance loans - 80,565						
Intercept	12.020	***		15.119	***	
Loan amount	0.003	***	4.79	0.001	***	2.23
HPA: First year of the loan	(8.384)	***	(7.42)	(7.717)	***	(6.71)
HPA: Difference between 2st and 3nd year of the loan	0.427		0.41	1.393	***	1.25
Change in employment growth	(2.965)	***	(1.00)	(7.628)	***	(2.35)
DTI ratio missing	0.005		0.02	0.015		0.08
DTI ratio less than 35 percent	0.079	***	0.45	(0.010)		(0.06)
DTI ratio greater than 41 percent	0.031		0.18	0.018		0.11
FICO score, low range	(0.005)	***	(0.64)	(0.005)	***	(1.28)
FICO score, middle range	(0.009)	***	(2.33)	(0.006)	***	(1.83)
FICO score, high range	(0.008)	***	(3.58)	(0.010)	***	(2.89)
CLTV ratio less than 80	(0.550)	***	(1.50)	(0.526)	***	(2.88)
CLTV ratio between 80 and 90	0.302	***	1.22	0.239	***	1.22
CLTV ratio equal to 90	0.547	***	3.67	0.513	***	2.81
CLTV ratio between 90 and 100	0.568	***	3.24	0.676	***	1.62
CLTV ratio greater than or equal to 100	0.869	***	3.04	0.237		0.14
Full documentation	(0.212)	***	(1.26)	(0.276)	***	(1.63)
Reported income if full documentation	(0.003)	***	(2.34)	0.000		0.24
Reported income if limited documentation	(0.003)	***	(2.29)	0.000		0.30
High cost spread, less than 3 percent	(0.215)	***	(1.08)	(0.054)		(0.26)
High cost spread, between 4 and 5 percent	0.021		0.10	0.083	**	0.40
High cost spread, between 5 and 6 percent	0.116	***	0.59	0.110	**	0.57
High cost spread greater than or equal to 6 percent	(0.041)		(0.21)	0.101	**	0.56
2-year Treasury constant maturity rate	0.225	***	2.81	0.271	***	3.67
Spread over 2-year Treasury constant maturity rate	0.109	***	1.65	0.198	***	3.45
High incidence of less than high school education	0.048	*	0.21	0.028		0.13
High incidence of more than college education	(0.389)	***	(0.85)	(0.229)	***	(0.51)
Low incidence of wealth	0.504	***	2.81	0.147	***	0.80
High incidence of wealth	(0.330)	***	(0.76)	(0.134)	*	(0.28)
High incidence of old housing	0.302	***	1.48	0.127	***	0.63
High incidence of vacant units	0.275	***	1.03	0.098	***	0.34
Asian	(0.122)	**	(0.32)	(0.065)		(0.14)
Black or African-American	0.367	***	2.22	0.102	***	0.61
Other race	(0.007)		(0.01)	(0.104)		(0.17)
Hispanic or Latino	(0.160)	***	(0.71)	(0.071)	**	(0.31)

Source: GAO analysis of CoreLogic LP, HMDA, FHFA, Census, and BLS data.

Note: In the "Significance" columns, the symbols *, **, and *** indicate statistical significance at the 10 percent, 5 percent, and 1 percent levels, respectively. A blank cell in these columns indicates that the coefficient for the variable was not statistically significant at these levels.

Table 7. Estimation Results for Longer-term ARMs for Owner-Occupants.

	Purchase loans			Refinance loans		
	Coefficient	Significance	Marginal effect	Coefficient	Significance	Marginal effect
Number of observations: Purchase loans - 227,066 Refinance loans - 127,675						
Intercept	14.625	***		17.372	***	
Loan amount	0.001	***	1.59	0.0009	***	0.90
HPA: First year of the loan	(7.409)	***	(2.35)	(7.719)	***	(1.99)
HPA: Difference between 1st and 2nd year of the loan	3.433	***	1.26	2.739	***	0.78
Change in employment growth	(7.745)	***	(0.79)	(9.297)	***	(0.80)
DTI ratio missing	0.045	*	0.09	0.059	*	0.10
DTI ratio less than 35 percent	(0.070)	***	(0.12)	(0.142)	***	(0.21)
DTI ratio greater than 41 percent	0.042	**	0.08	0.069	**	0.11
FICO score, low range	(0.006)	***	(0.43)	(0.007)	***	(0.62)
FICO score, middle range	(0.009)	***	(0.89)	(0.010)	***	(0.79)
FICO score, high range	(0.011)	***	(0.69)	(0.012)	***	(0.54)
CLTV ratio less than 80	(0.856)	***	(0.92)	(0.757)	***	(1.13)
CLTV ratio between 80 and 90	(0.564)	***	(0.39)	0.218	***	0.25
CLTV ratio equal to 90	(0.428)	***	(0.44)	0.487	***	0.48
CLTV ratio between 90 and 100	0.330	***	0.56	0.757	***	0.94
CLTV ratio greater than or equal to 100	0.706	***	1.81	1.143	***	1.29
Full documentation	(0.634)	***	(1.17)	(0.705)	***	(1.06)
Reported income if full documentation	(0.0005)	**	(0.16)	0.0002		0.05
Reported income if limited documentation	0.0002	*	0.11	0.001	***	0.25
High cost spread indicator	0.158	***	0.25	(0.036)		(0.05)
5-year Treasury constant maturity rate	0.205	***	0.52	0.199	***	0.41
Spread over 5-year Treasury constant maturity rate	0.404	***	1.35	0.265	***	0.83
High incidence of less than high school education	0.020		0.02	(0.041)		(0.03)
High incidence of more than college education	(0.299)	***	(0.42)	(0.337)	***	(0.39)
Low incidence of wealth	0.108	***	0.10	0.096	*	0.07
High incidence of wealth	(0.236)	***	(0.33)	(0.208)	***	(0.26)
High incidence of old housing	(0.043)		(0.04)	0.040		0.03
High incidence of vacant units	0.237	***	0.23	0.184	***	0.14
Asian	0.214	***	0.25	0.094	**	0.08
Black or African-American	0.496	***	0.66	0.092	**	0.10
Other race	0.075	*	0.05	0.141	**	0.07
Hispanic or Latino	0.596	***	1.18	0.398	***	0.57

Source: GAO analysis of CoreLogic LP, HMDA, FHFA, Census, and BLS data.

Note: In the "Significance" columns, the symbols *, **, and *** indicate statistical significance at the 10 percent, 5 percent, and 1 percent levels, respectively. A blank cell in these columns indicates that the coefficient for the variable was not statistically significant at these levels.

Table 8. Estimation Results for Fixed-rate Mortgages for Owner-Occupants.

	Purchase loans			Refinance loans		
	Coefficient	Significance	Marginal effect	Coefficient	Significance	Marginal effect
Number of observations: Purchase loans – 350,486 Refinance loans – 621,968						
Intercept	16.255	***		15.972	***	
Loan amount	0.002	***	1.82	0.002	***	1.42
HPA: First year of the loan	(7.574)	***	(2.05)	(6.240)	***	(1.85)
HPA: Difference between 1st and 2nd year of the loan	3.161	***	1.05	2.504	***	0.81
Change in employment growth	(5.744)	***	(0.57)	(7.156)	***	(0.68)
DTI ratio missing	0.039	*	0.08	(0.035)	**	(0.07)
DTI ratio less than 35 percent	(0.002)		0.00	(0.050)	***	(0.08)
DTI ratio greater than 41 percent	0.135	***	0.25	0.084	***	0.16
FICO score	(0.011)	***	(2.17)	(0.010)	***	(1.95)
CLTV ratio less than 80	(0.912)	***	(1.08)	(0.592)	***	(1.05)
CLTV ratio between 80 and 90	(0.268)	***	(0.21)	0.076	***	0.11
CLTV ratio equal to 90	(0.086)	***	(0.09)	0.337	***	0.39
CLTV ratio between 90 and 100	0.330	***	0.56	0.468	***	0.56
CLTV ratio greater than or equal to 100	0.662	***	1.64	0.835	***	0.84
Full documentation	(0.444)	***	(0.86)	(0.306)	***	(0.56)
Reported income if full documentation	(0.003)	***	(0.66)	(0.003)	***	(0.75)
Reported income if limited documentation	(0.001)	***	(0.23)	(0.001)	***	(0.23)
High cost spread indicator	0.176	***	0.34	0.014		0.03
10-year Treasury constant maturity rate	0.125	***	0.18	0.130	***	0.18
Spread over 10-year Treasury constant maturity rate	0.275	***	1.46	0.231	***	1.22
High incidence of less than high school education	0.058	**	0.06	(0.013)		(0.02)
High incidence of more than college education	(0.268)	***	(0.30)	(0.202)	***	(0.19)
Low incidence of wealth	0.271	***	0.28	0.019		0.02
High incidence of wealth	(0.277)	***	(0.34)	(0.122)	***	(0.13)
High incidence of old housing	0.207	***	0.22	0.117	***	0.12
High incidence of vacant units	0.172	***	0.15	0.032		0.03
Asian	0.002		0.00	(0.125)	***	(0.09)
Black or African-American	0.520	***	0.80	(0.035)	**	(0.05)
Other race	0.210	***	0.12	0.026		0.02
Hispanic or Latino	0.241	***	0.41	0.063	***	0.10

Source: GAO analysis of CoreLogic LP, HMDA, FHFA, Census, and BLS data.

Note: In the "Significance" columns, the symbols *, **, and *** indicate statistical significance at the 10 percent, 5 percent, and 1 percent levels, respectively. A blank cell in these columns indicates that the coefficient for the variable was not statistically significant at these levels.

APPENDIX II. MATCHING CORELOGIC LOAN PERFORMANCE AND HOME MORTGAGE DISCLOSURE ACT RECORDS

Data Sources

To describe the race, ethnicity, and reported income of nonprime borrowers, we matched loan-level records from two primary data sources—CoreLogic LoanPerformance's (CoreLogic LP) Asset-Backed Securities Database and Home Mortgage Disclosure Act (HMDA) data compiled by the Federal Financial Institutions Examination Council (FFIEC). The CoreLogic LP database provides extensive information about the characteristics and performance of securitized nonprime mortgages. However, it contains relatively little information about borrowers, providing only credit scores and debt-service-to-income ratios.[61] In contrast, HMDA data contain limited information about loan characteristics and nothing about performance, but they do provide information on borrowers' race, ethnicity, and reported income. HMDA data are estimated to capture about 80 percent of the mortgages funded each year and cover all major market segments, including nonprime loans. HMDA data, therefore, should capture most of the loans in the CoreLogic LP database.

While the CoreLogic LP and HMDA data emphasize different kinds of loan and borrower information, they do have some information in common. These common data items—including loan amount, loan purpose, loan origination date, property location, and loan originator—allow the two data sets to be matched on a loan-by-loan basis. Using the methodology that we developed in previous work, we matched records from the CoreLogic LP database for loans that were originated from 2004 through 2006 to HMDA data files for those same years.[62] We focused on loan originations from this period because there were large numbers of nonprime originations in those years.

The CoreLogic LP data set that we used for the matching process contained records for 9,292,684 loans. The data set included records for conventional first-lien purchase and refinance loans to owner-occupants, investors, and owners of second homes. The data excluded records for loans for units in multifamily structures, and for manufactured housing; loans in Guam, Puerto Rico, and the Virgin Islands; and loans with terms other than 15, 30, or 40 years.

The HMDA data set that we used for the matching process contained records for 24,227,566 loans. As with the CoreLogic LP data, we focused on first-lien purchase and refinance loans. The HMDA data set excluded loans for properties other than one- to four-family residential units. Because the CoreLogic LP database contained only conventional loans in private label securitizations, we also excluded from the HMDA data set loans that involved government programs—such as mortgages guaranteed by the Federal Housing Administration or the Department of Veterans Affairs—and conventional loans that were indicated as sold to Fannie Mae, Freddie Mac, Ginnie Mae, or Farmer Mac.

Steps Taken to Make the Data Sets Compatible

Matching the loan records from the two data sources required us to make the common data items compatible. We were able to use a straightforward process for the loan amount and purpose that required only rounding the CoreLogic LP loan amount to the nearest $1,000 and aggregating the three CoreLogic LP refinance categories into one category. However, the process was more complicated for origination date and property location.[63] We determined that the name of the loan originator was not particularly useful for making initial matches of loan records because this information was missing for a substantial percentage of the CoreLogic LP records. However, the originator's name was useful in assessing the quality of the matches that we made using other data elements.

Loan Origination Dates

About 15 percent of the loans in our CoreLogic LP data set had an origination date that was the 1st day of a month.[64] This distribution pattern was inconsistent with the distribution of origination days in HMDA, which showed a much more even pattern throughout the month, with an increase in originations toward the end of each month rather than the beginning of each month. Because of this inconsistency, we relied on the origination month rather than the origination month and day to match loan records.

Property Location

The CoreLogic LP and HMDA data provided different geographic identifiers for loans, with the CoreLogic LP data providing the ZIP code and the HMDA data providing the Census tract. To facilitate record matching on the basis of property location, we related the Census tract information in the HMDA data to a corresponding ZIP code or ZIP codes in the CoreLogic LP data, using 2000 Census files and ZIP code boundary files from Pitney Bowes Business Insight. Using mapping software, we overlaid Census tract boundaries on ZIP code boundaries to determine the proportion of each Census tract's area that fell within a given ZIP code area. For each Census tract, we kept all ZIP codes that accounted for at least 5 percent of that tract's area. About 60 percent of the Census tracts were associated with only one ZIP code (meeting the 5 percent threshold), and almost all Census tracts (97.5 percent) included no more than four ZIP codes. When a Census tract was associated with only one ZIP code, all HMDA records in that Census tract were candidates to match CoreLogic LP records in that ZIP code. All HMDA records in tracts with more than one ZIP code were candidates to match CoreLogic LP records in those ZIP codes.

Matching Methodology

We matched loan records in the CoreLogic LP and HMDA data sets as follows. First, for each loan origination year (2004, 2005, and 2006), we made initial matches by identifying CoreLogic LP and HMDA loans with the same property location,[65] origination month, loan amount, and loan purpose. After finding all possible HMDA matches for each CoreLogic LP record, we classified these initial matches as either one-to-one matches (CoreLogic LP records with one corresponding HMDA record), one-to-many matches (CoreLogic LP records with more than one corresponding HMDA record), or nonmatches (CoreLogic LP records with no corresponding HMDA record). One-to-one matches accounted for about 55 percent of the loans in our CoreLogic LP data set, one-to-many matches accounted for about 25 percent, and nonmatches accounted for about 15 percent. Our match rates were highest for 2004 originations, about 85 percent, and lowest for 2006 originations, about 82 percent.

The quality of the matches was particularly important because we were examining statistical relationships between borrower characteristics and loan performance. To provide reasonable assurance that the matches were robust, we performed three types of quality checks on our initial one-to-one and one-to-many matches. First, we used information about the loan originator—information that was included in both the CoreLogic LP and HMDA data. The HMDA data clearly identified loan originators—referred to as "HMDA respondents"—using a series of codes that corresponded to a list of standardized originator names. However, in more than 40 percent of the CoreLogic LP records in our data set, the originator name was marked as not available. In other cases, the originator was listed by a generic term, such as "conduit," or was an entity that appeared to be involved in the securitization process but was not necessarily the originator. Originators that were listed were often referred to in a number of ways—for example, "Taylor Bean," "Taylor Bean Whitaker," "Taylor, Bean & Whitaker," "TaylorBean," "TBW," and "TBW Mortgage Corp." all referred to the HMDA respondent "Taylor, Bean & Whitaker." For CoreLogic LP loans with originator information, we standardized the originator names in the CoreLogic LP data, and we used these same originator names for the HMDA data. We compared the standardized originator names in matched records and if the standardized names matched, we classified the match as a robust match, and deleted any other HMDA records that might have matched to that CoreLogic LP record.

Second, for CoreLogic LP loans with no originator name, we examined the relationship between the HMDA loan originator and the issuer of the securities associated with the loan. Many institutions, such as Countrywide and Ameriquest, originated and securitized large numbers of nonprime loans. While some of these institutions identified themselves as the originator of a loan, others typically did not make the originator information available. In these cases, if the CoreLogic LP securitizer matched the HMDA originator, we classified an initial match as a robust match. If the issuer did not originate substantial numbers of nonprime loans, or also relied on other originators to provide loans for its securitizations, we developed criteria to check for evidence of business relationships between the issuer and various originating institutions. This check had two components. First, if within the CoreLogic LP data set we identified an originator-issuer combination, we defined that combination as a business relationship. Second, we considered combinations of originators from the HMDA data and issuers from the CoreLogic LP data. For an originator-issuer combination to be a business relationship, a combination had to appear at least 250 times in our set of initial one-to-one matches, or meet one of two additional criteria. Specifically, if the combination appeared at least 100 times, the originator must have made 10 percent of the issuer's securitized loans, or if the combination appeared at least 50 times, the issuer had to have securitized 33 percent of the loans made by the originator. We classified initial matches for which such business relationships existed as robust matches.

Additionally, if none of these tests resulted in a robust match, we examined the loan origination day in the CoreLogic LP and HMDA data sets. If the days matched exactly, we classified an initial match as a robust match. Finally, for some one-to-many matches that shared originator, issuer, or business relationship characteristics, we examined the CoreLogic LP and HMDA characterizations of whether the borrower was an owner-occupant. In some cases, we were able to classify an initial match as a robust match if CoreLogic LP and HMDA owner-occupant characteristics matched. Overall, we produced high-quality matches for about 73 percent of the records in our CoreLogic LP data set, including about 75 percent of the loans originated in 2004, about 73 percent of the loans originated in 2005, and about 72 percent of the loans originated in 2006 (see table 9).

A potential concern with constructing a data set using a matching process is that records that do not match may differ systematically from records that do match, thereby making it difficult to make inferences from the matched data. However, we believe that the CoreLogic LP records that we were unable to match to HMDA records were similar in important respects to CoreLogic LP records that we could match. For example, loans in subprime pools represented 61.5 percent of the overall CoreLogic LP sample, and 62.3 percent of matched loans. Purchase loans represented 44.8 percent of the overall CoreLogic LP data set, and 46.0 percent of matched loans. In terms of geography, state shares of unmatched and matched loans were similar. Loans in California represented 23.1 percent of the full CoreLogic LP data set and 22.5 percent of matched records. Furthermore, nonprime borrowers with matched and unmatched records had similar FICO scores. For example, subprime borrowers with matched records had median FICO scores of 617, 620, and 617 for loans originated in 2004, 2005, and 2006, respectively; the corresponding scores for subprime borrowers with unmatched records were 617, 617, and 615. Likewise, Alt-A borrowers with matched records had median FICO scores of 708, 709, and 703 for 2004, 2005, and 2006, respectively; the corresponding scores for Alt-A borrowers with unmatched records were 706, 707, and 702. In addition, as shown in table 10, for each loan origination year and mortgage product type, median initial interest rates were identical or similar for borrowers with matched and unmatched records.

Table 9. Results of the Matching Process (CoreLogic LP Loan Records to HMDA Loan Records).

Loan origination year	Number of CoreLogic LP records	Initial matches to HMDA records		Robust matches to HMDA records	
		Number	Percentage	Number	Percentage
2004	2,750,030	2,292,747	83.4%	2,053,999	74.7%
2005	3,630,993	3,000,004	82.6	2,640,799	72.7
2006	3,029,202	2,471,231	81.6	2,191,156	72.3
Total	**9,410,225**	**7,763,982**	**82.5%**	**6,885,954**	**73.2%**

Source: GAO analysis of CoreLogic LP and HMDA data.

Table 10. Median Initial Interest Rates, by Loan Origination Year, Mortgage Product Type, and Match Status.

Mortgage product type	Median initial interest rate, by loan origination year					
	2004		2005		2006	
	Matched	Unmatched	Matched	Unmatched	Matched	Unmatched
Short-term hybrid ARMs	7.000	6.990	7.350	7.375	8.375	8.375
Fixed-rate mortgages	6.625	6.500	6.500	6.500	7.400	7.450
Longer-term ARMs	5.625	5.625	6.125	6.125	6.875	6.875

Source: GAO analysis of CoreLogic LP and HMDA data.

End Notes

[1] The subprime segment of the nonprime loan market generally serves borrowers with blemished or limited credit histories, while the Alt-A market segment serves borrowers whose credit histories are close to prime, but the loans have one or more high-risk features.

[2] GAO, *Characteristics and Performance of Nonprime Mortgages,* GAO-09-848R (Washington, D.C.: July 28, 2009).

[3] GAO, State-Level Information on Negative Home Equity and Loan Performance in the Nonprime Mortgage Market, GAO-10-633R (Washington, D.C.: May 14, 2010); Loan Performance and Negative Home Equity in the Nonprime Mortgage Market, GAO-10-146R (Washington, D.C.: Dec. 16, 2009); and GAO-09-848R.

[4] See GAO, Nonprime Mortgages: Data on Loan Performance by Cohort Year, Product Type, and Location, an E-Supplement to GAO-10-805, GAO-10-806SP (Washington, D.C.: Aug. 24, 2010). For a discussion of our methodology for estimating performance by congressional district, see GAO-09-848R.

[5] Nonagency mortgage-backed securities (MBS), also known as private-label MBSs, are backed by nonconforming conventional mortgages securitized primarily by investment banks. Nonconforming mortgages are those that do not meet the purchase requirements of Fannie Mae or Freddie Mac because they are too large or do not meet their underwriting criteria. About 75 percent of subprime and Alt-A mortgages originated from 2001 through 2007 were securitized. For the period of January 2001 through July 2007, the CoreLogic LP database contains information covering, in dollar terms, an estimated 87 percent of securitized subprime loans and 98 percent of securitized Alt-A loans. Researchers have found some evidence that nonprime mortgages that were not securitized (mortgages that lenders held in their portfolios) may have less risky characteristics than those that were securitized. See Christopher L. Foote and others, "Reducing Foreclosures," Federal Reserve Bank of Boston Public Policy Discussion Paper No. 09-2 (April 2009).

[6] The CoreLogic LP database has a loan-level indicator for loan class (subprime or Alt-A), but it is not well populated. Therefore, we used the pool-level classification. According to mortgage researchers, some of the loans in subprime pools may not be subprime loans, and some of the loans in Alt-A pools may not be Alt-A loans.

[7] Unless otherwise noted, we treated delinquent loans, loans in default, and loans in the foreclosure process as mutually exclusive categories. We considered a loan to have completed the foreclosure process if it was in real-estate-owned status as of a particular date, or was paid off after being either 90 or more days delinquent, in the foreclosure process, or in real-estate-owned status.

[8] A loan cohort is a group of loans that originated in the same year.

[9] GAO-10-806SP.

[10] The period of 2004 through 2006 covers the peak years of nonprime mortgage lending, and the performance window includes periods of both house price appreciation and depreciation. Additionally, we focused on this period because data limitations complicated our efforts to produce robust matches between the CoreLogic LP and HMDA databases for loans originated in other years.

[11] Although the HMDA data provide information on borrowers' race, ethnicity, and reported income, they contain limited information about loan characteristics and no information about performance. HMDA data are estimated to capture about 80 percent of the mortgages funded each year and cover all major market segments, including nonprime loans. HMDA data should therefore capture most of the loans in the CoreLogic LP database, which provides extensive information about loan characteristics and performance.

[12] More than 90 percent of loans in the CoreLogic LP database was for properties located in metropolitan areas covered by FHFA's HPIs. We excluded loans for properties outside of these areas.

[13] There is no uniform definition of default across the lending industry. For the purposes of this report, we use the definition provided unless otherwise noted.

[14] GAO-10-146R.

[15] GAO, *Information on Recent Default and Foreclosure Trends for Home Mortgages and Associated Economic and Market Developments,* GAO-08-78R (Washington, D.C.: Oct. 16, 2007).

[16] As we have previously noted, the data we used for our analysis do not cover the entire nonprime market but do cover the large majority of nonagency securitized mortgages within that market.

[17] By comparison, as of the first quarter of 2007, active nonprime loans originated from 2000 through 2005 had a serious delinquency rate of 7 percent. Although defaults and foreclosures also increased in other market segments, the serious delinquency rate for the mortgage market as a whole was substantially lower. According to the Mortgage Bankers Association, the serious delinquency rate for the broader mortgage market was approximately 2 percent as of the first quarter of 2007 and 10 percent at the end of 2009.

[18] Active loans can move in and out of serious delinquency status over time. For example, if a borrower makes one or more payments on a loan that has been in default (more than 90 days past due), its status could improve to delinquent (30 to 89 days past due) or current.

[19] GAO-09-848R.

[20] GAO-10-806SP.

[21] The CLTV ratio is the amount of the first mortgage and any second liens divided by the value of the home at loan origination.

[22] In a prior report, we examined the relationship between these types of variables and the likelihood of default to assess the implications of proposed legislation intended to strengthen consumer protections for mortgage borrowers. See GAO, *Home Mortgages: Provisions in a 2007 Mortgage Reform Bill (H.R. 3915) Would Strengthen Borrower Protections, but Views on Their Long-term Impact Differ*, GAO-09-741 (Washington, D.C.: July 31, 2009).

[23] Earlier in this report, we used the term "in default" to refer only to loans that were delinquent by at least 90 days. For efficiency of language, henceforth we use the broader definition stated in this section of the report.

[24] In GAO-09-741, we used a similar model to estimate mortgage defaults. However, the results presented in that prior report and this report are not directly comparable, in part because we did not match the CoreLogic LP data to HMDA data in the prior report. Therefore, we did not include information on borrowers' race, ethnicity, or reported income. Also, for that study, we estimated default probabilities for loans originated from 2000 through 2006.

[25] We present the results for purchase and refinance loans to owner-occupants in the body of this report and results for loans to investors in appendix I.

[26] Michelle A. Danis and Anthony Pennington-Cross, "The Delinquency of Subprime Mortgages," *Journal of Economics and Business*, vol. 60 (2008); Andrew Haughwout, Richard Peach, and Joseph Tracy, "Juvenile Delinquent Mortgages: Bad Credit or Bad Economy?," *Journal of Urban Economics,* vol. 64 (2008); Shane M. Sherlund, "The Past, Present, and Future of Subprime Mortgages," *Finance and Economic Discussion Series,* no. 2008-63, Federal Reserve Board (November 2008); and Yuliya S. Demyanyk, "Quick Exits of Subprime Mortgages," *Federal Reserve Bank of St. Louis Review*, vol. 91, no. 2 (2009).

[27] When we use the phrase "all else being equal" in describing the marginal effect of changes in a particular variable, we mean that we estimated default probabilities using two different values for that variable, setting the values for all other variables to their means for the respective product type and loan purpose.

[28] We used FHFA's metropolitan HPIs, which are broad measures of the movement of single-family house prices in 384 metropolitan areas. The HPIs are published by FHFA using home price data provided by Fannie Mae and Freddie Mac on the basis of sales and refinancings of the same properties at different points in time.

[29] That is, house prices and employment growth tended to move in the same direction. Specifically, the correlation coefficient between our measures for house price changes and employment growth in the first 24 months of the loan was 0.66. (The Pearson's correlation coefficient is a statistical measure of association, ranging in value from negative 1 to positive 1, with negative 1 indicating a perfect negative correlation, 0 an absence of correlation, and positive 1 a perfect positive correlation.)

[30] Other research has found similar associations. See Danis and Pennington-Cross, "The Delinquency of Subprime Mortgages"; Haughwout, Peach, and Tracy, "Juvenile Delinquent Mortgages: Bad Credit or Bad Economy?"; Sherlund, "The Past, Present, and Future of Subprime Mortgages"; and Demyanyk, "Quick Exits of Subprime Mortgages."

[31] In our statistical model, we split the initial interest rate into two variables, representing the relevant interest rate index and the interest rate spread, and found that both variables had a positive association with default probabilities. Other research examining the influence of those two interest rate components together also found a positive association with default probabilities. See Demyanyk, "Quick Exits of Subprime Mortgages."

[32] The DTI ratio represents the percentage of a borrower's income that goes toward all recurring debt payments, including the mortgage payments. The higher the ratio, the greater the risk that the borrower will have cash-flow problems and will miss mortgage payments.

[33] For a further discussion of this hypothesis, see Foote and others, "Reducing Foreclosures."

[34] Anthony Pennington-Cross and Giang Ho, "The Termination of Subprime Hybrid and Fixed Rate Mortgages," *Federal Reserve Bank of St. Louis Working Paper Series,* no. 2006-042A (July 2006); Danis and Pennington-Cross, "The Delinquency of Subprime Mortgages"; and Haughwout, Peach, and Tracy, "Juvenile Delinquent Mortgages: Bad Credit or Bad Economy?."

[35] This pattern reflects the fact that loans with limited documentation of income were typically associated with the Alt-A market, which serves borrowers with credit histories better than those of subprime borrowers.

[36] To produce these estimates we used a statistical model similar to the one used to produce the other estimates in this report, except that the model excluded the documentation variable. We estimated default probabilities separately for loans with and without full documentation using the documentation-level-specific means for credit score, reported income, and CLTV ratio and the mean values for all loans for all other variables. The mean loan amount was higher for loans with limited documentation (about $265,000) than for loans with full documentation (about $200,000). To control for the tendency of the higher loan amount to increase the default risk for loans with limited documentation, we used the mean loan amount for all loans (about $230,000) in this example.

[37] In this report, we use the race and ethnicity categories defined in the HMDA data. When we refer to white borrowers, we exclude borrowers who identified their ethnicity as Hispanic or Latino. When we refer to black

or African-American borrowers, we include borrowers of all ethnicities. When we refer to Hispanic or Latino borrowers, we include borrowers of all races.

[38] To produce these estimates, we used a statistical model similar to the one we used to produce the other estimates in this report, except that the model excluded the race and ethnicity variables. We estimated default probabilities separately for white, black or African-American, and Hispanic or Latino borrowers using the mean values for all variables for the respective group.

[39] For example, among owner-occupants, about 60 percent of black homeowners and 55 percent of Hispanic homeowners were first-time buyers, compared with 40 percent of all homeowners in 2007, according to the American Housing Survey. See U.S. Census Bureau, Current Housing Reports series H150/07, *American Housing Survey for the United States: 2007* (Washington, D.C.: 2008), p. 158.

[40] In 2006, for example, the average unemployment rate was 8.9 percent for the black or African-American civilian population, 5.2 percent for the Hispanic population, and 4.0 percent for the white population, according to BLS.

[41] For example, in 2007, 51 percent of nonwhite and Hispanic families reported that they had saved in the preceding year and 87 percent reported owning any financial assets; the corresponding percentages for non-Hispanic white families were 59 percent and 98 percent, respectively. See Brian K. Bucks and others, "Changes in U.S. Family Finances from 2004 to 2007: Evidence from the Survey of Consumer Finances," *Federal Reserve Bulletin* (February 2009).

[42] In 2007, the median assets for nonwhite and Hispanic families having any assets was $9,000, compared with $44,000 for non-Hispanic white families, according to the *Survey of Consumer Finances.*

[43] William P. Alexander and others, "Some Loans Are More Equal than Others: Third-Party Originations and Defaults in the Subprime Mortgage Industry," *Real Estate Economics,* vol. 30 (2002); and Carolina Reid and Elizabeth Laderman, "The Untold Costs of Subprime Lending: Examining the Links among Higher-Priced Lending, Foreclosures and Race in California," (a paper presented at the Institute for Assets and Social Policy, Brandeis University, April 2009).

[44] William C. Apgar and Allegra Calder, "The Dual Mortgage Market: The Persistence of Discrimination in Mortgage Lending," in *The Geography of Opportunity: Race and Housing Choice in Metropolitan America,* ed. Xavier deSousa Briggs (Washington, D.C.: Brookings Institution Press, 2005).

[45] GAO-09-741.

[46] As we have previously noted, we focused on data sources that are widely available. As a result, we did not include proprietary data maintained by lending institutions and other mortgage market participants in our scope.

[47] As we have previously explained, nonagency securitized loans are nonconforming conventional mortgages securitized primarily by investment banks. Nonconforming mortgages are those that do not meet the purchase requirements of Fannie Mae or Freddie Mac because they are too large or do not meet their underwriting criteria.

[48] The prime market segment serves borrowers with strong credit histories and provides the most attractive interest rates and mortgage terms. The government-guaranteed market segment primarily serves borrowers who may have difficulty in qualifying for prime mortgages but features interest rates competitive with prime loans in return for payment of insurance premiums or guarantee fees. FHA and the Department of Veterans Affairs operate the two main federal programs that insure or guarantee mortgages.

[49] Agency securitized loans are conforming conventional mortgages that meet the requirements for purchase and securitization by Fannie Mae or Freddie Mac.

[50] HUD provides aggregated and some loan-level data on its Web site (see http://www.hud.gov/offices/hsg/hsgrroom.cfm (accessed July 6, 2010) and https://entp.hud.gov/sfnw/public/ (accessed July 6, 2010)).

[51] For example, HMDA data on mortgages made in 2009 are not available until September 2010. HMDA data can be ordered through the FFIEC Web site (see http://www.ffiec.gov/hmda/ (accessed July 6, 2010)).

[52] The data sources may have different definitions for certain data elements. Some data fields in the HMDA database may be unavailable to the public to protect borrowers' privacy, and some data fields in nonprime data sources may not be well populated.

[53] Information in figure 13 is current as of July 2010. The availability of different data elements may change over time. The data elements shown in the figure are those available to data users outside of the companies or agencies that maintain the data.

[54] The HMDA data, however, do provide information on the spread between the annual percentage rate—a measure of credit cost to the borrower that takes account of the interest rate, points, and certain lender charges—and the rate on Treasury securities of comparable maturity for loans with prices above designated thresholds. A point is a loan charge, usually paid at loan closing, expressed as a percentage of the loan amount (1 point is 1 percent of the loan balance).

[55] The study examined pricing in terms of interest rates for subprime loans originated from 2004 through 2006. See Andrew Haughwout, Christopher Mayer, and Joseph Tracy, "Subprime Mortgage Pricing: The Impact of Race, Ethnicity, and Gender on the Cost of Borrowing," Federal Reserve Bank of New York Staff Paper No. 368 (April 2009).

[56] CoreLogic LP offers a separate data product that provides information on other mortgage debt. HMDA data contain records on first and junior liens but do not identify whether two or more loans are related to the same property. However, using a record-matching process, it is possible to identify pairs of loans used to finance the same property. See GAO, *Federal Housing Administration: Decline in the Agency's Market Share Was Associated with Product and Process Developments of Other Mortgage Market Participants,* GAO-07-645 (Washington, D.C.: June 29, 2007).

[57] We requested and obtained the date fields from FFIEC, which compiles and publishes the HMDA data, to conduct studies requested by Congress. Under GAO's disclosure regulations, set forth at 4 C.F.R. Part 81, we do not provide members of the public with records that originate in another agency obtained in connection with our work. Instead, we refer members of the public requesting information to the agency that originated the record. 4 C.F.R. § 81.5(a). Additionally, under our regulations, we do not disclose to the public records containing confidential financial information, see 4 C.F.R. § 81.6(e), nor do we disclose records containing private or personal information, which, if disclosed to the public, would amount to a clearly unwarranted invasion of the privacy of a person, see 4 C.F.R. § 81.6(f).

[58] Some firms offer databases that draw on public records and may be used to track properties or borrowers over time. For example, researchers used historical registry of deeds records for the entire state of Massachusetts to track homeownership experiences of subprime borrowers. See Kristopher Gerardi, Adam Hale Shapiro, and Paul S. Willen, "Subprime Outcomes: Risky Mortgages, Homeownership Experiences, and Foreclosures," Federal Reserve Bank of Boston Working Paper No. 07-15 (May 2008).

[59] Pub. L. No. 111-203, 124 Stat. 1376 (July 21, 2010).

[60] We used the FHFA metropolitan HPIs, which are broad measures of the movement of single-family house prices in 384 metropolitan areas. The HPIs are published by FHFA using home price data provided by Fannie Mae and Freddie Mac on the basis of sales and refinancings of the same properties at different points in time.

[61] The debt-service-to-income ratio is the borrower's total monthly debt service payments divided by monthly gross income.

[62] GAO, *Loan Performance and Negative Home Equity in the Nonprime Mortgage Market,* GAO-10-146R (Washington, D.C.: Dec. 16, 2009).

[63] For privacy reasons, the origination date is omitted from each HMDA record when it is publicly released. We requested and obtained the date fields from FFIEC, which compiles and publishes the HMDA data. Under GAO's disclosure regulations, set forth at 4 C.F.R. Part 81, we do not provide members of the public with records that originate in another agency obtained in connection with our work. Instead, we refer members of the public requesting information to the agency that originated the record. 4 C.F.R. § 81.5(a). Additionally, under our regulations, we do not disclose to the public records containing confidential financial information, see 4 C.F.R. § 81.6(e), nor do we disclose records containing private or personal information, which, if disclosed to the public, would amount to a clearly unwarranted invasion of the privacy of a person, see 4 C.F.R. § 81.6(f).

[64] This pattern reflects CoreLogic LP's practice of imputing the origination month for some loans on the basis of the month in which the first payment is due. In these cases, CoreLogic LP records the origination date as the 1st day of the imputed origination month.

[65] Property location is reported at the Census tract level in HMDA and at the ZIP code level by CoreLogic LP. We used the spatial relationships between Census tracts and ZIP codes to assign each Census tract to those ZIP codes associated with it.

INDEX